THE 8-WEEK CHOLESTEROL CURE

A revolutionary three-pronged approach to lowering blood cholesterol levels based on modified diet and special foods and vitamins.

THE 8-WEEK CHOLESTEROL CURE

How to lower your blood cholesterol
by up to 40 per cent without
drugs or deprivation

by

Robert E. Kowalski

THORSONS PUBLISHING GROUP

First published 1987 in the USA by Harper & Row, Publishers, Inc.,
10 East 53rd Street, New York, NY 10022.

Revised UK edition first published 1988

British Library Cataloguing in Publication Data

Kowalski, Robert E.
   The 8-week cholesterol cure.
   1. Man. Cardiovascular system. Diseases.
   Therapy. Low cholesterol diet
   I. Title
   616.1'0654

   ISBN 0-7225-1580-4

*Published by Thorsons Publishers Limited,
Wellingborough, Northamptonshire, NN8 2RQ, England.*

Printed in Great Britain

10 9 8

I dedicate this book to my father with loving memories of the past, and to my children, Ross and Jenny, with the joys and memories of the present and future.

CONTENTS

TABLES

ACKNOWLEDGEMENTS

Full acknowledgement of all those who contributed to the development of this book would be impossible, as they include my teachers and mentors through the years, the doctors and nurses who helped me stay around in this world to write it, and all those whose lives have touched mine in ways reflected throughout these pages. I'm particularly grateful, however, to Dr Albert A. Kattus, both for his medical ministrations and his personal support and confidence in the research documenting the basic premise of this book. My thanks also to the nurses at the Santa Monica Hospital Medical Centre who contributed their time to our research project. I also deeply appreciate the confidence of all those involved in the process of bringing the manuscript dream to the published reality.

FOREWORD

by Albert A. Kattus, MD
Director, Cardiac Rehabilitation, Santa Monica Hospital Medical Center, Santa Monica, California
Honorary Professor of Medicine, University of California School of Medicine, Los Angeles, California

In the last century the concept of preventive medicine had its first big triumph when the ravages of bacterial infective disease began to come under control. Pasteur taught how to destroy the germs of tuberculosis and typhoid fever and other diarrhoeal organisms in the milk supply. Pure water and uncontaminated foods, vaccination, and, at length, antibiotics brought many of the great scourges of the world under control, with the saving of innumerable lives.

The big recent triumph of disease control is highlighted by the mortality statistics of cardiovascular disease over the years from 1950 to 1980. The mortality rate due to diseases of the heart and blood vessels has fallen 40 per cent in the United States over the past thirty years. Whereas infectious disease was the leading cause of death in the first half of our century, the leading causes of death in the second half of the century have been arteriosclerotic diseases of the heart, brain, and other vital organs.

The fact that the mortality of these diseases has been reduced by 40 per cent, however, does not mean that this epidemic is now under control. The fact is that cardiovascular disease (clogging of the arteries of the heart and other vital organs) is still the leading cause of death in our time. Thus, in order to complete the victory over this disease, it is necessary that the entire population of the country cooperate to develop lifestyles that will minimize the likelihood of progression of the interior chemistry that results in clogging of the arteries of the body.

How did it happen that the mortality rates fell by 40 per cent in the years from 1950 to 1980? The key to understanding that big drop is found in an analysis of what happened during those years. At the peak of the mortality rate for heart disease, the Second World War was just over. People were looking for a better break. But a surprising number were having heart attacks, and many who had avoided bullets, shrapnel, and grenades were now falling victim to heart disease.

At about that time, the federal government took partial responsibility for the nation's health by establishing the National Institutes of Health, whose work is involved with pure food and drugs, vaccination, and pure water. Now that it was clear that heart and blood-vessel diseases were killing more Americans than any other disease, it didn't take long before the National Heart Institute was born. This organization developed and financed research programmes on campuses, in university medical school laboratories, and in major non-university medical centres.

At about the same time, the American Heart Association began to promote heart disease research by funding investigators, some of the eminent scientists and others promising young researchers and teachers, from private donations.

Thus a strong surge of scientific investigation began regarding the basic causes of heart disease and what might be done to reduce the terrible toll, much of it among young persons in the prime of life. Some of the fruits of the effort were the development of coronary care units, the heart-lung pump for open-heart surgery, cardiopulmonary resuscitation, drugs for controlling lethal abnormalities of the heart rhythm which often lead to cardiac arrest and sudden death, and electronic heart pacemakers to keep the heart from beating too slowly. Many lives were saved among those presenting with heart disease. Mortality from heart attack (myocardial infarction) was significantly reduced. But the cost was enormous and the underlying disease of the arteries was still there, likely to strike at another time. No cures could be claimed. The magic formula for cleaning out the arteries was not discovered.

The basic need was understanding the chemical mechanism resulting in the deposit of atherosclerotic plaque that clogs the arteries and leads to stroke and heart attacks. The idea is that if the mechanism is known and understood it may become possible to prevent the disease process before it has a chance to start. It may be much easier on the patient to avoid the disease that could kill him and it is likely to be much less expensive to prevent the disease rather than to treat it after it has done severe damage to health and longevity.

The research of the years of the fifties and sixties provided the information that paved the way to preventive cardiology. Discovery of the three major risk factors that are the most reliable predictors of coronary heart disease provided clues to prevention. These factors are high blood pressure, cigarette smoking, and elevated blood levels of cholesterol. When these characteristics are present in an individual, that person has a ten times greater risk of having coronary heart disease than those in whom the factors are absent.

Epidemiologists have studied the statistics of the falling rate of heart disease and have reached the conclusion that the remarkable reduction of heart disease death cannot be due to better doctoring by the physicians who treat the disease after it is diagnosed. The answer is that the adoption of a more healthful lifestyle has taken place in a large segment of the population. The public has learned about the risk factors and has taken it upon itself to find out how it can help itself to a heart-disease-free future.

We know that in the years from 1963 to 1977 tobacco use fell by 30 per cent and 40 million Americans stopped smoking. In recent years, consumption of animal fats and oils has dropped by 47 per cent and butterfat intake has gone down by 33 per cent. These data indicate that the public is taking action to improve health habits and has succeeded to a remarkable extent.

Smoking can be stopped by an act of the will. Nothing complex there: either you do it or you don't.

Blood-pressure control may depend on maintaining appropriate body weight, avoiding too much sodium, and, if necessary, use of medicines which can lower the pressure.

Control of the blood cholesterol is the most complicated problem. Each person's own body chemistry determines how much cholesterol that body will make. We know that some people can lower the cholesterol manufactured and the amount in the blood just by cutting down the amount of fat they eat. However, some people have high levels even though they eat almost no fat. Some people respond well to certain medicines for cholesterol reduction and some do not. The problem is to be sure that the cholesterol which is so important in forming the blockage material in the arteries can be brought to a low enough level in the blood to assure that it won't deposit in the arteries and yet will be present in enough quantity to fulfil the basic jobs that it has to do — that is, to help build the membranes that form the walls of the body cells and to aid in the synthesis of a number of the body hormones vital for human function. Previous efforts have been largely unsuccessful.

Mr Kowalski has provided the information needed for lowering one's cholesterol. It is a 'how-to' book. How to find the foods that are least likely to bring about a cholesterol excess. How to avoid the foods that are most likely to yield a cholesterol excess. How to use special foods with special properties for lowering cholesterol. How to use the vitamins that tend to lower cholesterol.

This is a comprehensive work on how to deal with the chemistry of cholesterol so that it will enhance good health and avoid the diseases that are caused by clogged-up arteries.

Adherence to the programme described in this book has resulted in lowering the serum cholesterol in a series of volunteer test subjects. Surprisingly these subjects also had the additional bonus of a significant rise in the level of high density lipoprotein, a protective component of cholesterol further lowering the risk of coronary artery obstructive disease.

I have watched the programme evolve and I have seen the gratifying reduction in heart disease risk of most of the volunteer participants in the research. The results have indicated that the consumption of a low-fat diet, along with oat bran and niacin (one of the B-complex vitamins) is both safe and effective. I believe that this programme will become a useful method for self control of the serum cholesterol level, thus further reducing the risk of coronary heart disease by preventive measures.

INTRODUCTION

On Monday, 5 October 1987, six months after the first American publication date of this book, the US Federal government and more than twenty health organizations declared war on cholesterol and heart disease. In a much publicized press conference, they issued America's first detailed guidelines for both physicians and the public.

I was extremely gratified to see that they unequivocally stated that cholesterol levels should never exceed 5.2 mmol/l, regardless of age or sex. That's considerably lower than the previously accepted levels, and in keeping with the recommendations I had earlier published in my book.

In order to bring information regarding the identification and treatment of elevated cholesterol levels to both the public and doctors, a major thrust was initiated in the press and elsewhere. Diet, the authorities said, was first on the agenda for those whose levels were above the cut-off point. And, if necessary, drugs could be used to bring this risk factor under control. Interestingly, in the many reports following that noteworthy press conference, the use of oat bran and niacin were mentioned as excellent ways to reduce cholesterol levels. In other words, the concepts first put down in this book were receiving widespread endorsement.

There have been a vast number of developments since the first publication of *The 8-Week Cholesterol Cure*, and I've brought all this information together in revising the manuscript for this edition.

There's no doubt that publishing this book was the single most important event in my career if not in my entire life. The response was spectacular. During my media tour, whenever I appeared on a television or radio interview show in which viewers and listeners could phone in questions and comments, the lines were jammed. Time and time again producers and hosts told me that no interview in the past ever evoked so many calls.

Here's one example. Dr Art Ulene featured the book and its programme on *The Today Show* on NBC TV. It was one of ten transmissions over a two-week period dealing with various aspects of health. Viewers were invited to write for a printed summary of the report. They received 25,000 requests, setting a record at NBC. Extra staff had to be hired to respond to those requests.

The public obviously had been waiting for practical information on how to deal with this major risk factor in the disease which results in the deaths of so many. The recommendations issued in the past had not been satisfactory. That fact is driven home in many of the literally thousands of letters I receive.

A great number of my readers in America have told me that they never expected a problem because they were already following the advice they'd heard for cutting back on fats and cholesterol. They were shocked when their test results came back with elevated cholesterol levels. They were also horrified when, all too often, their doctors were not aware that such levels were extremely dangerous. But, naturally, they were pleased when, after following the simple recommendations in this book, their cholesterol levels fell to completely safe levels, thus totally eliminating this major risk factor.

The book became a major American bestseller, remaining at the top of the list in the *New York Times* for months. But it wasn't only members of the public who were reading the book. I'm very pleased that the medical community has responded so favourably. I've received dozens of letters from doctors and other health professionals telling me how they were using the book and its programme both for themselves and for their patients. For many doctors, this was the way to work more effectively with their patients. They could prescribe reading the book, and would then continue to monitor progress and answer individual questions regarding specific needs.

Needless to say, there are some authorities who are not in complete agreement. While virtually everyone who has read and reviewed the book has pointed to its accuracy, thoroughness, and practical approach, some are concerned about recommendations regarding the use of the vitamin niacin to lower cholesterol levels. You'll read more about this in Chapter 5. Their concern is that people may take large doses without medical supervision, even though I specially emphasize that such supervision is best.

It seems pretty obvious to me that people would not undertake a cholesterol-lowering programme on their own. If nothing else one needs to have blood tests done in order to determine cholesterol levels both at the beginning and after attempting to lower those levels. That's true even for those *not* using niacin.

Happily, however, most doctors and other health professionals welcome the book as a major step forward in our battle against heart disease. I've been invited to speak at major medical centres, hospitals, clinics, and annual meetings of medical societies across America. One cardiologist, in his introduction to the medical college at which I was to speak, said: 'I'm only sorry I didn't write this book myself.'

But you already know how important cholesterol levels are in determining your own health. That's probably why you're now reading this book.

Many of my readers to date have been women, and that's because this is not just a man's disease. While most of the research in the area of heart disease has focused entirely on men, coronary heart disease (CHD) is far from the exclusive domain of the male of our species.

Since the first publication of the book, an article has been published in the *New England Journal of Medicine* which casts new light on the relation of menopause to the risk of CHD. The number of women suffering heart attacks is growing, and the same risks that affect men must be considered for women, especially after menopause.

I've included the details of that report dealing with women in Chapter 2. Similarly, I've brought other parts of the book up to date regarding new research developments, foods which have been found to lower cholesterol levels, new products that have come onto the market recently, and a number of other details that have come to light since the book was first published.

Asked what will be the number one health problem in western countries in the year 2000, over 200 scientists and doctors immediately pointed to cardiovascular disease. The study of particularly eminent authorities was conducted by Louis Harris and Associates for the Bristol-Myers Company. While they were optimistic about developments in medical and surgical progress, those authorities recognized that people need to be informed and need to make some lifestyle changes in order to reduce their own risks of heart disease.

To a very large extent, your health is in your own hands, and I sincerely hope you'll follow the programme, thus substantially reducing the risk of heart disease for yourself. You *can* beat the odds!

1. THE PROGRAMME'S PROMISE

By starting to read this book you've already taken the first step toward vastly improved health and vitality. The rewards to be gained by following the Ultimate Lifestyle Programme outlined here are tremendous. Consider these promises:

- You'll be able to control your weight without feeling at all deprived.
- You'll eliminate a major heart disease risk factor from your life. Your cholesterol level will plunge dramatically, without drugs or deprivation diets.
- You'll vastly improve your chances for living a long, long life. The Fountain of Youth is a fantasy. This promise is a reality.

Probably the most astounding thing about this programme is how really easy it is to follow. This is the programme that says 'yes, yes, yes' instead of 'no, no, no'. You can eat to your heart's content, knowing that you won't gain weight. Yes, you can go to restaurants. Yes, you can enjoy really taste-tempting foods. Yes, you can involve your entire family and all your friends—who wants to live like a monk, watching the world go by?

You'll look great and feel great. Think of how long you've wanted to lose those extra pounds. Now you can do so with confidence. And you'll have a vitality and exuberance you never knew possible. You'll wake up in the morning ready to face the day and all its challenges.

Remember Ponce de León and his search for that elusive Fountain of Youth? Practically everyone would like to live to a ripe old age. Biology books say the human lifespan should be one hundred years. The Bible states that the life of man is 'three score and ten', but many men and women never reach that promised seventy. Yet science has methods to offer to achieve longevity, and you *can* use them.

No one can promise you won't be hit by a bus tomorrow. Or be struck dead by lightning. But you *can* cut the risk of heart disease and other life-shortening diseases. That's a promise. The chapters to come explain how you can eat to live, following this Ultimate Programme for Cholesterol Control and Longevity.

As Mr Spock says on *Star Trek*: 'Live long and prosper.'

Looking for the silver lining — a personal introduction

At 41 years of age I'd already had one heart attack and two coronary bypass operations. I had been denying my problem for years, but suddenly came to the realization that something had to be done to improve my chances of survival. I began to search for alternative approaches and therapies that finally led me to the formulation of a complete, thoroughly enjoyable lifestyle, which I'm quite sure will help me live for decades to come, deriving full pleasure from all that life has to offer. Simply enough, I've found the silver lining in the black cloud, and I want to share it with you.

I sincerely hope that you'll follow the suggestions this programme offers so that you can reap its benefits. Before going on to describe the programme and how it can turn your life around for the better, I'd like to introduce myself and tell you *my* story in a bit more detail.

For the past several years I've specialized in writing about medicine. At Iowa State University I received my B.S. and M.S. degrees in Science Journalism, with additional study in medical physiology. During the next few years I had the opportunity to work in the pharmaceutical industry, with a medical association, and in the food industry. Finally in 1980 I became a freelance medical writer.

But during the time when I was writing about health, my own was deteriorating. Fast.

Heart disease was rampant in my family. My father died of a coronary attack in 1969. And, when I was only 29, a free blood analysis at a medical convention revealed that my cholesterol level was 6.5 millimols per litre. The national adult average is about 5.4, and experts were starting to say at that time that even 5.2 millimols per litre was too high. But I ignored the findings.

Then in 1978, on Memorial Day, I had a myocardial infarction. A heart attack. Subsequent testing showed badly clogged coronary arteries, and it was time for my first coronary artery bypass surgery. A triple.

Still I denied the problem. I told friends that all was well, and that my 'new pipes' were as clean as a baby's. I did very little to stop or slow the progress of the disease that had led to the clogging in the first place.

Sure, the doctors told me to cut down on fats and cholesterol. But when I did so, following the American Heart Association's guidelines at the time, my cholesterol level changed very little. Besides, I kept telling myself, the whole idea of cholesterol and its effect on heart disease was still 'controversial'. So I stopped having my blood tested and passed the next six years in ignorant bliss.

Then came the shocker.

After my annual treadmill stress-test examination, a cardiologist told me that the results were not encouraging. How could that be? I asked. I had been regularly swimming a mile of laps in the pool, usually three to five times a week. My weight was completely in control. I wasn't smoking cigarettes. Still, the doctor suggested another angiogram.

Like the guy who closes the barn door after the proverbial horse has run off, I suddenly became very diet conscious. Maybe there *was* something to the idea after all. And my cholesterol level was now 7.3 millimols per litre. Not good.

I went on a very strict fat- and cholesterol-lowered diet for the next two months. The American Heart Association would have been proud of me. But, after cutting out all egg yolks, all red meat, practically all cheese (and all the other foods I loved), the tests showed my cholesterol level had dropped only 13 points. Discouraging, to say the least.

Then came the finishing note: the angiogram showed the need for another coronary bypass, this time a quadruple. The surgeon agreed with the need, but wasn't encouraging. He told me the mortality rate for 're-dos' was 5 to 6 per cent. I went home and cried like a baby.

I had so much to live for! I adored my very young children; Jenny was 3 and Ross was 6 at the time. They needed me! Never before had I wanted so badly to live.

Well, the surgery went particularly well. I wasn't one of the mortality statistics. In fact, the experience wasn't nearly as bad as the first. My recovery was spectacular, and within a couple of weeks I was back at the typewriter.

But this time I decided, in effect, enough was enough. *Something* had to be done about the cholesterol problem. I was absolutely determined that this was one risk factor that I would get rid of. But how?

Diet hadn't done the job in the past, and my readings in the medical literature bore out the conclusion that some people—like me—just couldn't properly metabolize cholesterol. Even with just a bit in the diet, it seemed the blood levels would be high.

There seemed to be only two alternatives, and neither was terribly appealing.

First there was the Pritikin Programme. I had read Nathan Pritikin's books and heard about the good results some adherents had while scrupulously following this strict regimen. While I have a great deal of respect for this approach and its founder, for me this seemed like a life of deprivation.

I loved eating in restaurants, and Pritikin said to avoid eating out. I loved a wide variety of foods, and he said stick almost exclusively with steamed rice and vegetables. Here's what Pritikin says in his chapter titled 'Hanging In While Dining Out'. It's on page 196 in the paperback edition:

> Dietary sabotage away from home is impossible to avoid, but it can be countered successfully. Confronted with this kind of terrorism, many people simply give up. . . . Don't get into the habit of eating out too often. It can get wearying to make a production of ordering your foods in the enemy camp.

When I read this I was really discouraged. One of the true pleasures of my life has always been experiencing delicious foods in a variety of restaurants all over the country. But I was willing to give it all up if that's what it took to get my cholesterol down and give myself a fighting chance.

The other alternative was one of the cholesterol-lowering drugs. They *had* been demonstrated to be effective. But think of what they do to your life. First, the cost is out of sight. A month's supply of cholestyramine, one of the most prescribed drugs in this category in the U.S., runs to more than $100. I could think of lots of ways to spend that $1,200 a year more pleasantly. Second, you not only have to buy the drug, you have to take it. Now, I was never a very good medicine taker, even as a child. I'm probably worse now. But this drug sounded like something out of a horror script. It comes in little packets, looking like gritty sand. You stir the granules into a glass of juice or water and gulp it all down before the mixture settles out. Four times a day. But that's just the beginning. Reading about the adverse reactions listed in the *Physician's Desk Reference*. I learned that the most common problem is constipation. But one can also develop 'abdominal discomfort . . . flatulence, nausea, vomiting, diarrhoea, heartburn, anorexia, indigestive feeling and steatorrhoea'. That last one means your bowel movements may have the consistency of grease, since the drug acts by binding fats coming through the digestive tract. Not a very appealing alternative at all.

But what else could I do?

Because of the nature of my work as a medical writer, I had ready access to the medical literature. Never was I more motivated to 'do my homework'. And I was well rewarded. There was a viable alternative after all. People have elevated, high-risk cholesterol levels for three reasons. First, their diets contain too much fat and cholesterol, which their bodies are unable to properly handle. Second, they do not excrete sufficient amounts of cholesterol through bile acids in the colon. Third, they produce a large amount of cholesterol in their livers. Put the three together, and the cholesterol count soars. It seemed logical, then, to consider all three aspects of the problem.

You've probably heard that sometimes 'the whole is greater than the sum of its parts'. Well, I read about three quite different approaches to lowering cholesterol, all of which had been demonstrated to be somewhat effective, but none of which did the trick completely. My hypothesis was that if I put the three together they would work synergistically to achieve the total effect I was hoping for.

Bingo!

From a dangerously high serum cholesterol level of 7.3 (that's millimols per litre, the designation typically used in medicine) my rate went to a comfortably safe 4.4! In just eight weeks. My doctors and nurses were amazed and delighted. Results like these had never before been achieved in such a short time, especially without drugs or an extremely restricted diet. The magic I'd been looking for seemed to be within my grasp: the combination of a common breakfast cereal, over-the-counter vitamins, and a reasonable and healthful diet, along with a programme of exercise. Best of all, there was no reason why everyone in the world couldn't share the benefits. No impossible-to-follow dietary restrictions. No unpleasant drugs to take. No superhuman athletic demands.

Next, working with my cardiologist, I put the concept to a test to see if other men and women could benefit to the same degree. They did. The results of that study are in another chapter, and they are quite dramatic.

Needless to say, I was ecstatic over my own results. Now that my cholesterol level was only 4.4, one of the major risk factors had been removed. I could stop worrying about my arteries clogging up so quickly again.

But there were other rewards I hadn't even counted on. I had lost about twelve pounds during and after my surgery, which I expected would come right back when I started to follow a normal eating pattern and my appetite returned.

My appetite did return, and I did start eating a great deal of food every day. But I did not gain the weight back. So I started to eat even more. *Still* no weight gain. On top of everything else, it appeared that my programme had a special weight-control bonus.

Digging further into the medical literature, I found out there was a scientific explanation for all this. Part of the programme calls for including oat bran in one's diet in the form of muffins and also cooked into other foods. Not only does this cereal whisk fats and cholesterol through the digestive system, but it also creates tremendous feelings of fullness—not the bloated feeling some fad diet drugs give, but a nice satisfied feeling. You just don't feel hungry between meals. You have no desire for snacks. Scientists call this 'satiety'. I call it wonderful.

But there's still more good news. With my old eating habits, I had used antacids pretty often to relieve indigestion and heartburn. With my new programme, I could throw those antacids in the trash, or save them for friends who hadn't seen the light yet.

Speaking of friends, we all know how people feel sorry for those on diets. It seems dieters have no fun at all; they must feel deprived and hungry all the time. But my friends, even those who didn't have to worry about their weight, were eager to try my programme, asking for recipes and sampling my muffins. I'm a walking testament to how *good* a person can feel!

Finally, a word about longevity. To tell the truth, I had never thought much about the long-term future. My father and many in my family died young, and I had assumed that I had inherited that legacy. Now my cholesterol level is way down, my blood pressure is low-normal, my weight is completely under control, and I'm looking forward to a long life.

This programme does more than just protect against heart disease. In the coming chapters, I'll tell you what medical authorities have learned about longevity and how the programme puts you ahead of the game.

Read the book, follow its recommendations, and start on your way to a long, healthy life. Nothing like this programme has ever been offered to the public before. Since it is truly new and revolutionary, I'd love to hear about your own result. I'd greatly appreciate your taking a few moments to tell me a bit about yourself and how the programme has worked for you.

In the meantime, good luck and good health!

2. CHOLESTEROL: NO MORE CONTROVERSY

Ironically, cholesterol has affected my own life over and over again during the past twenty years.

I first heard of cholesterol in college, when the professor simply described the substance as he would any other chemical covered in the course. Cholesterol, he said then and and it remains true today, is an organic chemical compound in the family of alcohols. It looks and feels like soft wax. Cholesterol is just one of a whole group of compounds in the body known as sterols, all of which are essential to life. Cholesterol enters the body through the foods, specifically the animal foods, we eat. It is also manufactured by the body in the liver. On the one hand, if the body doesn't have enough cholesterol to form vital hormones and metabolic products, we would not be able to survive. On the other hand, if the body has too much cholesterol, the excess begins to line the arteries, leading to atherosclerosis.

A long time ago, scientists noticed that in cultures where very little saturated fat and cholesterol were consumed, there was a parallel lessening of heart disease. But did the eating of cholesterol *lead* to the heart disease, or was it just another of the many aspects of the modern lifestyle that could be blamed? Thus began the controversy, the so-called diet/heart debate that raged for many years.

On a holiday when I was home from college, my father mentioned that his doctor had noticed that his cholesterol level was elevated and had advised staying away from certain foods that had a lot of cholesterol. Of course, not much was known about dietary modification back in 1965. Dad and I had a number of discussions about cholesterol. I pointed out that Eskimos eat a lot of blubber and they don't get heart disease. There just was no proof about the whole thing. Just to be on the safe side, Dad avoided oysters, then thought to be high in cholesterol, when we ate out in restaurants. He ate fish because he actually preferred seafood over steaks. But, without much guidance, he still ate a lot of cheese and drank whole milk, and his cholesterol level as affected not a bit. One day in 1969 I got a phone call that

Dad had died, at the age of 57, of a massive coronary.

Should I blame cholesterol? Well, Dad also had very high blood pressure. He was under a great deal of stress the year he died. And there was a family history of heart disease. Actually, I thought it was too bad that he had missed out on the oysters.

Two years later, while working for a medical association in Chicago, I attended a medical meeting where a new computerized blood-analysing device was being unveiled. All of us attending the meeting got free blood tests, and I learned from mine that while everything was in the 'normal' range my cholesterol level was a bit high. One of the doctors at the association said that 6.5 mmol/l was too high for someone only 29 years old.

I shrugged it off and went on with my normal, all-American eating habits. There was no proof, I reasoned, that changing my diet would lower my cholesterol level.

My career path led, in 1973, to a job as a science writer at the National Dairy Council. Over the next seven years I became Director of Communications, managing a great number of projects designed to improve the public's nutrition in general, and to increase the consumption of dairy products in particular by stressing their high calcium content.

During that seven-year period of time I read extensively about the cholesterol issue and met most of the scientists conducting research on the topic. Of course a great deal of my time was spend defending dairy foods against those who brought up the cholesterol problem. Even though I knew I had an elevated cholesterol level myself, I still felt there was no proof that diet could affect cholesterol levels, no reason to recommend altering the eating patterns of the entire nation. It was a 'controversy'. There was room for 'debate'.

A number of research studies during those years swayed many individuals, including me, to believe that altering the diet was not the proper course of action to reduce cholesterol levels. First, those who did change their eating habits found that their cholesterol levels did not decrease significantly. Second, the 'average' cholesterol level in adult men was in the low to middle range of 5.2 to 6.5 millimols per litre of blood. If that was average, therefore 'normal', why try to change anything? Third, studies showed that people with low levels of cholesterol did not increase those levels when fed an extra-large load of cholesterol. Even the American Medical Association, after reviewing these data, concluded that there was no reason to give a blanket prescription of dietary modification to the general public. Many other medical and scientific organizations agreed.

Then, in 1978, at the age of just 35, I had that heart attack. After

I recovered from the attack, the doctors recommended a triple coronary artery bypass; three of the arteries supplying blood to the heart were blocked and needed to be bypassed with bits of vein taken from my legs.

Yes, they took samples of my blood. Yes, the cholesterol levels were elevated. But even after the surgery I didn't really alter my diet. You might ask why.

The answer is very simple, or at least it appeared simple to me at the time. When I did try to alter my diet somewhat by cutting back on butter, whole milk, steaks, and the like, the results were so minimal that I concluded that I was just one of those unlucky people who didn't respond to dietary modification. This was the cholesterol level my body had 'chosen' to maintain no matter how much or how little cholesterol I ate. Besides, the surgery had 'cleaned up' my system and I was as good as new. So I thought. Six years later, I had my second bypass operation; this time a quadruple. I was only 41 years old. Not a very good record, and not a very good omen for the future.

It was time for a re-examination of the situation. Diet still did not seem to be the answer in my own case. Just before the surgery my cholesterol level was 7.3 mmol/l. By rather strict dieting over the next two months I was able to achieve only a drop to 7.0. During that time, I drank only skimmed milk, ate no butter or red meat, and forgot the egg entirely.

Still, the evidence that cholesterol levels in the blood are a major risk factor in heart disease was building up faster than ever before. In 1984 even *Time* magazine ran a cover story on cholesterol, picturing a typical breakfast plate of eggs and bacon forming a frowning face. No more controversy, the article read. Cholesterol must be reduced to decrease the risk of heart disease. A crucial piece of data had been delivered in the scientific community after years of study. There was no longer any question about it: lowering cholesterol significantly reduced the incidence of heart disease.

For me, this began, rather belatedly, a comprehensive review of the medical and scientific literature dealing with cholesterol, heart disease, and what could be done. What I read led to an awakening, albeit a rude one. I'd like to share with you the most important data and recommendations I found in the vast library of available literature. I think you'll agree when you read the data that some action should be taken about cholesterol—and that the approach needed has not been available before. A new, safe, effective, and not unpleasant method of cholesterol reduction is needed.

Diet and coronary heart disease

The first indications ever put down on paper that diet might be linked to heart disease, as well as to other diseases, came from observations of the eating habits of a wide variety of populations. Comparisons were made, for example, between Japanese men living in Japan and relatives who had come to the United States. More than thirty such studies have been done over the years, and the conclusions remain the same each time. Those groups consuming less saturated fat and cholesterol have less coronary heart disease. [1*]

Parenthetically, it's also worth mentioning that similar studies were performed in terms of sodium consumption. Again the results are conclusive. The more salt and other forms of sodium in the diet, the higher the incidence of hypertension, high blood pressure. [1]

Certainly other factors must also be considered, as practically nothing in science and medicine is perfectly cut and dried. For example, in a study done with accountants, cholesterol levels rose tremendously during the stressful months just before the annual filing of income-tax returns. Those cholesterol levels drop back down after the due date passes. Thus stress has a great deal to do with cholesterol levels. In fact, Dr. Meyer Friedman first postulated that the Type A—or high-strung, anxious—individual is more prone to heart disease and elevated cholesterol levels than is the more relaxed Type B person. Friedman and his partner, Dr. Ray Rosenman, in their book *Type A Behavior and Your Heart,* [2] recommend finding ways of changing behaviour—of avoiding anger and time-driven stress factors—in order to reduce cholesterol levels.

It is also known that certain individuals have a definite genetic pre-disposition to elevated lipid levels of all sorts. Simply enough, this appears to be a genetic metabolic disability to handle dietary fats and cholesterol. Even in animal studies, some are able to consume large amounts of cholesterol with no problem, while others need just a trace in their diets to cause havoc. The bottom line seems to be that many people, *but not all*, have the cholesterol problem. Some people, despite a diet filled with sinful goodies, nonetheless maintain low cholesterol levels. My brother Tom, for example, is one of those lucky ones. Tom eats everything he wants, with no regard to anything but taste. He watches calories only to stay fashionably slender. Tom loves eating in fine restaurants, and views the baked potato as a vehicle for butter and sour cream. Double portions, at that. Yet every time he has a blood test the result show that his cholesterol level is actually on the low side!

This is the same guy I grew up with. My mother fed us the same foods. We've had practically parallel lives. Yet his system handles dietary

* Notes will be found beginning page 233.

fats perfectly while mine goes wild. No one ever said life was fair.
Anyway, back to the literature.

In studies at the University of Illinois and elsewhere pigs were fed
a variety of diets. Pigs are used because their vascular systems are
very similar to those of human beings. The pig's aorta, the large artery
coming out of the heart, is practically the same as ours. No doubt
about it, diet can alter the accumulation of the so-called atherosclerotic
plaque that lines the aorta and other arteries. Pigs with a predisposition
to a high cholesterol diet will clog up their arteries rather quickly. Many
studies have shown this to be true.

Certain groups of people, even those living in the affluent United
States, have a very low level of heart disease. And the diet is involved.
Such a group is the Seventh Day Adventists, whose lives are built
around a vegetarian diet. [3] But even those data are not clear. Yes, they
have little heart disease. Yet, they avoid meat. But they follow what
is known as a lacto-ovo vegetarian diet, which includes lots of cheese
and eggs almost every day. Yet eggs and cheese are where a large
amount of dietary cholesterol is found. It appears, to me at least, that
some other factors are operating for the Seventh Day Adventists.
Probably this comes down, once again, to simple genetics. They tend
to be a rather closed group of people, with individuals marrying within
their religion. Perhaps the trait of handling dietary fats properly has
been handed down through the generations. On the other hand, if
a Seventh Day Adventist were to have a genetic problem, reducing
saturated fat and cholesterol by avoiding red meats would be important.

It is such conflicting and confusing data and information that have
developed the controversy over the years. But, as we're about to see,
that discussion is really moot for those who *do* tend to develop high
cholesterol levels.

Does any controversy still exist regarding diet and heart disease?
To answer that question, Dr Kaare Norum of the University of Norway
in Oslo sent a questionnaire to more than two hundred of the leading
authorities all over the world. These were the men and women doing
the cutting-edge research dealing with dietary fat and coronary heart
disease. He asked them whether they believed there is a connection
between diet and the development of coronary heart disease. Ninety-
seven per cent said yes. Asked whether they thought there is a
connection between diet and blood cholesterol level, 98 per cent said
yes. And when asked whether there is a connection between plasma
cholesterol and the development of coronary heart disease, 98 per cent
again said yes. The conclusion anyone can reach is that there is no
more controversy.

A survey conducted by the Food and Drug Administration in 1984 indicated that cholesterol and salt are the two top health threats as perceived by the American public. The Roper Organization survey found that 65 per cent of those contacted considered cholesterol a significant health concern. That number was 10 per cent higher than the year before.

The month before the 1984 survey was published, the National Institutes of Health strong advised Americans to reduce dietary fat and cholesterol because of their direct link with the rate of heart attacks. The government panel reported that 60 per cent of all Americans have high cholesterol levels and should make significant efforts to reduce the fat and cholesterol content of their diet.

The problem has always been, however, that while the link between the cholesterol levels in the blood and heart attacks has been well established, the connection to the diet has been less clear. In other words, while it may be true that reducing cholesterol levels in the blood will reduce the threat of heart disease, will a reduction in dietary fat and cholesterol lower that threat? The hang-up has been that, for the most part, attempts to reduce fat and cholesterol in the diet have not shown tremendous success in lower cholesterol in the blood. Actually, early intervention studies looked only at the amount of cholesterol, not the fat, in the diet. Later, both fat and cholesterol were viewed together as responsible for raising serum cholesterol levels. And, as time went on, it was found that saturated fat has more impact on serum cholesterol than does cholesterol itself.

A major four-year study by the National Institutes of Health—the 'Multiple Risk Factor Intervention Trial' (MR FIT)—was conducted primarily to zero in on nutrition intervention for individuals at high risk of heart disease.[4] Cholesterol levels of those persons in the study were 5.7 mmol/l or higher. The 'mmol/l' stands for millimols of cholesterol per litre of blood. The diet suggested to the men in the study contained 300 milligrams or less of cholesterol, with 35 per cent of calories as fat.

How successful was the test? At the end of the first year there was an overall decrease of only 6 to 7 per cent from initial cholesterol levels. For those who did particularly well, also losing weight during the year, there were reductions up to 10 per cent. After four years, the MR FIT programme achieved an average cholesterol reduction of 6.7 per cent.

Clearly this level of success is just not enough. For those men and women at risk, with, say, cholesterol levels of 6.5 mmol/l or higher, even a full 10 per cent drop is not sufficient.

Another study was published, also in 1984, by the National Heart, Lung, and Blood Institute. This was the result of the Lipid Research

Clinics Coronary Primary Prevention Trial.[5] In that particular investigation, scientists tried to determine whether lowering cholesterol levels could actually reduce the incidence of coronary heart disease.

Recognizing that diet alone probably would not bring cholesterol levels down significantly, the researchers decided to increase the likelihood of success by adding a cholesterol-lowering drug to the programme. The drug was cholestyramine, frequently prescribed by doctors to bring down dangerously high cholesterol levels.

This drug lowers cholesterol levels by binding fats in the intestine, causing them to be excreted in the faeces. To be effective, the drug often must be taken three to four times a day. It comes in packets of granules which can be mixed with water or fruit juice. Taking the drug is rather unpleasant, and not everyone is willing to stick with it.

Subjects in the study were asked to follow a modified diet with reduced fat and cholesterol. They received either the drug or a placebo. No one knew which. Results were published in the *Journal of the American Medical Association*. Altered diet alone produced a 3.4 per cent decrease in cholesterol levels. Altered diet along with cholestyramine brought the decrease to 14 per cent during the first year. Not surprisingly, the placebo had little if any effect. Over the succeeding years of the study, the cholesterol levels slowly rose back up, for a total decrease of only 6.5 per cent. Compliance was a problem.

However, some of the subjects did stick with the programme. They achieved significant lowering of their cholesterol levels over the eight-year period of time. And their risk of coronary heart disease dropped proportionately.

Medical authorities believe that while the total level of cholesterol is an important indicator of risk, an even more precise measurement is the so-called LDL cholesterol levels. This stands for low-density lipoprotein cholesterol. A more complete discussion of LDL cholesterol is found later in the chapter.

Within the cholestyramine-treated group, patients experienced a 0.6 mmol/l drop in LDL cholesterol levels. This was associated with a 17.2 per cent reduction in the actual incidence of coronary heart disease.

In other words, those individuals who were able to significantly reduce cholesterol levels experienced far less heart disease. Conversely, those who did not drop their cholesterol levels during that eight-year period had far more heart disease.

Moreover, the authors of the published study state that for subjects taking the full amount of cholestyramine LDL cholesterol levels fell by 35 per cent. Total cholesterol levels dropped 25 per cent. This much of a reduction, they say, would reduce the incidence of coronary heart disease by 49 per cent. Consider the incredible implications of that statement: *The risk of coronary heart disease is cut in half by lowering LDL cholesterol levels 35 per cent!*

Another way of looking at these data was discussed by a panel of the National Institutes of Health. Those experts said unequivocally that each 1 per cent reduction in blood cholesterol levels produces a 2 per cent reduction in coronary heart disease. For example, a 5 per cent reduction in total blood cholesterol should reduce disease rates by 10 per cent. Combinations of diet, drugs, and reduction of other risk factors can reduce disease by up to 50 per cent, they said. Feeling strongly about their findings, the NIH set out to convey this information to physicians, to educate them as to the value of cholesterol reduction for their patients.

But, once again, we're faced with the dilemma of just how to achieve that 35 per cent LDL reduction. The study's authors point out that it can be done with diet and drugs. But is this reasonable to expect for the entire population? Millions of people are at risk from heart disease, but it's highly unlikely that these millions would or could take the drugs used in the study.

An alternative might be strict dietary restriction. Nathan Pritikin has published a number of books detailing his approach to dietary control of cholesterol.[6] It is an effective programme. To reduce cholesterol significantly with the Pritikin Program, fat and protein are each kept to only 10 per cent of total calories. Compare this with even the recommendations given by the American Heart Association of limiting fat to 30 per cent, or even 20 per cent. Meat, fish, and poultry combined must not add up to more than one pound per week. The result is practically a vegetarian diet. Again, not many individuals could comply with this programme—especially for the rest of their lives.

These were the choices available to me when I determined that it was essential to reduce my own cholesterol levels. Neither the radical dietary programme nor the drugs seemed appealing. That's why I developed the programme by which I lowered my own levels by not just 30 per cent, or even 35 per cent, but a full 40 per cent.

Now that you've seen how effective cholesterol lowering can be in reducing the incidence of heart disease, and knowing that there *is* a safe, effective way to do so pleasantly, let's learn a bit more about cholesterol chemistry. You've probably heard the terms and names before, but it's good to have a firm understanding so that you can take better control over your own life.

Cholesterol and lipid terminology

Actually, cholesterol is just one of a number of fats, also called lipids, found in the blood. Some of those fats are harmful when levels rise too high. Other lipids, the neutral sterols, are chemically related to cholesterol but have no detrimental effects. Finally, cholesterol itself is a broad term referring to a number of fractions.

The term we hear most often, *cholesterol*, usually refers to *total cholesterol*, the total amount of all cholesterol in the blood. The amounts are measured in milligrams per decilitre, abbreviated as mg/dl or mg/dL. This is the number most people and most doctors talk about when trying to 'keep the cholesterol down'.

A number of years ago, researchers found that the total cholesterol in the blood could be broken down into a number of fractions, determined by the *lipoproteins*, which carry cholesterol: low-density lipoprotein cholesterol (LDL), very-low-density lipoprotein cholesterol (VLDL), and high-density lipoprotein cholesterol (HDL).

Low-density lipoprotein cholesterol (LDL) is generally regarded as the real culprit in coronary heart disease.[7] LDL carries cholesterol through the blood and deposits it in the arteries in a concretion of calcium, fibres, and other substances collectively referred to as plaque. The formation of such plaque is called atheroma, and the disease is atherosclerosis. It is this atherosclerosis which we commonly call heart disease. Actually, the heart usually is healthy, but the arteries are blocked. So a more proper term is coronary heart disease, with the word coronary referring to the coronary arteries supplying the heart with blood. The higher the level of LDL in the blood, the greater the risk of heart disease occurring.

Very-low-density lipoprotein (VLDL) is the substance used by the liver to manufacture LDL. Scientists refer to VLDL as a precursor of LDL. In other words, the higher the level of VLDL, the more LDL can be produced by the liver.

High-density lipoprotein cholesterol (HDL) is the protective fraction of cholesterol. HDL actually acts to draw cholesterol away from the linings of arteries. The higher the HDL level, the more protection against heart disease.

The ratio between total cholesterol and HDL cholesterol, or between LDL cholesterol and HDL cholesterol, is extremely important. The higher the ratio, the greater the risk of heart disease, since there is far more LDL trying to line the arteries than there is HDL trying to keep the cholesterol away from the arteries.

Blood tests prescribed by doctors will usually include information about levels of *triglycerides*. These fats in the blood have quite a different pattern from that of cholesterol. Some people may have normal levels of cholesterol but very high levels of triglycerides, and vice versa. Scientists generally agree that there is, however, an association between elevated triglycerides and elevated cholesterol. Lowering triglycerides can help bring down cholesterol as well.

In total, then, it's best to have low levels of total cholesterol, LDL cholesterol, VLDL cholesterol, and triglycerides, as well as low cholesterol ratios, while keeping a high level of protective HDL.

How much is too much?

Until fairly recently, the majority of doctors were not concerned if one's cholesterol level fell into the normal/average range for adult men and women. The problem with being 'average', however, seems to be that most people—including many children—have levels much too high. The 'normal' level may not be a safe level. This is especially true when comparing those levels with profiles of other ethnic groups. The conclusions are clear from dozens of studies: those cultural groups with lowest levels of cholesterol have the lowest incidence of heart disease.

The attitudes and opinions of doctors as to how high is too high began to change in 1983 with the publication of an article by Drs Basil Rifkind and Pesach Segal in the *Journal of the American Medical Association*. [8] In the study reported, plasma cholesterol and triglyceride levels were established for more than sixty thousand participants in ten separate American populations. New definitions were set for those who are *hyperlipidemic* (with elevated fats in the blood in general) and *hypercholesterolemic* (with elevated cholesterol levels).

The tables toward the end of this chapter, from Drs Rifkind and Segal's paper, give breakdowns of cholesterol levels for men, women, and children. As an example, in Table 1, only 5 per cent of the population of males have a cholesterol level of 3.9 mmol/l or lower in the age group 40-44 years. Conversely, looking at the 75th percentile, 25 per cent of the same population have a level of 5.9 mmol/l or more. The average level for this group is 5.3 mmol/l. More and more authorities today are recognizing that safe levels are much, much lower than what has been accepted for the past twenty years, and intervention of one sort or another is called for whenever the level exceeds 5.2 mmol/l. Thus the *average* adult male, and many other people of both sexes and in all age groups, need to do something to reduce elevated cholesterol levels.

What about children? As seen in the tables, children's cholesterol levels also vary. Diet does seem to make a difference. A study of rural Guatemalan children showed that an increase in cholesterol in the diet for just one month resulted in a significant increase in cholesterol levels in their blood. [9] In an American study, when the average daily cholesterol level in the diet was decreased from 720 to 380 milligrams with total calories from fat decreased from 38 per cent to 33 per cent, there was an average decrease in cholesterol levels of 15.6 per cent. [9] The higher the original level, the greater the decrease. Thus some children have the tendency early in life to develop elevated levels, and those are the children who respond most to dietary changes.

Many children in elementary schools throughout America are learning that a diet lower in fats is better for them. My own son came home from school—first grade, at that—having learned that skimmed milk is better for him than whole. It's difficult to completely change the diets of youngsters. They still enjoy those lunches at McDonald's once in a while. But moderation should be the watchword.

Certainly diet is the first step toward controlling levels of total cholesterol in the blood. That, in turn, can help retard the process of atherosclerosis and the development of heart disease. But what about the levels of protective HDL cholesterol?

It has been definitively reported that the determination of HDL cholesterol levels can help identify persons at risk of heart disease. In one study, the vast majority of men with coronary heart disease had total cholesterol/HDL level ratios of six-to-one or more. [10]

But can one affect those HDL levels to improve the ratio? It appears that one can do so through diet and exercise. HDL levels rise when the diet is low in fats and cholesterol, reduced in total calories, and includes a moderate amount of alcohol. [11] While no one actually advocates alcohol consumption for the purpose of affecting HDL levels, it has been shown again and again that a moderate amount of alcohol, say a drink or two daily, does result in a higher HDL level. On the other hand, a diet high in refined sugars can make the HDL levels fall. [11]

A number of studies have proven that those who regularly take part in rigorous exercise have higher levels of HDL. The question, however, is whether those levels can be significantly changed by working out.

The recommendation from all authorities is that the place to start is the diet. The goal is to have a ratio of total cholesterol to HDL cholesterol below 4.5. The ratio can be affected by either raising the HDL or lowering the LDL. The latter is more practical. The 4.5 ratio is the level associated with the standard risk of women, who have far less heart disease than men. Even better is a ratio of 3.5, which is associated with half the standard risk for men. [12]

What might be some specific examples of such ratios?

$$\frac{5.2 \text{ mmol/l total cholesterol}}{1.3 \text{ mmol/l HDL cholesterol}} = 4.0 \text{ ratio}$$

$$\frac{4.5 \text{ mmol/l total cholesterol}}{1.4 \text{ mmol/l HDL cholesterol}} = 3.0 \text{ ratio}$$

$$\frac{6.5 \text{ mmol/l total cholesterol}}{1.1 \text{ mmol/l HDL cholesterol}} = 6.0 \text{ ratio}$$

$$\frac{5.4 \text{ mmol/l total cholesterol}}{1.5 \text{ mmol/l HDL cholesterol}} = 3.5 \text{ ratio}$$

As one works through a number of such possible equations, it becomes obvious that the best way to achieve a good ratio is by lowering the total cholesterol. If one were to have a greatly elevated cholesterol level of, say 7.8 mmol/l, one would be highly unlikely to achieve a beneficial ratio by increasing the HDL level without also lowering the total cholesterol level.

Lowering total cholesterol and LDL cholesterol levels sufficiently by diet alone, however, may not always be possible. The Council on Scientific Affairs of the American Medical Association states,

In carefully controlled metabolic ward situations, decreased cholesterol and saturated fat intake without altered energy intake (calories) results in a decrease of perhaps 30% in serum cholesterol concentration. In the more generally applicable circumstances of free-living subjects, the decrease in plasma cholesterol concentration is considerably less. [13]

In other words, most people will not achieve sufficient lowering of serum cholesterol through diet alone. Yet this does not mean one should ignore the diet. The Council points out that 'there is good reason to believe that the average cholesterol levels in persons in the United States may be higher than optimal due in part to the typical US diet.'

Adults in primitive and Oriental societies have an average total cholesterol level between 3.9 and 5.2 mmol/l. Remember that total cholesterol levels between 3.6 and 4.7 mmol/l are consistently found to be related to the lowest rates of atherosclerosis and coronary heart disease. [13]

As the average cholesterol level rises above 5.2 mmol/l, the incidence of coronary heart disease increases proportionately. Thus, the Council concludes, 'average total plasma cholesterol levels of 4.7 and 5.2 mmol/l in adult populations seem to be associated with a low incidence of both cardiovascular and other diseases and probably should be considered optimal.'

Where to begin? The American Heart Association has recommended three phases of dietary modification. Each is increasingly restricted, with increased expectations for success.

In Phase I, the diet would include no more than 300 milligrams of cholesterol daily. There should be a fat intake of not more than 30 per cent of total calories, with 10 per cent each from saturated, polyunsaturated and monounsaturated fats and oils. This approach will usually reduce cholesterol levels by from 10 to 15 per cent in normal individuals.

In Phase II, fat and cholesterol intake should not exceed 30 per cent of calories and 250 milligrams per day, respectively. Finally, in Phase III, the restricted diet would contain only 20 to 25 per cent of calories as fat, with less than 10 per cent coming from animal sources. Cholesterol intake should be kept under 100 milligrams daily.

In 1986 the American Heart Association refined and clarified its position on cholesterol intake for the general population. While 300 milligrams remained the daily limit, the AHA recommended a maximum of 100 milligrams per 1000 calories consumed daily. So 300 milligrams would be the limit for someone eating 3000 calories; someone consuming 2000 calories should limit cholesterol to only 200 milligrams.

This would obviously necessitate a proportionate drop in recommendations for Phases II and III, although those recommendations have not yet been formulated. Interestingly, however, the AHA seems awkwardly unable to face the increasing evidence that the 20 per cent-of-calories level of fat intake is best for everyone and that this goal *can* be achieved. An AHA principal spokesperson and policy formulator told me it could take years for the general population to lower intake to Phase I. Those with insight will make the changes much, much sooner.

The place to begin, it seems logical to assume, is with Phase I. This is the same approach advocated by many health and medical authorities. The U.S. Department of Agriculture and the U.S. Department of Health, Education and Welfare jointly published the official 'Dietary Guidelines for Americans' in 1980.[14] That report suggests eating a wide variety of foods, avoiding too much fat, saturated fat, and cholesterol, eating foods with adequate starch and fibre, and avoiding too much sugar and sodium. That seems like good advice everyone can live with without feeling like a martyr. Then, as needed, fat intake can be further reduced.

Medical and scientific authorities in America finally came to a national consensus in 1987 with the issue of the first guidelines for cholesterol. The maximum, the government-sponsored panel declared, is 5.2 mmol/l regardless of age or sex. That, of course, is a far cry from what doctors had believed to be 'normal' in the past.

The panel members said they hoped that cholesterol levels would be more strictly controlled, thus greatly reducing a major risk factor in heart disease. They pointed to a parallel situation in 1970. At that time physicians were told that all patients should be examined for hypertension, and that elevated blood pressure should be aggressively treated to eliminate or reduce that heart disease risk. Some optimistically voiced the feeling that in years to come the risk of cholesterol would similarly be cut back tremendously.

Yet even the 5.2 mmol/l maximum cited by the panel may not be low enough. A premier cholesterol researcher, Dr Jeremiah Stamler published unequivocal proof of the value of lowering cholesterol levels even further. The article in the *Journal of the American Medical Association* reported the latest findings of the MR FIT (Multiple Risk Factor Intervention Trials) programme, in which 356,222 men aged 35 to 57 were screened for heart disease risk. [15] As the years have gone by since the first screening in 1973, death rates have been compared. The cholesterol findings are striking.

Dr Stamler states:

The relationship between serum cholesterol and CHD is *not* a threshold one, with increased risk confined to the highest quintiles, but rather is a continuously graded one that powerfully affects risk for the great majority of middle-aged American men.

The eminent researcher has concluded that even levels of 5.2 mmol/l are not low enough. Deaths from heart disease, he says, are 'attributable to serum cholesterol levels equal to or greater than 4.6 mmol/l.' Clearly, Dr Stamler is saying that getting those cholesterol levels as low as possible is the goal to aim for.

Of course, in looking at the total lipid levels and their effect on heart disease, we cannot lose track of the importance of the protective levels of HDL. A person with a level of 4.6 and an HDL of 1.0 would have a 4.5 ratio. Very good. Another person might have a level of 5.2 with an HDL of 1.3, for a ratio of 4.0. That might be even better. But in either case, no one should be completely satisfied until the total cholesterol is less than 5.2 or at least until the ratio is less than 4.5. The programme of The 8-Week Cholesterol Cure can do both.

Interesting, also, is the case of those fortunate individuals whose total cholesterol level is very low. Dr William Connor of the University of Oregon studied a group in the mountains of Mexico. The Tarahumara Indians live a truly primitive life. Their diet is sparse and extremely limited in animal origin foods. They exercise extensively, often playing a game of kicking a ball while racing on foot for up to twenty-four hours at a time without stopping. Taking blood samples, Dr Connor and his group found cholesterol levels around 3.1 to 3.4. The HDL level in the Indians was also very low. But there was no trace of heart disease in the entire population. Dr Connor concludes that when the total cholesterol level falls to very low values, the importance of the protective HDL becomes less significant.

Most of the research done in the area of heart disease has focused entirely on men. But, as already indicated, CHD is far from the exclusive lot of the male of our human species. Women, too, have the standard risk factors to consider, including elevated levels of cholesterol. Many of the subjects of my own research at Santa Monica Medical Center were women, and I receive as many letters from women as from men in response to my book.

Most authorities agree, in fact, that the risk of heart disease in women is on the rise. They cite increased risk factors including stress, cigarette smoking, and hypertension. The statistics bear them out. The number of women suffering heart attacks and having bypass surgery is increasing annually.

An article published in the *New England Journal of Medicine* casts new light on the relationship of menopause to the risk of CHD.[16] A total of 121,700 women aged 30 to 55 years were monitored for six years, from 1976 to 1982. While there was no increase of risk following natural menopause, women who had undergone hysterectomy involving removal of both ovaries were at increased risk. But that risk could be removed by oestrogen replacement therapy.

This indirectly demonstrates the protective aspects of oestrogen in women. There appears to be a link between that hormone and the levels of protective HDL. When women have the standard risk factors operating—cigarette smoking, hypertension, and elevated cholesterol levels with reduced HDLs—heart disease incidence climbs.

Women who participated in my study with oat bran and niacin showed particularly striking results in terms of elevation of the HDL levels, producing wonderfully improved ratios. There's no doubt about it, heart disease is not at all just a man's disease.

Selecting a sound diet

The problem for most people trying to do something to change a lifetime of dietary habits is thinking, 'What do I have to give up?' Instead, the proper approach should be 'What are the thousands of delicious foods I should pick?'

First of all, what is the purpose of eating? Basically, we should eat to live. Too many have learned to live to eat. It's time to get back to basics.

The purpose of a good diet is to provide all the nutrients we need to live a hearty, robust life. Those nutrients help us maintain and, in the case of children, grow our bodies.

While the plan has been criticized from time to time for being too simplistic, the basic four-food-group approach remains an excellent guideline for selecting foods. This plan calls for a wide variety of foods.

Adults need a minimum of two servings from the meat and dairy groups and four servings each from the fruit-vegetable and grain groups. Is this plan possible and practical for a calorie-and-cholesterol-conscious person? It definitely is if one remembers the advice to consume a *wide variety* of foods from these groups. And the plan comes to life when one stresses the importance of the latter two groups of foods. Stress the word *minimum* in the four servings.

In order to get all the protein needed, two servings from the meat group are completely sufficient. Some prefer to call this the protein group, since it also includes protein sources such as poultry, fish, and beans.

Is there anything wrong with beef? Or with any of the other red meats? Absolutely not, if eaten in moderation. But what constitutes a 'serving' of meat? It's not a twelve-ounce steak! A serving of meat should be no more than four ounces. And it's really not asking that much to trim the excess fat from the edges.

But there's more to the meat group than just red meat. Actually, relying on just one type of food becomes boring. Don't forget poultry and seafood. Practically every great chef in the world prides himself on thinking of fantastic ways to serve a whole world of foods.

Next we come to the dairy group. Milk products are an excellent source of calcium, protein, and vitamins A and D. But those nutrients do not reside in the fat. Low-fat or nonfat varieties of milk, yogurt, and cheese have all the same nutrients. Often they cost less. And, if at first your taste buds don't respond favourably, give yourself a little time to get used to the idea of the light flavours of the reduced-fat dairy foods. After a while, believe it or not, one actually comes to prefer the more healthful types.

When it comes to the fruit-vegetable group, there's no limit at all to what you may eat as long as you don't start gaining weight. Orange juice, for all its vitamin C, is also pretty heavy on calories. On the other hand, if you've cut down on fats, you can make up for those calories with fresh fruits of all types. Go into a good food store, or a fresh-fruit-and-vegetable store and treat yourself to a shopping bag full of fresh treats. 'Mangoes, papayas, chestnuts from the fire . . .' So goes an old Rosemary Clooney song.

Finally, the grain group. Now you can forget all the old rules about avoiding those so-called 'fattening' starches. Eat rice and rolls and breads if you want to—every single day. Don't even worry about the calories. And remember, in some parts of Europe and other countries where bread is considered a staple of life and a source of national pride, no one puts butter on the bread. It takes away from the taste of the bread itself.

When it comes to pasta, go wild. Enjoy all the forms and varieties you can find. A little marinara sauce, a fresh salad, a chunk of sourdough bread, and a glass of wine all make that spaghetti dinner a memorable occasion.

Since I started to cut down on fats, I don't have to count calories. Now I can eat all the food I want, with practically no limits. Instead, I count the milligrams of cholesterol and the amount of fat in the foods I select. Following the recipes in this book will help you to get started. You'll also find that many recipes printed in today's magazines list the milligrams of cholesterol and the grams of fat in each serving. You can cut those levels even further by doing some simple alterations, such as using egg substitute for egg yolks and by using soft margarine instead of butter. And, although there's nothing wrong with enjoying beef, pork, lamb, and veal, spread your imagination beyond those types of meat. Substitute a turkey cutlet for a veal cutlet. Try ground chicken breast instead of beef in your burgers. Experiment with different types of seafood you may have avoided before. Shish kebabs made with large scallops are fantastic!

The aim is to keep your fat and cholesterol intake low, the lower the better. No matter what else one may do to reduce cholesterol levels in the blood, the place to start is with the diet.

To help you start counting those grams and milligrams, you'll find some charts of commonly eaten foods and the amounts of fats and cholesterol found in typical serving sizes in Chapter 3. 'Winning by the Numbers'. After just a little while, you'll begin to gravitate toward those foods with low levels of fats and cholesterol and you won't even need the guideline charts.

I love the little motto I saw on the refrigerator of a friend trying to keep her gorgeous figure. The motto read: 'A moment on your lips, forever on your hips'. As nice as it is to preserve that slim figure, think how much more important it is to keep those arteries clear and flowing.

Remember the conclusion of the medical authorities who state emphatically that a cholesterol reduction of 35 per cent cuts the risk of heart disease in half. It's worth it!

How to read these tables

In any population group or groups, there will be an average level of fats in the blood. Data are presented here in percentiles. Figures given in the 5 per cent category are presented to show what low levels would be. On the other hand, those in the 95th percentile (95 per cent) in the categories of total cholesterol and LDL cholesterol are at the greatest risk of coronary heart disease. To help put things into perspective, populations that have little or no atherosclerotic cardiovascular disease often have LDL cholesterol levels that average below 2.6 mmol/l. [15] The risk of heart disease relates clearly to increasing LDL cholesterol above the 50th percentile. [17] This would be higher than 3.9 mmol/l for adults.

As an example of reading these tables, look at Table 1. For adult males aged 40 to 44 years, the average total cholesterol level is 5.3. Only 5 per cent of men have levels of 3.9 mmol/l. On the other end of the scale, 25 per cent of men in this age group (75th percentile or 75%) have levels of 6.0 mmol/l or greater; 10 per cent (90th percentile or 90%) have levels over 6.5 mmol/l; 5 per cent (95th percentile or 95%) have cholesterol levels of 7.0 or more.

Bear in mind that according to these tables of data, when compared to current clinical medical opinion, half the adult male population aged 40 to 44 have cholesterol levels that should be reduced.

Remember also that clinical trials indicate that each 1 per cent reduction in blood cholesterol levels produces a 2 per cent reduction in coronary heart disease. For example, a 5 per cent reduction in blood cholesterol should reduce disease rates by 10 per cent. How many investments can you think of in which you can double your input?

For many individuals, diet alone can reduce a moderately elevated cholesterol level of, say, 5.4 or 5.6 down to less than 5.2. This, as we'll see, is made even easier now with the addition of oat bran to the diet, as fully described in Chapter 4, 'Getting the Scoop on Oat Bran'. For those with more highly elevated levels a programme of diet modification, oat bran, and niacin has been shown to be dramatically effective. We'll talk more abut niacin in Chapter 5.

How effective? As you'll read in Chapter 13, 'The Proof of the Pudding', the programme results in cholesterol levels dropping 30, 35, 40, 45, even 50 per cent or more. One's risk of coronary heart disease comes tumbling down on this practical programme.

Moreoever, the protective HDL levels rise just as dramatically. All participants in a research study conducted to demonstrate the efficacy of this programme showed an average rise of 35 per cent in their HDL levels. Again, read the 'Proof' chapter.

There no longer is any controversy regarding cholesterol and its deadly effect. Many people have a tendency toward elevated cholesterol levels, which are made even worse by a fatty, cholesterol-laden diet. But those cholesterol levels can be cut down to size quickly and easily, resulting in the virtual elimination of this major risk factor.

Do you know your own cholesterol level? If not, the place to start is your doctor's surgery. Before the test it's important to fast completely for 12 to 14 hours before blood is taken. Within a week you'll know your own level of risk. Be sure to ask for the *exact* numbers rather than accept the soothing advice that your cholesterol level is 'normal'. If your level is low, thank your lucky stars. If it's above 5.2 this is the time to do something about it.

Table 1. **Plasma total cholesterol (mmol/l) in adult males**[8]

Age/years	Average	5%	75%	90%	95%
0–19	4.0	3.0	4.4	4.8	5.2
20–24	4.3	3.2	4.8	5.3	5.7
25–29	4.7	3.5	5.2	5.8	6.3
30–34	4.9	3.6	5.6	6.2	6.6
35–39	5.2	3.7	5.8	6.5	7.0
40–44	5.3	3.9	5.9	6.5	7.0
45–69	5.6	4.1	6.1	6.7	7.1
70 +	5.3	3.9	5.9	6.5	7.0

Table 2. **Plasma low-density lipoprotein cholesterol (mmol/l) in adult males**[8]

Age/years	Average	5%	75%	90%	95%
5–19	2.5	1.7	2.7	3.1	3.4
20–24	2.7	1.7	3.1	3.6	3.7
25–29	3.0	1.8	3.6	4.0	4.3
30–34	3.2	2.1	3.8	4.3	4.8
35–39	3.5	2.1	4.0	4.5	4.9
40–44	3.5	2.2	4.0	4.5	4.8
45–69	3.8	2.3	4.3	4.9	5.3
70 +	3.7	2.3	4.3	4.7	4.8

Table 3. **Plasma high-density lipoprotein cholesterol (mmol/l) in adult males**[8]

Age/years	Average	5%	10%	95%
5–19	1.4	0.9	1.0	1.9
15–19	1.2	0.8	0.9	1.7
20–24	1.2	0.8	0.8	1.7
25–29	1.2	0.8	0.8	1.7
30–34	1.2	0.8	0.8	1.7
35–39	1.2	0.8	0.8	1.5
40–44	1.2	0.6	0.8	1.7
45–69	1.3	0.8	0.8	1.8
70 +	1.3	0.8	0.9	1.9

Table 4. Plasma total cholesterol (mmol/l) in adult females[8]

Age/years	Average	5%	75%	90%	95%
0–19	4.1	3.1	4.5	4.9	5.2
20–24	4.4	3.2	4.9	5.6	5.9
25–34	4.5	3.4	5.0	5.7	6.1
35–39	4.8	3.6	5.3	5.9	6.3
40–44	5.0	3.7	5.6	6.1	6.6
45–49	5.3	3.9	5.8	6.5	7.0
50–54	5.7	4.3	6.2	6.8	7.4
55 +	5.9	4.4	6.5	7.1	7.6

Table 5. Plasma low-density lipoprotein cholesterol (mmol/l) in adult females[8]

Age/years	Average	5%	75%	90%	95%
5–19	2.6	1.7	2.8	3.2	3.6
20–24	2.7	1.4	3.1	3.6	4.1
25–34	2.8	1.8	3.2	3.7	4.1
35–39	3.1	1.9	3.6	4.1	4.4
40–44	3.2	1.9	3.7	4.3	4.5
45–49	3.4	2.1	3.9	4.5	4.8
50–54	3.6	2.3	4.1	4.8	5.2
55 +	3.9	2.5	4.4	5.0	5.6

Table 6. Plasma high-density lipoprotein cholesterol (mmol/l) in adult females[8]

Age/years	Average	5%	10%	95%
5–19	1.4	0.9	1.0	1.8
20–24	1.4	0.9	0.9	2.1
25–34	1.4	0.9	1.0	2.1
35–39	1.4	0.9	1.0	2.1
40–44	1.5	0.9	1.0	2.3
45–49	1.5	0.9	1.0	2.2
50–54	1.5	0.9	1.0	2.3
55 +	1.5	0.9	1.0	2.5

Table 7. Plasma triglycerides in males[8]

Age/years	Average	5%	90%	95%
0–9	0.6	0.3	0.9	1.1
10–14	0.7	0.3	1.1	1.4
15–19	0.9	0.4	1.4	1.7

Table 7. Plasma triglycerides in males[8] (cont'd)

Age/years	Average	5%	90%	95%
20–24	1.1	0.5	1.9	2.3
25–29	1.3	0.5	2.3	2.8
30–34	1.5	0.6	2.4	3.0
35–39	1.6	0.6	2.8	3.6
40–54	1.7	0.6	2.8	3.6
55–64	1.6	0.7	2.7	3.3
65 +	1.5	0.6	2.4	2.9

Table 8. Plasma triglycerides in females[8]

Age/years	Average	5%	90%	95%
0–9	0.7	0.4	1.1	1.2
10–19	0.8	0.5	1.3	1.5
20–34	1.0	0.5	1.6	1.9
35–39	1.1	0.5	1.8	2.2
40–44	1.2	0.5	1.9	2.4
45–49	1.2	0.5	2.1	2.6
50–54	1.4	0.6	2.1	2.7
55–64	1.4	0.6	2.3	2.8
65 +	1.5	0.7	2.3	2.7

Table 9. Plasma cholesterol and triglycerides in children before puberty[15]

	5%	50%	95%
Total cholesterol	3.2	4.0	5.2
LDL cholesterol	1.7	2.5	3.5
HDL cholesterol	1.0	1.4	1.9
VLDL cholesterol	0.1	0.3	0.5
Triglycerides	0.3	0.6	1.2

3. WINNING BY THE NUMBERS

More than twelve separate clinical trials have established that lowering levels of blood cholesterol can reduce the incidence of cardiovascular disease. Adults should aim for a total cholesterol level of less than 5.2 mmol/l. The National Institutes of Health in January 1985, stated that 'one-half of the U.S. population is at risk of coronary heart disease, with blood cholesterol levels above 5.2 mmol/l.'

The programme in this book is designed—and proven—to lower cholesterol levels by 20, 30, even 40 per cent or more. That's because this is the only programme to consider all three reasons for elevated cholesterol. You've been eating too much fat and cholesterol, so I'll show you some delicious ways to cut back on those culprits. Your body doesn't excrete sufficient cholesterol in the form of bile salts and bile acids through your intestine, so eating oat bran will increase the amount of cholesterol excreted. And your liver has been producing too much cholesterol, so by taking some niacin you'll short-circuit that production. By considering all three aspects, the programme is effective although it calls for only moderate dietary modification, a small amount of oat bran, and reasonable doses of niacin.

It's fairly straightforward to suggest eating three oat-bran muffins a day. And you can count the niacin tablets you swallow daily. But for most people, when it comes to percentages and figures and numbers about nutrition, the eyes just glaze over. Who can understand or remember all those numbers?

For example, the American Heart Association says that everyone in the United States should limit their cholesterol intake to no more than 300 milligrams a day. And the fat intake should be no more than 30 per cent of total calories, with 10 per cent each coming from saturated fat, polyunsaturated fat, and monounsaturated fat. Confusing? You bet. What does all that mean in the real world of shopping for and eating food?

Most people find it tough just to remember how many calories different foods have; it's difficult to memorize calories charts. The majority of us just learn that some foods are more 'fattening' than others.

Even then, there are tons of misconceptions. For example, that butter has more calories than margarine; actually they're identical. Or that pasta and baked potatoes are fattening; actually, it's only the fats we may put on those foods that add up the calories.

But, even if we don't known *anything* about calories, we can see the results in the mirror and on the bathroom scale. It's not quite so simple with cholesterol. Too many people don't know their levels are dangerously high until the doctor says it's time for bypass surgery.

Before we get into the actual details of how to win by the numbers, I want you to think about something obvious. We all learn things a little bit at a time. Today we can all tell the difference between an inch and a mile, and between an ounce and a gallon. We know that something weighs 'about a pound', and that another thing is 'about six inches long'. We've learned those things by experience over the years.

It'll take a little time, but you can also learn the numbers that can help you live a long life. It's worth the effort. So let's start with something very basic: how to figure out how much food to eat to stay healthy and at ideal body weight.

As adults, we're no longer growing in the same way children grow. Our bones, skin, and muscles are pretty much developed. Therefore, we need far less food, in proportion, than we did when we were younger. But how much?

Only two variables come into play: first, whether you're a man or woman; second, whether you're sedentary, moderately active, or very active. Then decide your ideal weight. The weight table (page 105) specifies weights most health authorities have accepted as beneficial for optimum health.

The next step is to decide to feed *only* your ideal weight, *not* the weight you have today—unless, of course, you are already at ideal weight. If you weigh, let's say, 175 lb (12½ stone) and should weigh only 150 lb (10¾ stone), then feed only your 150 lb (10¾ stone) self—let the other 25 lb (1¾ stone) slowly drift away.

An adult man with a moderately active lifestyle will require 15 calories for every pound of his weight. If he starts to become involved with a really strenuous exercise programme, he may need an extra calorie per pound. If he becomes sedentary, like so many men, he'll be able to burn even fewer than 15 calories per pound.

Despite all requests for equal rights, women unfortunately have different metabolisms, and, for the most part, they burn fewer calories per pound. A moderately active woman needs only 12 calories per pound of ideal body weight.

The calculations, then, are rather simple:

Moderately active man
150 lb (10¾ stone) × 15 calories/lb = 2250 calories/day

Relatively unactive man
150 lb (10¾ stone) × 13 calories/lb = 1950 calories/day

Moderately active woman
120 lb (8½ stone) × 12 calories/lb = 1440 calories/day'

Relatively unactive woman
120 lb (8½ stone) × 10 calories/lb = 1200 calories/day

Obviously, if you are greatly overweight, or if you get turned on to heavy-duty exercise, your caloric needs will be different Read Chapters 7 and 8, on weight loss and exercise, for more specifics. But, for the most part, these are the caloric needs for the male and female examples I've chosen. Now do the calculations for yourself.

Counting calories is fairly simple. Some foods today have very informative nutrition labels. Many magazines today provide complete nutrition breakdowns along with their recipes, listing the amount of fat, cholesterol, sodium, and calories provided per serving. *Good Housekeeping* and *Weight Watchers Magazine* are two good examples. The chart at the end of this chapter lists fat, cholesterol, sodium, and calories found in many commonly consumed foods. And you may wish to purchase a complete calories counter in booklet form. You'll quickly see that foods with the most calories also have the most fat.

Carbohydrates and proteins contain just 4 calories per gram. There are about 28 grams to an ounce, for those who don't 'think metric'. But fat contains 9 calories per gram! If you just cut down on the amount of fat you eat, you'll automatically and dramatically reduce calories.

Which brings us to the very important consideration of how to determine how much fat to include in our daily food intake.

First, the average diet is between 40 and 50 per cent fat. And every medical authority agrees that's too much. The UK Committee on Medical Aspects of Food Policy (COMA) recommends 30 per cent for the general population. Many feel that those with an elevated cholesterol level should cut down to less than 30 per cent. And those at real risk should cut down to just 10 per cent. With this complete programme. I was able to bring my own cholesterol level down by taking the middle-ground level of 20 per cent fat intake. Dozens of others have proved that anyone can do the same. So aim for that 20 per cent number, or 30 per cent if your cholesterol is not too high, and here's how to do your calculation for your own body.

Let's take the example of the 150 lb (10¾ stone) man who's moderately active. He needs 2250 calories daily in order to neither gain nor lose weight. And because he's on this programme to dramatically reduce his cholesterol level he's decided to consume only 20 per cent of calories as fat.

So we multiply 2250 calories by 20 per cent to get a total of 450 calories as fat. What does that mean? How can we tell how much food provides 450 calories as fat?

Fat, as you'll recall, provides 9 calories per gram. The man in our example wants to eat no more than 450 calories as fat. Therefore we divide 450 calories by 9, the number of calories per gram, to give us 50 grams. So our man can now limit himself to 50 grams of fat daily. That's a good target, even if he misses by a bit.

Personally, I have found the 20 per cent level, providing 50 grams of fat daily, to be right for me. It's right because my regular blood cholesterol tests indicate that my serum cholesterol remains in the safe zone. But will this be right for you? Each of us has a slightly different body, with its own metabolism. You may find that you can increase the percentage to, say, 25 per cent of calories as fat. Start with that 20 per cent level and go from there.

Again, it's the combination of the aspects of this programme that allows us to only moderately modify the diet. Other authorities including the late Nathan Pritikin say it is an all-or-nothing situation. Until this programme came along, they were right. And that deserves some explanation.

Researchers have found that the body has what they call a saturation level for fat and cholesterol intake. Some people have a relatively low blood cholesterol level even though they consume a lot of dietary fat and cholesterol. Others, including myself, don't metabolize fat and cholesterol as well. But dietary intake does have impact on everyone to one degree or another.

If one were to find a group of normal, healthy men and women whose cholesterol levels were, say, an average of 4.4 and feed them an extra egg daily, their cholesterol levels would go up. The same would apply if one added several extra grams of fat daily. But if another group had an already elevated level of, for example, 6.5, the extra fat or cholesterol would not have as much if any effect. Those persons would be at their saturation levels and it would take a considerable amount of additional fat and cholesterol to drive their levels in the blood higher.

The converse also applies. If one has an elevated cholesterol level and cuts back only a bit, there will be little or no effect. That's why so many people over the years have claimed that dietary cholesterol has little to do with serum cholesterol. Eliminate egg yolks, eat very little meat, and do all the other modifications, and there still will be an elevated level. It's only when one almost completely eliminates fat and cholesterol from the diet than an elevated cholesterol level can be brought back down to truly safe levels of between 3.9 and 4.7.

That's why the Pritikin diet and others require such strict adherence. For persons with elevated cholesterol levels which put them at risk, the saturation points are very low. The diet, therefore, must be all-or-nothing.

The 8-Week Cholesterol Cure, however, considers all three aspects of elevated cholesterol. Diet is only one of those three aspects. While it is still very important to modify the diet, eating oat bran and supplementing the diet with niacin will complete the cholesterol-lowering effect we all want.

The table at the end of this chapter clearly states the amount of both fat and cholesterol found in commonly used foods. Some shellfish have considerable amounts of cholesterol, though still much lower than previously believed. These foods, however, have very low levels of fat. So they can be enjoyed in moderation as long as they are not fried.

Do some other comparisons in the chart. Note that while turkey breast and beef cuts contain just about the same amount of cholesterol in a 3½-ounce serving, the difference in the amount of fat is enormous. One serving of turkey provides less than 2 grams, while the same weight of porterhouse steak gives you nearly 15 grams!

But does that mean you can't ever have a piece of beef? Certainly not. Just remember that you want to keep your total fat consumption and cholesterol intake down on a daily basis. If you want a piece of steak for the evening meal, cut down on fat in the rest of your foods that day. And choose the cuts of beef lower in fat content.

I grew up in Chicago, a city famous for its steaks. There the fine steak houses took pride in their 24-ounce sirloins, or the porterhouses they delivered on an oversized platter. That's just totally unacceptable for *anyone* today. There's no reason in the world to eat that much meat at one sitting—even the National Live Stock and Meat Board in Chicago agrees!

On the other hand, a 3½-ounce piece of meat may not be enough to satisfy that urge for an occasional rare steak. So double the amount. Sure it's o.k. to do it now and then. You'll be consuming 140 milligrams of cholesterol, and, for a T-bone steak, 28.4 grams of fat. Just know what you're doing. Then, to make up for that intake, avoid sour cream on the potato, pass up butter with your bread, and have just a touch of oil and vinegar dressing on your salad.

Take a few moments right now to calculate your own calories and fat intake for the day. Actually work with a piece of paper and a pencil to caculate the numbers for yourself. This is important, so don't skip it. Here's how to do your own determination of daily fat intake in grams.

Mark down the weight you would like to maintain

(ideal weight) . . . . . .

Now multiply that weight by the appropriate number of calories depending on the amount you exercise. Multiply by 10 calories if you are a sedentary adult woman, by 11 calories if you are a sedentary adult man, by 12 calories if you're a moderately active woman, and by 15 calories if you are a moderately active man. Those are the numbers of calories needed to maintain one pound of weight. So, by multiplying your ideal weight by the appropriate number of calories per pound, you'll have the number of calories you need to maintain that ideal weight. If you weigh more than the ideal weight, and still eat only enough calories to maintain the ideal weight, the extra weight will gradually disappear.

(ideal weight) × (calories per pound) = daily calorie intake
   in pounds

. . . .

Now let's determine how many of those calories will come from fat. Ideally, we want to consume 20 per cent of our calories as fat. So we multiply our daily calorie intake by 20 per cent.

(daily calorie intake) × .20 = daily calories as fat

. . . .   .20 = ...

What does that mean in terms of grams of fat? Each gram of fat provides nine calories. So we divide the calories eaten as fat by nine to determine the daily allowance of fat as measured in grams.

$$\frac{\text{(daily calories as fat)}}{9} = \underline{\text{daily allowance of fat in grams}}$$

$$\frac{\rule{3cm}{0.4pt}}{9} = \underline{\rule{4cm}{0.4pt}}$$

Now that you know how many grams of total fat you should limit yourself to, remember that there are three kinds of fat to choose from. Medical authorities recommend that you divide your fat intake evenly among saturated fats, polyunsaturated fats, and monounsaturated fats. Table 10 at the end of this chapter shows where those fats are found. You'll notice that not many foods provide monounsaturated fats. So for all practical purposes, and this is a practical book, you can really divide your fat grams between animal and plant sources. Emphasize vegetable fats. With one little exception: watch for the labels that tell you the oil is from coconuts or palm or that the oil is 'partially hydrogenated'. Those fats are saturated and belong in the same category as fats from animal sources.

There are so many terrific alternative recipes around that you'll wonder why anyone would ever complain about modifying the diet. This is modification, far, far, far, from deprivation!

Even if recipes don't specifically list the fat and cholesterol, it's fairly easy to see if the foods in question are o.k. Just use Table 10 at the end of this chapter.

What if you see recipes that are particularly appealing but are laden with no-nos? Or what about those cherished family recipes that you really love? Do you have to give them up? Never! Just substitute ingredients.

There are very few foods that don't have very acceptable low-fat, low-cholesterol substitutes. And you'll find that, if a recipe calls for ½ cup of oil, ¼ cup will do just as well. Maybe you'll even be able to get by with just ⅛ cup. As your tastes start to change, and believe me and everyone else who's done it, they will, you'll actually *prefer* the lighter, lower-fat versions.

Here are some helpful tips for substitutions in your recipes:

One whole egg = two egg whites
Cream = evaporated skimmed milk
Whole milk = nonfat milk
Butter = soft margarine or corn oil
Oil to fry = grilling
Shortening in baking = substitute ripe banana for half the shortening

You'll find many more hints about how to fill your pantry shelves with terrific foods and food substitutes in Chapter 12, 'Let's Go Shopping'. There are a number of fine foods available if you know what to look for in the supermarket. But by all means, when you go shopping, be sure you have the time to read those labels. Don't just rush out. Especially at the beginning when you're learning to recognize the hidden fats, schedule plenty of shopping time into the week.

Don't stop reading when you've finished a nutrient label. Find the ingredient listing on the side of the package. Ingredients are listed *in order of volume*. Don't forget that. If water is listed first, that means there's more water than anything else. If sugar tops the list, then you know you're getting a lot of sugar.

Pick up a number of foods to choose from. Look at the labels for both whole milk and nonfat milk. Not only do you have the problem of fat and cholesterol, a serving of whole milk provides 150 calories while nonfat milk has only 89. Now turn to the yogurt. Not all are the same, by a long shot. Opt for the low-fat or nonfat varieties. Look at the number of grams of fat contained in each.

Since few foods, however, list cholesterol content, take some time to learn where that cholesterol lurks. Remember that you are aiming for less than 250 milligrams daily. For some foods, that's a real problem while for others it's not at all. An egg yolk contains about 250 milligrams of cholesterol all by itself. You have two choices: either find an egg substitute, or eat just one egg yolk as your source of total cholesterol for the day. I personally don't feel that eating one egg yolk is worth giving up everything else for the day, so I've simply cut egg yolks out entirely. But my shopping cart is always loaded with eggs. I just use the whites.

You'll be surprised how quickly you'll learn the cholesterol levels of foods so that you won't have to consult the chart every time you bite into something. At the beginning, though, you'll also be surprised to see cholesterol in foods you never even thought of as culprits.

You'll have to know how *much* you're eating to successfully modify your diet. How big is a serving? For many people a steak, no matter how large, is a serving. In realistic terms, a serving of meat should be about four ounces. Don't forget: that's a whole quarter of a pound! Some hamburgers brag about being that large. If you don't know how much four ounces is, make a small investment in a food scale for the kitchen. After a while your eye will become trained to make accurate estimates.

Many individuals must also restrict the amount of sodium in the diet owing to high blood pressure, hypertension. The role of sodium is discussed fully in Chapter 6 (see page 95).

And nutrition isn't just a matter of learning what *not* to eat. This also means increasing the amounts of certain foods. Most women, for example, need far more calcium and iron than their present diets offer. That's spelled out in Chapter 11.

You'll be amazed, as time goes by, how easy it will be to choose one food over another because of the numbers you'll learn. Whether eating at home, in a restaurant, or at friends' homes, you'll come out a winner. There's nothing like the feeling of satisfaction you'll get when the doctor announces how dramatically your cholesterol level has dropped. *That's* winning by the numbers!

Type of fat found in foods
Saturated fat
Most fat from animal sources: beef, pork, lamb, veal, poultry, and fish

Coconut oil
Palm oil
Hydrogenated or partially hydrogenated vegetable oil

Monounsaturated fat
Olives and olive oil
Peanuts and peanut oil
Avocados

Polyunsaturated fat
Vegetable oils other than those listed above.

Note: Cholesterol is found only in animal sources.

These charts give a representative look at the foods you probably eat regularly. Don't try to memorize them, but do become familiar with trends in composition for types of foods. Certainly, it is not possible to list all the thousands of foods in the supermarket.

Table 10. Calorie, fat, cholesterol, and sodium content of foods

Food	Serving Size	Calories	Fat (grams)	Cholesterol (mg)	Sodium (mg)
Cheese					
Blue	1oz	107	8.3	25	402
Camembert	1oz	88	6.6	20	399
Cheddar	1oz	120	9.5	19	173
Cottage	1oz	27	1.1	4	127
Cream	1oz	125	13.4	27	85
Edam	1oz	90	6.5	20	278
Parmesan (grated)	1oz	118	8.4	25	215
Stilton	1oz	131	11.4	34	326
Dairy Foods					
Butter	1oz	210	23	65	245
Channel Islands Milk	1oz	22	1.5	5	14
Cow's Milk	1oz	19	1	4	14
Cream (single)	1oz	60	6	19	12
Cream (double)	1oz	125	14	40	8
Cream (sterilized)	1oz	64	6.5	21	16
Evaporated Milk	1oz	44	2.5	10	51
Longlife Milk	1oz	18	1	4	11
Skimmed Milk (whole)	1oz	10	0.03	0.63	15
Skimmed Milk (dried)	1oz	100	0.4	5	156
Sterilized Milk	1oz	18	1	4	11

Table 10. Calorie, fat, cholesterol, and sodium content of foods

Food	Serving Size	Calories	Fat (grams)	Cholesterol (mg)	Sodium (mg)
Eggs					
Boiled	one egg	74	5	225	70
Fried	one egg	116	10	Depends on fat used	110
Poached	one egg	78	5.5	240	55
Omelette	one egg	95	8	205	515
Scrambled	one egg	123	11	205	525
Fish					
Cod (steamed)	4oz	100	1	68	113
Haddock (steamed)	4oz	120	0.75	68	136
Halibut (steamed)	4oz	148	4.5	68	124
Lemon sole (steamed)	4oz	102	1	68	136
Plaice (steamed)	4oz	105	2	79	135
Whiting (steamed)	4oz	104	1	124	147
Herring (grilled)	4oz	225	15	90	192
Kipper (baked)	4oz	232	13	90	1118
Mackerel (fried)	4oz	212	13	100	170
Salmon (tinned)	4oz	175	9	100	644
Sardines	4oz	245	15	113	735
Trout (steamed)	4oz	152	5	90	99
Tuna	4oz	326	25	73	475
Crab (tinned)	4oz	91	6	113	418
Lobster (boiled)	4oz	135	4	170	373
Prawns	4oz	121	2	226	1797
Scampi (fried)	4oz	357	20	124	429
Shrimps	4oz	132	3	226	4339
Cockles	4oz	54	0.3	45	3978
Mussels	4oz	75	2	113	327
Oysters	4oz	58	1	57	576
Whelks	4oz	103	2	113	305
Winkles	4oz	84	1.6	113	1288
Fish fingers	4oz	263	14	57	396
Meats					
Bacon (fried)	4oz	531	48	96	2113
Bacon (grilled)	4oz	475	40	86	2260
Beef	4oz	300	29	93	340

Table 10. Calorie, fat, cholesterol, and sodium content of foods

Food	Serving Size	Calories	Fat (grams)	Cholesterol (mg)	Sodium (mg)
Lamb	4oz	183	10	124	99
Pork	4oz	166	8	113	86
Chicken	4oz	142	6	113	101
Duck	4oz	214	11	181	109
Turkey	4oz	193	7	70	59
Rabbit	4oz	202	9	78	36
Liver - calf	4oz	173	15	373	192
- lamb	4oz	262	16	452	215
- ox	4oz	225	10	271	124
- pig	4oz	215	9	328	147
Heart - lamb		135	6	158	158
- ox	4oz	203	7	260	203
Kidney - lamb	4oz	175	7	689	305
- ox	4oz	194	9	778	452
- pig	4oz	173	7	790	420
Corned beef	4oz	245	14	96	1074
Ham	4oz	136	6	37	1413
Luncheon meat	4oz	354	31	60	1187
Black pudding	4oz	345	25	77	1367
Faggots	4oz	303	21	89	927
Haggis	4oz	350	25	103	870
Liver sausage	4oz	350	30	136	972
Beef sausages	4oz	304	20	47	1243
Pork sausages	4oz	359	28	60	1158
Beefburgers	4oz	298	20	77	994
Cornish pastie	4oz	375	23	55	667
Pork pie	4oz	424	11	59	813
Sausage roll	4oz	523	9	34	655
Puddings					
Fruit cake	3.5oz	350	11	50	170
Gingerbread	3.5oz	375	13	60	210
Rock Cake	3.5oz	395	16	40	480
Sponge Cake	3.5oz	464	27	260	350
Eclairs	3.5oz	375	24	90	160
Cheesecake	3.5oz	420	35	95	260
Custard (from powder)	3.5oz	118	4	16	76
Ice cream	3.5oz	165	7	21	80
Lemon meringue	3.5oz	320	15	90	200

Table 10. Calorie, fat, cholesterol, and sodium content of foods

Food	Serving Size	Calories	Fat (grams)	Cholesterol (mg)	Sodium (mg)
Pancakes	3.5oz	300	16	65	50
Suet puddings	3.5oz	333	18	4	470
Trifle	3.5oz	160	6	50	50

4. GETTING THE SCOOP ON OAT BRAN

Other than a few hermits living in caves up in the hills, I don't imagine there's a single man, woman, or child who hasn't heard about the benefits of fibre in the diet. Everywhere you turn, someone's telling you to increase your fibre intake.

In case you haven't paid really close attention, the whole thing began in 1972 when Dr Dennis Burkitt, who had been studying primitive tribes in Africa, wrote a landmark paper published in *The Lancet*.[1] He observed that when the diet contains a lot of roughage, stools are softer and larger, and bowel movements are far more frequent. His conclusion, comparing the health of Africans with that of Westerners, was that dietary fibre has a role in the prevention of certain large-intestine diseases, including cancer of the colon and diverticulitis. He also noted that 'the serum-cholesterol rises when fibre is removed from the diet. Eating a fibre-rich diet or adding cellulose to the diet lowers the serum-cholesterol.'

That began a series of scientific discussions and research studies that have continued to this day. Dr David Kritchevsky, working at the Wistar Institute in Philadelphia, found that alfalfa did a good job of keeping cholesterol levels down in rabbits. Of course, humans couldn't eat alfalfa, but the work went on.

The story of fibre became a favourite with the media. There were high-fibre recipes in magazines and newspapers and pep talks on TV. Books were published on how to get more fibre into practically everything we eat. Quickly responding to the strong public demand, the food industry began actively marketing fibre in a wide variety of foods. Advertizing pointed out the fibre benefits of breads and cereals, especially breakfast cereals.

But, while a rose is a rose is a rose, not all fibre is the same. It's not that any harm can be done by consuming one fibre rather than another. Rather, different fibres accomplish different health benefits. For example, wheat fibre is excellent for speeding up the 'transit time' it takes for food to move through the digestive tract.[2] Such fibre is the ultimate natural laxative. In fact, a number of different kinds of fibre from a wide variety of food sources will achieve that same goal.

Unfortunately, however, the same does not hold true for the ability of all fibre to lower cholesterol levels. Research findings have been building over the past few years until now we have conclusive evidence that oat bran is the fibre of choice for those who want to keep their cholesterol levels out of the risk zone. It's a fascinating story that's worth telling.

Most of us are familiar with oatmeal, or rolled oats. That oatmeal is made by treating the whole grain with steam and then passing the grains between rolls to produce flakes. Grinding the oat flakes and sifting results in two milling fractions. There's a fine fraction, flour, and a coarse fraction known as oat bran. For a long time oat bran was available only in health-food stores, but because of greater demand you can now find it in some supermarkets as well.

The difference between oat bran and wheat bran is that oat bran contains a large portion of soluble fibre whereas wheat has mainly insoluble fibre. It's the soluble fibre that is capable of lowering cholesterol levels. [3]

Table 11 on page 68 lists the fibre content of various foods. Note that wheat bran has the most total plant fibre, but most of it is insoluble. Oat bran, on the other hand, has more soluble fibre than any other food.

But fibre is only part of oat bran's appeal nutritionally. A look at the nutrition information on the side of the oat-bran packet shows that a 100g serving has a substantial amount of protein, energy-providing carbohydrate, and the B-vitamin thiamin.

Before describing in detail what oat bran does and the research studies that back up its claims, here's an overview of just what can be expected by making oat bran a part of the daily diet. Oat bran significantly lowers both total cholesterol and LDL cholesterol while not at all lowering the protective HDL levels. As a side benefit, oat bran helps maintain a normal glucose level in the blood of diabetic patients.

Investigations regarding oat bran have been conducted all over the world. Both animal and human studies have consistently demonstrated the significant effect oat bran has on cholesterol levels in the blood. As is true with almost all breakthroughs in human nutrition and medicine, the first discoveries about the benefits of oat bran took place in laboratories where researchers studied animals. The first observation, made in the Netherlands in 1963, showed that rolled oats significantly lowered the cholesterol levels of rats. [4]

Then in 1967 scientists at Rutgers University in New Jersey determined that it was the fibre in oatmeal that was the effective portion.[5] Quaker Oats in the US, understandably interested in these findings, began doing its own studies and found that the specific element that lowered cholesterol was the gum fraction of oat bran. Over the years, numerous investigations on a wide variety of animals confirmed the initial discovery: that oat bran has a strong hypo-cholesterolaemic effect—it lowers cholesterol. One of the most active researchers during the early animal studies was Dr James Anderson at the Department of Medicine at the University of Kentucky in Lexington. His work and that of his colleagues really laid the foundation for human investigations to follow.

Interestingly, Dr Anderson first looked at oat bran as a food for controlling glucose levels in diabetic patients. He found that those patients also benefited in terms of reduced cholesterol levels.

To look more closely at just how oat bran works, Dr Anderson has done a number of metabolic studies with men who have high cholesterol levels. These are very tightly controlled investigations in which all individuals are fed exactly the same diet, the composition of which is known ounce-for-ounce and gram-for-gram each and every day.

One such study involved eight men given 100 grams of oat bran daily.[6] That's the equivalent of about one cup of cereal. They ate the bran in the form of muffins. Total cholesterol levels fell by 13 per cent and LDL levels went down by 14 per cent.

In another controlled study, six men were admitted to the metabolic ward and fed control diets for seven days, then switched to diets supplemented with 100 grams of oat bran for twenty-one days.[7] Serum cholesterol levels were stable on the control diets and averaged 280 mg/dl. That put the men at significant risk of developing heart disease. With oat-bran supplements, average serum cholesterol dropped to 77.8 per cent of the control values during the second week and were stable until the men went home after three weeks. At home, they ate a high-fibre diet containing 50 grams of oat bran daily, and were able to maintain a 23.5 per cent decrease from their original cholesterol levels. These results are comparable to those obtained using drugs such as colestipol or cholestyramine.

Using other experimental conditions, Dr Anderson showed that oatbran feeding reduced serum LDL cholesterol concentrations by 36 per cent while increasing HDL by 82 per cent.[8] He notes that feeding other water-soluble fibre forms such as pectin or guar will lower serum cholesterol concentrations, but both cause intolerable nausea and vomiting as common side effects.

Most recently, Dr Anderson showed that oat-bran diets decreased total serum cholesterol concentrations by 19 per cent and LDL cholesterol by 23 per cent.[9] Interestingly, even after the men went home, continuing to eat oat bran daily, their cholesterol levels fell even further, down a total of 24 per cent. This indicates that the longer one stays on a diet including oat bran, the greater the effects. The men ate 50 grams of oat bran daily, the equivalent of three muffins.

The total diet fed the men in this recent study is also striking in that it is typical of the average American diet. Twenty per cent of calories came in the form of protein, 43 per cent as carbohydrates, 37 per cent as fat, with approximately 430 milligrams of cholesterol each day. That diet, in other words, is not restricted at all. Note that the American Heart Association recommends keeping the cholesterol intake down to 300 milligrams daily for the entire population. For those with elevated cholesterol levels the AHA advises cutting down to as low as 150 milligrams daily. Bear in mind that one egg yolk contains about 250 milligrams of cholesterol. Even a very lean three-ounce serving of beef contains nearly 100 milligrams. Think of what the results might have been if Dr Anderson had combined his oat-bran regimen with a more modified diet!

What do these findings and statistics mean to the average person? Simply stated, even without restricting the diet radically, one can expect considerable lowering of cholesterol by simply eating three oat-bran muffins a day. Assuming the same results Dr Anderson found, some simple arithmetic shows that a person with a 6.9 mmol/l cholesterol level can anticipate dropping that number down under the 5.2 mmol/l level. Most authorities agree that keeping total serum cholesterol counts down under 5.2 greatly protects against heart disease. That encouragement makes those muffins taste even more delicious!

Can the same results be achieved with oatmeal? Since oat bran is one fraction of the oat flake, it would take more oatmeal than oat bran to achieve the same levels of lowering. There's no question, however, that oatmeal also exerts a cholesterol-lowering effect.

How does oat bran work?

No one knows for certain how oat bran works. Most papers written on the subject point to the fact that, when oat bran is included in the diet, the excretion of bile acids increases.[7,8,9] What does that mean? Bile acids are formed by the liver from cholesterol. The more bile acids are excreted, the more the liver has to make. The more acids are made, the more cholesterol is drawn out of the blood, and eventually out of other parts of the body. Thus there is less chance of cholesterol being deposited in the arteries. This could very well be the reason oat bran reduces levels of cholesterol.

A comparison of oat bran with drugs such as colestipol and cholestyramine is interesting and informative. Both of these drugs are resins which cling to bile acids in the intestine, causing them to be excreted and thus lowering the cholesterol level. This is not to suggest that oat bran is a drug but rather that the drugs seem to mimic the activity of this natural cereal food.

In one of Dr Anderson's studies, two diets fed to eight men during a ten-day period of time differed only in that one contained 100 grams of oat bran. It has been shown that results will begin to appear in this short a period of time, but that maximum results develop over a longer time span. Again in this study, the diet was not restricted; a relatively large amount of fat and cholesterol were included on a daily basis. The results showed that low-density cholesterol levels dropped 14 per cent, while HDL levels remained the same.

Additional benefits of oat bran

It shouldn't come as any surprise that oat bran has a number of benefits beyond the lowering of cholesterol levels. High-fibre diets such as those including oat bran actually lower insulin requirements for diabetic patients and help control blood sugar. Dr Anderson's research has documented that high-fibre, high-carbohydrate diets brought insulin requirements down by 25 to 50 per cent,[10] and also greatly helped those diabetic patients who previously required drugs other than insulin to control their disease. Using the high-fibre, high-carbohydrate diet, Dr Anderson was able to discontinue drug therapy for 90 per cent of non-insulin-dependent diabetic patients.

This same approach to the diet, with high intake of fibre such as oat bran, has been demonstrated to lower blood pressure by about 10 per cent.[11] Additional studies are under way to further investigate this advantage.

There is a very special added benefit that may come as a pleasant surprise: eating a diet rich in oat-bran fibre virtually assures weight control. Some of the reasons for this are relatively obvious. First, eating a high-fibre apple is more satisfying than gulping a glass of apple juice. The simple act of chewing is more enjoyable than swallowing. Second, the fibre replaces other high-fat and high-calorie foods, resulting in a reduction of calories.

Most significantly, when one eats a lot of oat bran, say three muffins a day, one just doesn't feel hungry. This is more than a matter of simply filling the stomach and saying, 'I'm full'. Personally, after having my three muffins and a fruit-milk shake in the morning, I never even think about food until well past noon.

Oat bran keeps you satisfied. Compare this with the familiar story of being hungry an hour after eating a Chinese meal. There's a scientific reason for this. Chinese food typically is low in fat, especially true for Cantonese specialities. The vegetables and rice don't provide long-term satisfaction, so people get hungry faster than after a hamburger or steak dinner.

In addition to the fat content of food, satisfaction depends very largely on how quickly the food moves through the digestive tract. As it happens, oat bran slows down the rate of the so-called 'gastric emptying', the time it takes to move out of the stomach. This adds to the feeling of fullness. Additionally, high-fibre foods provide more food mass in the small intestine and alter intestinal hormone secretion.

Certain nutrients such as carbohydrates are absorbed more slowly after high-fibre meals than after meals of low-fibre, refined foods. This slow absorption of nutrients for hours after fibre-rich meals contributes to that satisfied feeling.

Dr Anderson reports three reasons as to why oat bran may help in weight reduction.[11] First, there is a certain amount of loss of calories directly through the faeces. Second, carbohydrates are not fully metabolized. And third, fibre-rich foods such as oat bran require more energy to digest, thus actually increasing the rate at which calories are burned. Obviously, for those individuals who have a few pounds to lose, this is a tremendous benefit. For me personally, the diet plan including oat bran has meant that I can eat virtually as much food as I want. In fact, if there are a couple of days in a row when I don't make a point of eating as much as usual, I'll lose a pound or two. I actually have to eat more food, far more food, than I used to in order to maintain my weight.

Virtually every nutrition and medical authority has stated unequivocally that people should increase their fibre intake. COMA published its guidelines on diet in 1984.[12] The advice given has been very well publicized in the media. In essence the guidelines call for eating a wide variety of foods, avoiding too much fat, saturated fat, and cholesterol, eating foods with adequate starch and fibre, and avoiding too much sugar and sodium.

To achieve those goals the authorities recommend eating more complex carbohydrates in place of simple starches and sugars. This can be done by selecting foods high in fibre such as whole-grain breads and cereals and fruits and vegetables. A logical choice would be oat-bran cereal, since in addition to the benefits usually associated with fibre there are a number of other highly significant health advantages, as we've seen.

Are there any reasons not to eat oat bran? Only one caution was

ever expressed about eating a lot of fibre such as oat bran. Some
authorities worried whether certain nutrients might be lost because
of the effect on the intestine. I'm happy to report, however, that research
has shown no such ill effects from oat-bran and other high-fibre diets. [11]
In one recent study fifteen patients were given a high-fibre diet for
nearly two years. Their levels of nutrients, including calcium,
phosphorus, iron, magnesium, vitamin B_{12}, folic acid, and vitamins
A, D, and K, were studied and found to be absolutely unaffected.
Follow-up studies showed similar results after more than four years.

The conclusion is simple: there are lots of good reasons to start
eating oat bran and other fibre-rich foods, and no good reasons not
to. If an apple a day keeps the doctor away, a few oat-bran muffins
appear to do the same for cardiologists!

Will you notice any difference after you start eating oat bran
regularly? Unless you're already eating quite a bit of fibre in your
diet, oat bran will greatly improve your regularity. Constipation will
never be a problem. In fact, you may even expect more than one bowel
movement daily. Dr Burkitt's orginal observations in Africa indicated
that frequent bowel movements are, in fact, beneficial, and doctors
no longer tell patients that it's perfectly normal not to move one's
bowels daily.

While you're eating oat bran, the stools will be larger and softer.
Not runny or unpleasant, but much softer and more easily passed.
As might be expected, however, with the increased bowel activity comes
a certain amount of flatulence. Rest assured, this does lessen over time,
and it's perfectly normal.

Taking that first bite

Oat-bran cereal is available in some supermarkets and health-food
stores. As time goes on, you can expect to see it more and more.
Generally, oat bran comes as a breakfast cereal.

But cereal is just the beginning. You can use oat bran as a main
ingredient to make delicious oat bran muffins (see page 170).

I found that, while oat bran is very different from other flours and
cooking ingredients I had used before, it's really quite easy to work
with. Since I'm not particularly fond of hot cereal, muffins seemed
the logical way to go.

Personally I find myself on a tight schedule almost every day. I just
don't have time to sit down and eat a nice little breakfast or brunch
while reading the newspaper. Almost always it's a matter of eating
on the run, often gulping my food right over the sink to save clean-up

time. For me, and I think for millions of other busy men and women, muffins are the perfect fast food. That's not to say that such a fast-paced life is best. Sure, I prefer a relaxed breakfast with time to read the morning newspaper. But a somewhat rushed breakfast is far better than none at all. Frequently, also, I'll take the muffins with me in the car—you can't do that with bacon and eggs!

The beauty of muffins is that it's practically impossible to get tired of them. One day it's apple-cinnamon, the next day banana-date, the next day pineapple, with a shake to match. To make them even more delicious, I pop my muffins into the microwave oven for just 30 seconds to warm them. This is particularly useful since I store the muffins in the refrigerator to keep them from spoiling.

Some people like to add fibre such as oat bran to a blender shake. This adds a bit of 'chewiness' to the drink. If you like this way of getting oat bran into your diet, that's fine. But a word of warning: the raw oat bran is rather harsh on the stomach, and you could get a bit of bloating if you start off with too much *too fast*.

On the other hand, you can't eat too much oat bran when it's baked in muffins, breads, rolls, cakes, biscuits, and other foods naturally suited to it. Try the recipes I've supplied in Chapter 14. Then think of your own favourites. Whenever a recipe calls for breadcrumbs or coatings, try oat bran instead.

If you happen to be a baker, or are lucky enough to live with one or have one as a good friend, oat bran offers a whole world of delicious possibilities. When I first began restricting my diet to things that were 'good for me', I did rather miss the goodies. But as time has gone on, I've found so many alternatives that I don't feel a bit deprived. I eat cakes, biscuits, and all sorts of other treats. To make it all even better, I don't even have to worry about the calories. For once, the things you *should* eat taste as good as the things you *want* to eat.

To get started, buy a packet of oat-bran cereal. This will be enough to make about two dozen muffins. Sometime over the weekend, when you have about fifteen minutes, mix up a batch or two. Start out, perhaps, with twelve basic muffins and twelve apple-cinnamon. Allowing three muffins daily, that'll be more than enough to last for a full week. Even if you never baked a thing in your life, muffin making is simple and foolproof. All you need to start is a 12-cup metal muffin baking pan and a supply of paper muffin cup liners.

In addition, take a look at the recipes and see what ingredients you'll need to start making the ones that sound best to you. Probably you already have most or all the ingredients you need already. And you'll find that practically any fresh, dried, frozen, or canned fruit makes a delicious variety of muffins.

Table 11. Fibre content of various foods[2]

	Total Plant Fibre	Insoluble Fibre	Soluble Fibre
		g/100g wet weight	
Wheat bran	42.2	38.9	3.3
Oat bran	27.8	13.8	14.0
Oats (rolled oats)	13.9	6.2	7.7
Corn flakes	12.2	5.0	7.2
Grapenuts	13.0	7.4	5.6
Pinto bean	10.5	6.0	4.5
White bean	8.7	4.0	3.7
Kidney bean	10.2	5.5	4.7
Lima bean	9.7	6.4	3.3
Corn	3.3	1.5	1.8
Sweet potato	2.5	1.4	1.1
Kale	2.6	2.0	0.6
Asparagus	1.6	1.1	0.5
Cucumber	0.9	0.5	0.4
Apple	2.0	1.1	0.9
Orange	2.0	1.4	0.6
Banana	1.8	1.0	0.8
Peach	1.4	1.1	0.3

If you have a food mixer, that's all the better for mixing the liquid ingredients. And it's lots faster to mash bananas, for example, in the mixer than by hand. This is a small investment if you don't already have one.

The other thing that I would very highly recommend is an oven thermometer; you just can't trust the dial on your oven to set the temperature. Again, this is a very small investment, and one that you'll wonder how you ever got along without. Foods—all foods—come out a lot better when you follow the recipe to the letter, especially when it comes to cooking times and temperatures.

Oat bran is as effective eaten raw or cooked or baked. But you may experience some gastric upset including a bloated feeling from eating it raw. This is especially true for those not used to a high-fibre diet. Some, on the other hand, have no problem with uncooked oat bran. Try it for yourself to see if you can tolerate it. Add some to a non-fat milkshake. Or sprinkle it on other foods.

What about taking oat bran on the road when you travel? First, oat bran muffins will last unrefrigerated in a hotel room for up to five days. Also, you may wish to enjoy some oat bran cereal on your trip.

Place into individual plastic sandwich bags one-half cup of oat bran, one-quarter cup of raisins or other dried fruits, and some brown sugar or other sweetener. Make up as many bags as you'll need for the trip. In the hotel room you can use one of the mini-coffee makers that make one or two cups. Just set it to make hot water. Pour the cereal, fruit and sugar into a bowl, mix with $1\frac{1}{3}$ cups of hot water, and let the mixture set for two minutes. Or take the bag with you into the restaurant, and order some hot water along with your coffee, juice, and fresh fruit. I travel extensively and this has never been a problem.

When you get the results showing how much your own cholesterol has fallen with this programme, you'll be pleased to go out of your way just a bit to stay on the programme and eat some of that oat bran every day.

I was very pleased to learn from Dr James Anderson, the man we all owe a great debt to for discovering the benefits of oat bran, that the National Institutes of Health has given him a million-dollar research grant to directly compare the cholesterol-lowering potential of a diet with oat bran against the standard recommendations of the American Heart Association. I'd put my bet down that oat bran will come out the undisputed leader!

Bon appetit! Good health!

5. THE AMAZING STORY OF NIACIN

For many years I've been reading and writing about the needless and sometimes dangerous use of megadoses of vitamins. For the most part, a well-balanced diet appears to provide all the vitamins anyone needs. An 'insurance policy' in the form of a multiple vitamin and mineral pill probably does lots more good than harm. This is especially true for the majority of people, whose diets are far from optimal in the first place, or for those who, because of their lifestyles, may require more than the Recommended Dietary Allowances set down by the Department of Health and Social Security. But, when it comes to taking massive amounts of any one particular vitamin, there just doesn't seem to be any justification.

So, when I first heard about niacin and its effect on high cholesterol levels, I was, to say the least, sceptical. Then, coincidentally, I read an article by the Council on Scientific Affairs published in the *Journal of the American Medical Association*. This was an overview of what was generally accepted as effective dietary and drug therapy for heart-disease risk factors. Lo and behold, there it was in black and white: 'Nicotinic acid in doses of three to twelve 500-mg tablets daily will also lower the plasma LDL levels some 15% to 30%, and it is also effective in the reduction of VLDL levels. It also increases HDL levels.'[1]

Amazing. Here was the medical community, the experts from the American Heart Association and the American Medical Association, actively advocating megadose vitamin therapy for a condition I was very personally interested in. This niacin or nicotinic-acid business deserved deeper investigation. So began my extensive search through medical literature, finding everything I could that had been written about the vitamin.

Niacin and nicotinic acid are interchangeable terms for the same water-soluble B vitamin. It was first discovered by a physician who found that diets deficient in some mysterious substance led to the condition known as pellagra. That was in 1917. It took another twenty years of research before niacin was identified, at the University of Wisconsin.

As with all vitamins, the amount recommended for the general population is based on the level needed to prevent a deficiency state. In the case of niacin, 20 milligrams daily will prevent pellagra. Even in multivitamin preparations in which other vitamins are doubled or tripled, niacin or its metabolic form, niacinamide, is kept to a minimum. Niacin is metabolized by the body to form niacinamide. It's the latter form that's useful in terms of the body's nutrient needs. **But only the niacin, not the niacinamide, lowers cholesterol.** Perhaps this is due to the cholesterol-lowering action occurring at the time of metabolism from niacin to niacinamide in the liver.

The first discovery that niacin could reduce cholesterol levels was made in 1955 by Dr R. Altschul. He gave patients three grams a day—hundreds of times the RDA—and the results were excellent.

But, for whatever reason, the scientific and medical communities didn't jump on the bandwagon. It wasn't until 1962 that two other researchers reported that niacin could not only reduce cholesterol levels, but also make triglyceride levels fall. [2]

Dozens of reports of research studies came to the same conclusions. Niacin very effectively lowers total cholesterol, LDL cholesterol, and triglycerides while actually elevating the protective HDL levels in the blood. [2] In fact, the results of the Coronary Drug Project in 1975 showed that niacin could be singled out as being responsible for a 29 per cent reduction in nonfatal heart attacks. In 1980, a Swedish study revealed that risk factors for heart disease were significantly reduced in patients receiving niacin.

Just why this information hasn't been widely disseminated by the medical community to patients like me and millions of others who could profit by it, I don't know. But the facts are there, buried in dozens of rather obscure medical journals read by a handful of research scientists. I'm obviously delighted that I was able to discover the benefits of niacin for myself, and I'm equally pleased to share my findings with you.

How does niacin work?

If you recall, cholesterol is manufactured by the liver. Happily, that's exactly where niacin exerts its unique action. Even the experts are uncertain as to the exact mechanisms, and probably more than one mode of action is involved. However, most authorities concur that niacin lowers VLDL (very-low-density lipoprotein) levels by decreasing the liver-'s production of it. And, since the worst offender, LDL (low-density lipoprotein), depends on VLDL for its production, the levels of LDL in the blood drop. [3]

This all makes sense when one realizes that the whole cholesterol problem probably comes down to a metabolic deficiency. That's why one person can gobble egg yolks and butter and keep his cholesterol level down while another has to watch every bite. An example of another metabolic deficiency would be diabetes, whereby the pancreas does not release enough insulin into the blood to break down sugars for the body's use. For years, researchers have been looking at the metabolic process of cholesterol manufacture by the liver to see if they could 'short-circuit' the process. Niacin appears to do just that.

Niacin also appears to have a strong effect on the manufacture of the prostaglandins, minute amounts of hormone-like chemicals involved in practically every bodily function. In this case the prostaglandin in question is called PGI_2, and niacin stimulates the formation of PGI_2.

Why is that good? PGI_2 has been shown conclusively to be involved with platelet aggregation in the blood; without enough PGI_2 the blood has more of a tendency to clot. And the larger the chance of clotting, the greater the risk of vascular occlusion. By increasing the body's PGI_2, niacin can inhibit the progression of the atherosclerotic processes. [2]

The next benefit of niacin is that it removes triglycerides from the blood through a process called 'lipoprotein lipase activity.' [3] Again, just how this happens is not clearly understood. But you will recall from Chapter 1 that when triglycerides are reduced in the blood LDL levels are reduced as well.

And there's more. Those taking niacin at therapeutic levels have demonstrated increased HDL concentrations. By now you know that HDL has a strong protective influence, acting to draw cholesterol away from the lining of the arteries. This counters the effect of LDL, which draws cholesterol into the lining of the arteries, resulting in the atherosclerotic build-up of occluding plaque.

So there you have it. Niacin acts to lower LDL and VLDL production in the liver, to increase the amount of PGI_2, to decrease levels of triglycerides, and to increase the amount and proportions of the protective HDL in the blood.

Research results with niacin

The medical literature is filled with success stories in which cholesterol levels fall anywhere between 10 and 25 per cent for those taking niacin alone or in combination with other approaches. Just taking niacin alone, without any changes in diet or lifestyle, is enough to produce a significant lowering of total cholesterol levels. And when taken along with a sensible, modified-fat diet niacin produces even more dramatic results.

Reporting from the University of Minnesota Medical School, Dr Donald B. Hunninghake states that 'Of all the lipid-lowering drugs, nicotinic acid probably produces the greatest elevations in high-density lipoprotein cholesterol levels, with many studies reporting rises of between 0.3 and 0.4 mmol/l. When given within the usual dosage range of 3 to 6 grams, most studies report between 20 and 30 per cent reductions in low-density lipoprotein levels.'[4]

In the book *Vitamins in Human Biology and Medicine*, Dr Mark L. Wahlqvist writes that niacin achieves cholesterol-lowering results 'at least comparable to those of the other principal lipid-lowering drugs clofibrate (Atromid-S), and the resin cholestyramine (Questran).'[3] He cites reductions of cholesterol concentration of 10 to 25 per cent and, again, 'consistent increase in high density lipoprotein.'

Italian researchers reporting in the *American Journal of Cardiology* declare that 'Treatment with large doses of nicotinic acid is generally associated with a marked reduction in both plasma cholesterol and triglyceride levels of about 15 to 20 per cent and 45 to 50 per cent respectively.'[5] Using a form of niacin, these doctors noted a 20 per cent increase of the protective HDL levels.

But most of the reports deal with using niacin in combination with other drugs. Writing in the *New England Journal of Medicine*, Drs John P. Kane and Mary J. Malloy give the results of long-term treatment of patients with high levels of cholesterol in their blood.[6] Their study was done in three phases. Phase I compared the effects of the drug colestipol and a placebo. Phase II looked at the effects of colestipol with another drug, clofibrate. Phase III investigated the use of colestipol with niacin. In all cases cases, patients followed a diet with no more than 200 milligrams of cholesterol per day and no more than 10 per cent of calories as saturated fat. All patients had particularly high levels of cholesterol.

With colestipol alone, the average cholesterol levels decreased 16 to 25 per cent. Addition of the drug clofibrate produced an average fall of only 28 per cent. In bold comparison, serum cholesterol level fell *45 per cent* when colestipol was combined with niacin. Low-density lipoprotein cholesterol decreased 55 per cent with colestipol and niacin and HDL increased.

More recently, medical researchers at the University of Southern California performed a controlled study with the combined therapy of niacin, colestipol, and a fat-controlled diet in men who had undergone coronary bypass.[7] Some men received the actual drugs while others got only a placebo. Both groups followed the modified diet.

The control group, those men with placebos but on a modified diet, showed no significant decrease in blood cholesterol levels. On the other hand, those receiving the colestipol and niacin demonstrated a 29 per cent decrease in total cholesterol, a 41 per cent decrease in triglycerides, and a 69 per cent drop in LDL levels. The levels of HDL went up 33 per cent. Much of this success can be ascribed to the niacin component.

Drs Kane and Malloy also report an interesting phenomenon. 'Some patients,' they say, 'maintained on the combined drug regimen (colestipol and niacin) have sustained decreases of LDL cholesterol levels whether they are consuming diets rich in cholesterol and saturated fats or the restricted diet.'[8] However, they warn that other patients demonstrate an elevation in cholesterol levels when they go off the diet. They conclude that modified diet appears necessary for most individuals, and that colestipol and niacin, in their opinion, is the 'most potent combined-drug regimen yet described.'

We have already looked at how niacin achieves its cholesterol-lowering results. How about colestipol? This is a so-called 'bile-acid binding resin'. Colestipol and cholestyramine both act by binding the bile acids in the intestine. The drug is not absorbed by the body. Since cholesterol is necessary for the body to produce bile acids, the more bile acids are excreted the more cholesterol will be required and thus removed from the blood. Thus, by taking these resins three times daily, the cholesterol level drops.

Notice that colestipol and cholestyramine act in much the same way as we have seen that the naturally-occurring, better-tasting, and much cheaper oat bran does. The logical conclusion, therefore, is that the ultimate idea for reducing cholesterol would be a modified diet with the combined therapy of oat bran and niacin.

Again, Drs Kane and Malloy write that:
complementarity might be expected with drug combinations in which one agent (such as bile acid sequestrant) increases the catabolism (break-down) of LDL and the other agent (niacin) inhibits the secretion of the LDL-precursor lipoprotein VLDL . . . The complete normalization of LDL levels in compliant patients receiving colestipol with niacin indicates that the latter substance (niacin) has a potent complementary effect.[6]
Similarly, the oat bran and niacin combination should be expected to produce significant and beneficial cholesterol lowering.

Depending on the individual, the combination of oat bran plus niacin could be sufficient to keep cholesterol levels well within or even below normal limits, even without changing the diet at all. This is particularly true for the millions of people who already have begun to cut back moderately on high-calorie fatty foods.

In January 1986 the *Journal of the American Medical Association* published a 'Special Communication' to bring physicians up to date on the best approaches to lowering cholesterol levels. [9] The question of 'whether to treat', the authors wrote, has been changed to 'how best to treat'. Written by doctors from the National Heart, Lung, and Blood Institute, the article stated unequivocally that 'virtually all patients evaluated by a physician should be screened for hyperlipoproteinemia (high fat levels in the blood including cholesterol).'

How did these national experts advise physicians to help their patients? First, of course, the diet should be modified to cut back on fat and cholesterol. And to get individuals to 'the target values of 4.7 to 5.2 mmol/l for total cholesterol' they recommended niacin.

With all the drugs at the physician's disposal, why did these doctors conclude that niacin is the way to go? First, they write, 'niacin costs less than' the drugs. Second, niacin reduces LDL cholesterol levels. And third, 'niacin also appears to reduce the risk of cardiovascular disease. In the Coronary Drug Project, a secondary intervention trial, niacin reduced the rate of nonfatal myocardial infarction by 21%.'

When the American government-sponsored panel of health specialists met in Washington, D.C., in October 1987, to 'declare war on cholesterol' they pointed out that not everyone would be able to get their cholesterol levels under the desired 5.2 mmol/l limit by diet alone. Some may need to have drugs prescribed. They mentioned the bile-acid-binding drugs that I'd discussed in this book, and they also pointed out that niacin should be considered as a first-line of treatment. [10]

Considering the effectiveness of niacin which had been reported just a little earlier, that recommendation was indeed warranted. On 19 June 1987, a landmark medical article was published in the *Journal of the American Medical Association*. [11] That article not only demonstrated the dramatic benefits of lowering cholesterol levels, but for the very first time ever provided evidence that the atherosclerotic plaque build-up could actually be reversed!

Researchers at the University of Southern California worked with 162 non-smoking coronary bypass patients for two years. Each of the men was given an angiogram at the start of the study, and blockage in the arteries was carefully measured. Then the group was divided in two. The first group was given a fat-modified diet in which fat comprised about 20 per cent of total calories, the bile-acid-binding drug Colestipol, and niacin. The second group got a modified diet with placebo in place of the drug and niacin. At the end of the two-year period, there was a 26 per cent reduction in total plasma cholesterol, a 43 per cent reduction in LDL, and a 37 per cent increase in HDL. Studying angiograms done at the end of the study and comparing them with those done two years earlier, the researchers found that not only was the progress of the disease stopped in those on the diet/Colestipol/niacin programme, but also there was reversal of the atherosclerotic plaque build-up in more than 16 per cent of patients.

The authors concluded that, in their opinion, virtually every person undergoing bypass surgery should be given aggressive cholesterol-lowering treatment. I was pleased to note that the programme which demonstrated such powerful results was virtually identical to that recommended in this book. Instead of Colestipol, of course, I use oat bran and other water-soluble fibre-containing foods.

The USC researchers gave from 3 to 12 grams of niacin, with an average of 4.3 grams. I've found that far less than that can be extremely effective as part of the total programme of The 8-Week Cholesterol Cure.

But what about taking niacin over a long period of time? The results of a long-term study of methods of treatment show the benefits of niacin not only in lowering cholesterol levels but very importantly in extending life! The paper was published in the *Journal of the American College of Cardiology* in December 1986.

The study was first begun in early 1966 with men who had survived a previous heart attack. After the initial study period of 6.2 years, patients given niacin showed a 'significantly lower incidence of definite nonfatal myocardial infarction (heart attack) compared with patients in the placebo group.' And as reported in the current paper, after 15 years the results were even more dramatic.

There were 69 fewer deaths in the niacin group, representing an 11 per cent difference in mortality. Those receiving the niacin lived an average of 1.63 years longer than those not taking the vitamin.

The researchers also stated that 'treatment with niacin proved to be the best lipid-lowering regimen among the five Coronary Drug Project treatment regimens.' Of course, when combined with oat bran as in The 8-Week Cholesterol Cure, the cholesterol-lowering effects of niacin are even stronger.

So there you have it. The programme advocated in this book is the same recommended by some of America's most prestigious scientific and medical organizations. For some, diet, especially diet including oat bran and other water-soluble fibres, may be enough to get cholesterol levels down sufficiently. But, for many others, niacin is the treatment of choice.

How to take niacin

Niacin has long been available in practically every health-food store, chemist shop, and pharmacy. Most typically tablets come in

50-milligram, 100-milligram, and 500-milligram strengths. Time-release formulations are also available, and there is a brand-new formulation that I'll tell you about shortly. Happily, the vitamin is quite inexpensive.

Up until just recently, there has been only one safe way to begin taking niacin. The way I began, and the way I recommended to others for years, was to gradually increase the dosage. Most authorities in the past recommended starting with 100 milligrams three times daily, increasing the dose every third day until reaching a therapeutic level. [2,3,6]

Amounts of niacin prescribed by doctors in the past have varied from three to eight grams [6,7] and even up to twelve grams. [14] Most suggest a daily intake of three grams at first, with that level reached after a month's gradual build-up. If results are not adequate, patients can take more.

Combining a modified diet with oat bran, niacin dosage of only three grams was effective in my own case and for many individuals in a clinical setting. The details of that study are presented in Chapter 13, 'The Proof of the Pudding'. All those individuals had greatly elevated cholesterol levels to begin with.

Some individuals were able to maintain their reduced cholesterol levels even when they cut the niacin intake down to only two grams daily. And a report in *Family Practice News*, a doctors' newsletter in America, indicates that results can be obtained with as little as one gram of niacin. [12] Patients taking at least that amount each day for eight months experienced an 18 per cent drop in total cholesterol, while protective HDL levels rose by 40 per cent.

Researchers reported that even doses lower than one gram had effect, though not as much. This is particularly good news for those who might have adverse reactions, such as itching, with higher levels.

At the one-gram level, niacin had no side-effects whatever. This means that everyone other than those with specific contraindications can benefit from this vitamin.

How much will be right for you? If your cholesterol level is just a bit elevated, perhaps a modified diet including oat bran will be sufficient. Those with slightly higher levels may find one gram of niacin added to the diet daily will return cholesterol levels to safe values. And those with very high initial levels may need three grams of niacin daily. But, thanks to the unique combination of diet, oat bran, and niacin, the vast majority of people will need no more than three grams of the vitamin. And, as I'll discuss in detail, with a new formulation the dosage can be much lower indeed, and without the side-effects sometimes encountered with niacin.

The following table maps out the traditional manner of gradually building up dosages of niacin.

Dosage schedule for initiating niacin therapy

First three days: one 100-mg tablet three times daily = 300mg
Next three days: two 100-mg tablets three times daily = 600mg
Next three days: three 100-mg tablets three times daily = 900mg
Next three days: four 100-mg tablets three times daily = 1200mg
Next three days: one 500-mg tablet three times daily = 1500mg
Next three days: one 100-mg tablet plus one 500-mg tablet three times daily = 1800mg
Next three days: two 100-mg tablets plus one 500-mg tablet three times daily = 2100mg
Next three days: three 100-mg tablets plus one 500-mg tablet three times daily = 2400mg
Next three days: four 100-mg tablets plus one 500-mg tablet three times daily = 2700mg
From then on: two 500-mg tablets three times daily = 3000mg

A revolutionary new way to take niacin

When I first developed the programme in this book, only the traditional formulations of niacin that I've discussed thus far were available. Then in 1987 I learned of a revolutionary new formulation being made by a small company in Idaho.

The product, known as Endur-Acin, is a sustained-release niacin. The niacin very slowly trickles out of a wax matrix tablet, more smoothly than has ever been achieved before. Because of this smooth release pattern, two wonderful things occur. First, there is absolutely no flush. Second, the dosage needed to achieved dramatic effects is drastically slashed.

I learned that research was being conducted at Harvard University Medical School at the Channing Laboratories. I called and spoke with Dr Frank Sacks about his work and his results with the new formulation.

Dr Sacks was extremely enthusiastic. Yes, he said, there was absolutely no flushing with Endur-Acin. In fact, this would enable research to be done in a double-blind fashion, since no one would be able to know who was taking the niacin as the tell-tale flushing was completely absent. But even more importantly, Dr Sacks determined that only 1,500 milligrams achieved significant cholesterol lowering. This, he said, could be compared with the effectiveness of three grams of previously available niacin products. Think of it, only 1,500 milligrams of this vitamin could drastically lower cholesterol levels!

At that low level of dosage, one would expect little if any problem with side-effects. Dr Sacks confirmed that, saying that his patients tolerated the 1,500 milligrams with no side-effects whatever.

The Harvard researcher told me that he has been giving patients one 500-milligram tablet three times daily with meals. There is no need, he said, to gradually build up the dosage.

I'd prefer to see a more cautious approach. I've been telling people to start with one 500-milligram tablet with the evening meal. Assuming that there will be no difficulties or discomfort, after one week add another tablet with breakfast. Then after a week taking the 1,000 milligram total, you can go on to the three tablets, one 500-milligram tablet three times daily.

So, for those preferring to take this approach, the dosage schedule in this chapter can be completely ignored. And if you still prefer to start with even a smaller dosage, both the 500-milligram and 250-milligram tablets are available.

For most people this will be an unnecessary caution, but let me say that one should not chew the Endur-Acin tablets. Personally, I couldn't stand chewing any tablet, even an aspirin, but some people do so. In the case of Endur-Acin, you would spoil the sustained-release effect.

I mentioned earlier that niacin is incorporated into a wax matrix in the Endur-Acin formulation. Of course this is not a wax such as in candles, but a particular type of pharmaceutical substance that is not absorbed by the body. In the process of passing through the digestive tract, niacin slowly trickles out. The wax matrix typically disintegrates and is passed out of the system. Some people, however, might see part or even all of the tablet matrix in the stool. Such individuals have a particularly fast rate of evacuation through the intestine. But there is no need for concern; although the matrix remains, the niacin has leached out.

The possibilities posed by this revolutionary new approach to taking niacin are enormous. Needless to say I was excited to hear of this development. I've asked a number of physicians here in Southern California to try the Endur-Acin with their patients. One of those physicians, Dr Charles Keenan of Santa Monica, was particularly enthusiastic. He was one of the subjects himself in my original research with this programme, and subsequent to his own success in lowering his own cholesterol level, he has put hundreds of his patients on the programme. With the Endur-Acin he was able to prescribe the programme to many others since some people had previously been unable to tolerate the flush. And, as a physician, he was pleased that the potentially confusing gradual build-up could be eliminated.

An interesting side-note regarding the flush: while I personally have had little if any difficulty with the flush often associated with niacin, other people find this a major discomfort. Everyone's body is a bit different. My wife is a case in point. Several years ago she took a multivitamin preparation which contained a mere 50 milligrams of niacin, and she experienced, she recalls, a tremendous flush, turning her beet red. Although she has no problem with cholesterol, she took an Endur-Acin tablet just out of curiosity. Sure enough, even though that 50-milligrams of niacin had caused a tremendous flush years ago, the 500-milligram tablet of Endur-Acin brought on not even the tiniest blush or tingle. Many other people have reported the same experience.

And, of course, I wanted to try using Endur-Acin myself. In order to put it to the best possible test, I waited until I was able to completely duplicate my first personal experiment. In other words, I wanted to very carefully compare the benefits of Endur-Acin with the standard niacin tablets I had been taking.

For a full eight weeks, I monitored my diet closely to be certain I was eating the same amounts of fat and cholesterol as I had when I first began. Next, I consumed my half-cup of oat bran every day, either as muffins or as hot cereal in the mornings. And I took one gram of niacin with meals, three times daily, for a total of three grams a day. The results were very satisfying. I had a blood test done at Santa Monica hospital Medical Center where I had done the original research. My cholesterol level was a very respectable 161mg/dL.

The day I had my blood test done, I switched over to the Endur-Acin. I took one 500-milligram tablet three times daily with meals for a total of 1,500 milligrams each day. And, of course, I continued with the same diet and with my daily breakfast of oat bran.

Another eight weeks passed, and I had another blood test. When the results came back I felt there might have been some kind of laboratory error, even though I had the blood work done in the same hospital as always. My total cholesterol, the report said, was down to 3.5 mmol/l! To be certain that no error was involved, I repeated the test the following week. The report that time was 3.7 mmol/l, again, a spectacular response. And one can expect a small fluctuation in the number from week to week or even from day to day.

But the important thing here is that by taking *half* the amount of niacin I'd been taking for three years, I actually got *better* results!

Combining a modified diet with oat bran, niacin dosage of three grams was effective in my own case and for many individuals in a clinical study as reported in Chapter 13, 'The Proof of the Pudding'. All those individuals had greatly elevated cholesterol levels to begin with.

Since the time of first publication of *The 8-Week Cholesterol Cure*, thousands of people have used the programme to lower their own cholesterol levels. Some individuals were able to maintain reduced cholesterol levels even when they cut the niacin down to only two grams daily. Others, in keeping with the report mentioned earlier[12] found that only one gram of niacin daily provided sufficient results. And, of course, one could expect even greater benefits from lower doses when using the new formulation Endur-Acin. For many individuals one gram will be completely adequate.

How much will be right for you?

If your cholesterol level is just a bit elevated, perhaps a modified diet including oat bran will be sufficient. Those with slightly higher levels may find one gram of niacin added to the diet daily will return cholesterol levels to safe values. And those with very high initial levels, or with levels that have been resistant to dietary measures alone, will probably need to include niacin in the programme, either at the three gram levels from standard niacin, or with lower doses of Endur-Acin.

For those with extremely high cholesterol levels, or, again, highly resistant levels which have not responded to diet alone, Endur-Acin offers yet another benefit. If after taking 1,500mg of this sustained-release niacin the cholesterol levels are still higher than desired, one can take another 500-milligram tablet. For such indivdiuals the dosage pattern could be one 500-milligram tablet three times daily with meals, plus an extra 500-milligram tablet at bedtime. The total dosage of 2,000 milligrams is still well under the 3,000 milligrams I originally found effective, yet would be expected to produce far greater results.

Endur-Acin can be ordered directly from the manufacturer, Endurance Products Co in Idaho. They have made the product available to the public through a separate company for mail order sales. I'm particularly pleased that the cost for this very high quality product is extremely reasonable, often cheaper than ordinary niacin found in health food stores. If you're interested in obtaining a supply of Endur-Acin you may write for order information to:

> **Endurance Products Co.**
> **P.O. Box 2530**
> **Ketchum, Idaho 83340**
> **USA**

Possible side effects

Practically everyone taking standard formulations of niacin, and even sustained-release niacin tablets other than Endur-Acin, will experience a flush. This is a tingly, prickly sensation of the skin, primarily on the arms, shoulders, back, and chest. Often the skin will turn pink or red, as though one were blushing or had been in the sun. This flush is completely harmless.[2,3] Scientists say it has to do with release of prostaglandins. Some people become frightened by the first experience, thinking the flush is dangerous, even thinking it has something to do with the heart. Actually, it's limited strictly to the skin, and should be of no concern. Of course, those taking Endur-Acin will experience no flush at all.

For those taking standard formulations of niacin according to the dosage schedule printed in this chapter, the flush is strongest when first beginning to take niacin or when increasing the dosage level. After a few days of taking niacin at a given dose on a regular basis, the flush tends to diminish. Most people find that after a while even three grams daily, one gram with each meal, produces little if any flush.

In the past, people who had difficulty with the flush could reduce it significantly by taking half an aspirin tablet either with the niacin or thirty minutes beforehand. This will decrease the flush without influencing the effectiveness of cholesterol lowering.[2]

Some people react to the flushing experience more strongly than others. My printer, for example, started taking the tablets after we talked about the programme and his flushing was quite pronounced. In fact, after each dose he looked as though he had been in the sun for a couple of hours. He found that a sustained-release niacin helped to cut back on the flush. That was several years ago when I was first beginning to develop the programme. Today, of course, I'd simply advise him to take Endur-Acin.

Certain individuals, very few in my actual experience, have a bit of gastric upset when taking niacin or other vitamin preparations. Some of the older sustained-release niacin formulations did cause some gastric upset. Happily, the Endur-Acin causes no such problems at the lower dosage needed for effectiveness. To best ensure avoiding stomach problems, scientists recommend taking niacin with meals. This makes sense since most of us eat three meals a day, and this would fit the niacin dosage schedule perfectly.

The most troublesome side-effect reported in the literature—one that cropped up during the research reported later—has been an itching rash. There is no way to predict who will develop this adverse reaction. If it occurs at all, the rash will come on during the early period of niacin intake. Unlike the flush, the rash does not go away and it is the reason some people cannot take three grams of niacin. Don't confuse some initial itching with this rash, however. The itching, as part of the flush, passes, but the rash does not. Those who do develop the rash find that after discontinuing niacin the rash disappears within a few days. No such rash appeared in those taking one gram of niacin or less. And one would expect little if any incidence of rash with Endur-Acin.

Another side-effect that has been reported with high doses of niacin is blurred vision. Again, this disappears without residual ill effect after discontinuing the niacin. This, too, would not be a problem with the Endur-Acin.

Contraindications to niacin

As is the case for many if not all substances, certain people should not take niacin at all. Contraindications for taking this vitamin in large doses include active peptic ulcer, liver disease, severe heart arrhythmias, diabetes, and gout. Interestingly, however, doctors have told me they have given Endur-Acin to patients with diabetes and even mild cases of gout without difficulty. Certainly though, such patients should be closely monitored by their doctors.

Safety of taking niacin

The majority of people will be able to take even three grams of niacin without side-effects. All but those for whom niacin is contraindicated will experience no side-effects at the one-gram level. And few if any side-effects would be anticipated with 1,500 milligrams of Endur-Acin. The safety of taking niacin has long been documented.

The US Coronary Drug Project showed that niacin can be taken for prolonged periods of time with only the minor side-effects described above.[13] This study involved more than 8,000 individuals over the years 1969 through 1975.

Many doctors have been using niacin to treat patients with elevated cholesterol and triglyceride levels for years. Dr Louis Cohen, professor of medicine at the University of Chicago Medical Center, has been prescribing niacin in conjunction with the drug Probucol for the past twenty years.[14] He has had dozens of patients taking the vitamin for six years and more without any difficulties, and feels that niacin can be used for a lifetime.

Because niacin is metabolized by the liver, a bit of additional burden is placed on that organ. For some people, however, that little bit might be the straw that breaks the camel's back. If someone has been drinking heavily for many years, his or her liver has been compromised and is not functioning as well as it should. Similarly, if one has had diseases such as hepatitis or cirrhosis, again the liver has been damaged. The livers of such individuals may not be able to accommodate the niacin being taken, even at lower dosages.

That's why I recommend that after taking niacin for a period of time, say two months or so, one should have a blood-test, checking the function of the liver. Actually, this is not at all inconvenient since one will want to check the cholesterol level to determine progress by that time anyway.

The tests will show how well the liver is metabolizing the niacin. For the majority of people, there will be no problem at all. In fact, doctors, including those at Harvard, point out that a slight fluctuation in those liver function tests simply shows that the niacin is doing its job. But for those people whose livers have been damaged previously, the test might show that they should not take the niacin.

Once again, the value of doing this liver function test is another example of why it's important to work with your doctor in your efforts to lower cholesterol levels.

Don't let my recommendation for having the liver function test done frighten you. First, it's a very simple test. Second, the majority of men and women will show no problems whatsoever. Third, especially if you're using the Endur-Acin, the low dosages are expected to pose no difficulties as shown in the Harvard research. Fourth, the test need be done only one time to positively establish your own body's ability to metabolize niacin properly. And fifth, compare the recommendation for one liver test with the suggestions of the manufacturers of the much-publicized new cholesterol-lowering drug.

Mevacor® is the brand-name for lovastatin made by the Merck, Sharp & Dohme pharmaceutical company. It received US Food and Drug Administration approval in September of 1987, for prescription by physicians for lowering cholesterol levels. The drug has been much touted in the American press, and shares in the company soared when approval was granted.

But while the drug probably will have a legitimate role in lowering cholesterol levels for those patients needing it, there are a number of other considerations. First, there is absolutely no 'track record' of use with the substance. Many authorities are concerned that long-term side-effects will show up years down the road. Second, consider the company's recommendations regarding liver function tests for patients taking Mevacor® .

'It is recommended that liver function tests be performed every four to six weeks during the first 15 months of therapy and periodically thereafter in all patients.'[15]

That's quite a difference: one liver test for niacin versus a liver test every four to six weeks for Mevacor® . The reasons for suggesting such frequent liver testing for the new drug are enough to make many medical authorities very cautious about the use of the drug. Such authorities have frequently stated that they are concerned that the drug will be over-prescribed before attempting to lower cholesterol levels by dietary means and the use of more proven substances such as niacin.

As a side-note, you may be interested to know that the cost of Mevacor® will be as much as three thousand dollars annually. Compare that with the cost of some breakfast cereal and a bottle of vitamins!

Niacin as part of a complete programme

Niacin can be an important part of your programme to reduce serum cholesterol. Along with a modified diet including oat bran, niacin has been shown to be safe and effective. I'm pleased that since I developed this programme, many physicians have begun recommending it for their patients.

If you decide to include niacin in your programme to lower serum cholesterol levels, be sure to inform your doctor. Perhaps he or she would also like to read this book. By sharing the book with your doctor, you'll help bring the information about this effective programme to even more people.

A few words of caution

While niacin has been demonstrated to be quite safe for most people and is available in any health-food store or pharmacy, a few words of caution are in order. First of all, niacin should not be viewed as a substitute for good, healthful eating habits. Remember that the basis of any healthful diet is the reduction of fats and cholesterol and the increased consumption of complex carbohydrates.

Second, niacin should be considered part of the programme for those with quite elevated cholesterol levels. Does your serum level put you at risk? For those with moderately elevated cholesterol counts, say just twenty points over the desired level, modified diet alone, especially combined with oat bran, will probably be effective.

Third, there are definite medical contraindications for niacin. Some people should not attempt to take the vitamin at all. Those contraindications include gout and/or elevated levels of uric acid, ulcer, diabetes, and liver abnormalities. If you have any doubts at all, talk with your doctor. He or she is your best source of medical advice and supervision.

Fourth, niacin causes occasional minor side effects in some individuals. In addition to the flushing at the beginning of niacin consumption, some people develop a rash, skin itch, and possibly blurred vision. These effects disappear after one stops taking the niacin, within three to five days. There have been no reported long-term adverse reactions. As mentioned before, some people will not be able

to tolerate niacin. For those men and women, diet and oat bran are
still the best ways to control cholesterol levels.

For the vast majority, niacin can be taken for years and years to
reduce and maintain lowered cholesterol levels. Together, diet, oat bran,
and niacin form the most effective answer to the problem of elevated
cholesterol and heart-disease risk available for the general population.

As stated above, *if you decide to include niacin in your programme to lower
serum cholesterol levels, be sure to inform your doctor.* He or she will want to
include that bit of information in your personal records. If you have
any questions about using this vitamin, by all means discuss them
with your doctor.

6. OTHER MARVELS AND FABULOUS FOODS

In terms of cholesterol, one could classify foods into three groups: those that raise cholesterol levels, such as eggs and butter; those that have no effect on blood fats, such as carrots, lettuce, breads, and so on; and those that can actually lower lipid levels, such as oat bran. The really good news is that there are other marvels throughout the supermarket in that third cholesterol-lowering category.

Oat bran has beneficial effects because it contains a large percentage of water-soluble fibre termed 'gum'. There is more gum, ounce for ounce, in oat bran than in oatmeal, and that's why the bran works better. It makes sense then to think that other gums would work as well. And the medical literature indicates that, in fact, they do.

One such substance is guar gum, a type of carbohydrate found in cluster beans. Unfortunately, there is not enough in the beans. While isolated guar gum found as a powder has been shown to be effective in lowering cholesterol, it's difficult to incorporate into the diet as such. (First, cluster beans are not available as food. Second, guar gum content is low and must be extracted.) When mixed into foods such as soups and stews guar gum makes them extremely thick and heavy—five to eight times as much as cornstarch.

To see if they could get around this, scientists gave patients capsules containing guar gum rather than mixing it with foods. Patients lost no weight and followed normal eating patterns. After four weeks, guar gum lowered total serum cholesterol by an average of 16.6 per cent. Neither triglyerides nor HDL were affected. But to achieve this effect patients had to consume five capsules at breakfast, lunch, and dinner for a total of fifteen capsules containing nine grams of guar gum.

Guar gum comes both as capsules and as a powder to mix with water to make an orange-flavoured drink but is not very readily available in the UK. It is possible, however, to find it in some health food stores and pharmacies.

To achieve the therapeutic levels mentioned above, you'd have to take eighteen capsules daily, or two teaspoonsful of the powder. While you may not want to do this every day, the guar gum alternative may be useful for times when you're out of town and don't wish to bother with the oat bran or when you simply want a change of pace.

But, on a more practical level, we can all get the same effects by regularly consuming a variety of dry beans of legumes. Pinto beans, Great Northern beans, lima beans, lentils, red beans, haricot beans, and many others all over the world contain large amounts of water-soluble fibre. The same man who investigated the cholesterol-lowering effects of oat bran also looked into the possibilities of beans.

Dr James Anderson fed subjects a daily bean diet containing 115 grams of dried beans, based on dry weight before cooking, for three weeks. The participants in this study were given all their meals in the hospital so the researchers could determine exactly what was eaten. Pinto beans and haricot beans were served as cooked beans or bean soup. Cholesterol levels fell by an average of 19 per cent.

Now, granted, that's a lot of beans to eat each day. In fact, the study participants ate only 88 per cent of the beans served. It would be difficult to expect anyone to eat this amount of beans daily for the rest of his or her life. But there's no reason why one couldn't include dry beans as a regular part of the diet.

The possibilities are infinitely varied. In addition to soups and cooked beans, bean dips are a delicious and healthful alternative to high-fat snack dips. Try the bean recipes included in the recipe section and you'll soon turn into a real bean addict. One of my favourites is the dish called *hummus*, which is a staple food of people throughout the Middle East. I keep a supply in the refrigerator and use it as a snack along with pitta bread.

According to a survey conducted at the Baltimore Gerontology Research Center, in subjects of all age groups, from 30 to 79, each gram of dietary fruit fibre consumed corresponded with a mean 0.04 mmol/l decrease in serum cholesterol. Fruit-fibre intake among the 556 men in the study ranged from less than 1 gram to about 11 grams. There was a difference in cholesterol levels of about 0.4 mmol/l between the lowest and the highest fibre-intake groups. Isn't that a good reason to eat more apples and oranges?

Another excellent source of the water-soluble fibre which can lower cholesterol levels is rice bran. Just as oat bran is a part of the whole oat grain, so also rice bran is a portion of the whole rice grain.

You can use this rice bran to sprinkle over cereals, as a topping for yogurt and other foods which might need a bit of a crunchy texture, and as an ingredient in muffins and other baked goods. Is it a replacement for oat bran? Not at all. It's one more food to consider and to use in the diet. You'll find that rice bran isn't quite as versatile as oat bran in its cooking and baking potential, but it's nice to have for variety.

Remember the old-fashioned barley soup your mother or your grandmother used to make? For some reason we don't use as much of this grain any more, and it's time to get it back into our diets. First, the kind of barley you're likely to buy to be cooked into soups and stews contains about five grams of water-soluble fibre in a 100g (3½ oz) serving. So, by all means, it's another good food to include in the the the diet. Certainly you're not going to eat it daily, but it is yet one more source of that water-soluble fibre.

But there's more to the barley story. Some researchers at the University of Wisconsin's Cereal Institute have been looking at another aspect. I spoke with Dr David Peterson, the Institute's director, and here's what he had to say. Normally the outer portion of barley is removed in the process known as pearling. They have isolated two compounds in the protein-rich outer portion, which is normally discarded in processing, and which appear to have a potent cholesterol-lowering effect. And that effect is different from the bile acid-binding effect of water-soluble fibre. Instead, those barley-derived substances work on the activity of the enzyme HMG Co-A reductase which determines the amount of cholesterol made by the liver. Fascinating research, but unfortunately at this point in time the work has been done only with laboratory animals and the substances are not commercially available to us. In the meantime, however, you might want to seek out some unprocessed barley in your health food store.

Since Dr Anderson first did his research with the water-soluble fibre in oat bran, people have looked at other ways to work the substance into the diet. Surely rice bran and barley are excellent, natural sources. But there's another approach you might want to consider.

Metamucil is the best-known of a group of laxatives which are made from psyllium seeds. Those products have been on the market for many years. Recent research, however, has shown that the products are rich in soluble fibre and do have a cholesterol lowering effect. In fact, Dr Anderson himself did some investigation and found that three teaspoonsful daily are both safe and effective.

I hasten to point out that no one includes psyllium seeds on the shopping list, so these products should not be confused in any way with food, although they are 'natural'. I certainly would not recommend that people use laxatives rather than good, wholesome cereals. But there may be times, such as during travel, when this could be a consideration.

There's no question that we'll be seeing more and more research done in the years to come with new and exciting approaches to cholesterol control. One very novel effort involved the use of activated charcoal.

An article in the *Lancet* in 1986 continues to attract attention because of the finding that activated charcoal reduced cholesterol levels by an average of 41 per cent in seven patients. But don't rush out to the shops just yet. Here are a few things to consider.

First, to equal the amount given to those volunteer patients, you'd have to swallow 92 charcoal capsules daily. They took eight grams three times daily in a water suspension. The study lasted for four weeks. Personally, I don't think I'd enjoy gulping all that charcoal every day of my life.

Second, the long-term effects of such a radical idea haven't begun to be explored. Charcoal works by adhering to insoluble-particles and excreting them out through the colon. But we don't know whether the charcoal might also grab onto and get rid of vitamins and minerals.

A longer study with a larger group of subjects will be done to see if there might be some merit to the charcoal concept. In the meantime, it's nice to know that oat bran achieves the same goal of binding onto bile acids formed of cholesterol, thereby reducing the body's total supply of the culprit.

Another bit of research and development to keep your eye out for involves a synthetic fat being formulated by the Proctor & Gamble company. Called sucrose polyester, or SPE for short, this is a specially designed oil which contributes absolutely no fat to the diet.

Here's the way it works. The chemists at Proctor & Gamble took a molecule of sucrose, common table sugar, and added glycerol molecules until they built up a giant molecule so large that it can't pass through the lining of the digestive tract to enter the body's bloodstream. As a result, the SPE is totally non-absorbed by the body.

As is often the case, however, there's a fly in the ointment. SPE has not been shown to be completely free of side-effects, and there is concern about consuming large quantities of the artificial oil.

It now appears that SPE will be an ingredient along with other oils. Proctor & Gamble will probably market a product which will contain about 35 per cent SPE and 65 per cent vegetable oil. While that will offer a certain amount of fat savings, the product will still not be something to use as freely as water. A 35 per cent saving in fat will provide a product that will contain eight to nine grams of fat per tablespoon, rather than fourteen grams.

SPE will also be available for commercial use in the preparation of processed foods and in the restaurant industry. There a more concentrated form of the artificial oil mày be used. In any case, authorities remain concerned about heavy use of SPE over the long term before we know what, if any, side-effects may result.

Another area of product development to keep an eye on is pectin. Another soluble fibre, pectin has been shown to lower cholesterol levels. But common food sources contain little of the substance, and artificial sources have produced some ill-effects. However, work continues.

Researchers at the University of Florida in Gainesville have found that patients taking about three tablespoons of grapefruit pectin, either as capsules or as a food additive, experienced cholesterol reductions of an average of 7.2 per cent. The substance given was specifically derived from the rind and flesh of the grapefruit, rather than feeding grapefruit itself. This was a well-controlled study, with groups receiving first the pectin and later crossing over and receiving a placebo. Some of the 27 volunteer subjects got up to a 19 per cent lowering. The researchers' report also noted comparable results achieved by scientists at the U.S. Department of Agriculture using carrot pectin. But the authors pointed out that one pectin may work quite differently from another.

Some interesting research now being conducted indicates there may be another lipid-lowering vegetable category for us to consider. Some dietitians now believe that cruciferous vegetables, notably broccoli and cauliflower, can help lower cholesterol levels. These are preliminary observations; however, there are no reasons *not* to eat more of those vegetables. If they do help lower cholesterol, that's wonderful. If not, they still provide fibre in the diet as well as vitamins.

Next on the cholesterol-lowering food shopping list should be plenty of fish. Years ago people thought fish was brain food. Now, thanks to advances in nutrition, we know it's great for the heart.

Not too many years ago, dietitians and nutritionists placed certain seafood dishes on the list of foods to limit or avoid. Salmon, they said, was a fatter-than-average fish. The same went for mackerel. Shellfish, the common wisdom advised, was high in cholesterol. Avoid these if possible, the helpful manuals said. But times and techniques have changed and improved.

As for those fatty fishes, it turns out that the particular fat in salmon and mackerel is a tongue-twister called eicosapentaenoic acid, a polyunsaturated variety of fat found in most cold-water fish. This particular fish oil, termed EPA for short, has the remarkable ability to reduce both triglyceride and cholesterol levels. Some fish have more EPA than others. Salmon, mackerel, and menhaden store this fat in their flesh, while cod and shark store EPA in their livers. All cold-water fish, however, supply some EPA. And all fish, both salt and fresh water varieties, have far less saturated fat than beef.

German researchers fed healthy adult volunteers two eight-ounce cans of mackerel in addition to their other daily foods each day. They gave another group the same amount of herring, a fish without EPA in its fat content. After two weeks of the fishy diets, the mackerel group showed a 7 per cent drop in cholesterol and a 47 per cent dip in triglycerides. Blood pressure also fell, by about 10 per cent. No such benefits for the herring eaters, though.

I'll be the first to admit that sixteen ounces is a lot of fish to eat every day, and fish all by itself is not a very practical answer to the cholesterol problem, but by including fish in the diet at least once, preferably twice, a week, you will be helping to reduce your cholesterol level.

In fact, a very recent study reported in the *New England Journal of Medicine* indicated that the death rate from heart disease was more than 50 per cent lower among men who ate at least 30 grams—that's one ounce—of fish daily as compared with men who ate no fish at all. Just one or two fish dishes a week, the researchers wrote, may offer significant protection against heart disease.

When you look at Table 10 (see page 57), you see that some fish contain higher amounts of fat and cholesterol than others. Should one consume only those with low levels? First, as we have seen, the EPA which is largely responsible for high fat levels in fish is actually beneficial rather than detrimental. Second, in those fish with higher-than-average levels of cholesterol the fat content is often quite low. The conclusion reached by the medical authorities, then, is to eat a wide variety of many kinds of fish. There's no need to avoid any of them.

And what about those much-maligned shellfish? Well it turns out that, through no fault of their own, the original compilers of cholesterol data were in error on this one. Cholesterol is just one of a large family of chemical substances collectively termed the sterols. Other sterols include, for example, vitamin E (alpha-tocopherol) and precursors of vitamin D (ergosterol). The original testing methods could not distinguish among all the sterols. So the shellfish earned the undeserved reputation of having high cholesterol levels. Actually, scallops contain a mere 35 milligrams per 3½-ounce serving. That Alaskan delicacy king crab has only 60 milligrams. Clams, oysters, and mussels are particularly low in cholesterol. Lobster, once a distinct no-no for even those who could afford it, has a bit less than 100 milligrams. In fact, the only food from the sea that has a considerable amount of cholesterol is shrimp, which contains more than 100 milligrams per serving. Even so, when planning a 250-milligram-per-day programme, a serving of shrimp should be no problem.

Shellfish have the added benefit of being particularly low in fat.

Scallops have only 0.2 grams of fat per serving. Shrimp contains only 0.8 grams. And lobster provides just 1.9 grams. All those contributions are practically negligible. So while your selection of a given shellfish may provide the daily limits of cholesterol, the dish won't even be counted in terms of fat.

Is there anything to watch out for in the fish market? Yes, there's one exception which probably won't bother too many people. Caviar, that costly curiosity, tips the scales both for cholesterol and fat content. But consider the amounts you may actually eat and the frequency of having a nibble, and most of us won't have to worry.

As I often complained, when I ate little or no fish and lots of beef, the prices of fish were low and those of beef were high. Now the reverse is true. We can buy good steaks for much less than salmon or swordfish. But smart shoppers can enjoy seafood frequently without bending the budget at all.

First of all, all food prices are based on supply and demand. Many fish are in lesser demand. Try some of the less popular varieties such as monkfish, sand dabs, rockfish, and many others. Talk with the person behind the counter to find out some tasty treats you wouldn't have considered otherwise. 'Go with the flow' for fish that are in season and thus priced inexpensively.

Leave it to the Japanese to imitate some of the best things in life and bring them to those of us with champagne tastes and beer budgets. Their latest innovation is called *surimi*, an imitation crab product made from white fish such as pollock. Try it in salads and main dishes. And look for the soon-to-be-introduced imitation shrimp and scallops. These foods provide great nutrition with low fat and low cholesterol.

The next question is which oil to use to cook with. Does it really make any difference? The answer is yes. As we get into a discussion of cooking oils, I'll get a pet peeve off my chest. *No* vegetable oil of any kind has any cholesterol at all. Period. Cholesterol comes from animal sources only. Thus when a manufacturer claims that a brand of vegetable oil 'has no cholesterol' it makes about as much sense as saying that water is wet. So much for that. Only those cooking fats from animal sources, such as bacon grease, butter, and lard, contain cholesterol. Avoid these as you would poison.

The next part of choosing a cooking oil isn't as simple, and requires a bit of explanation. Every fat and oil contains the three types of fat: saturated, polyunsaturated, and monounsaturated. While it's not terribly important to understand the chemistry, the degree of saturation depends on how many hydrogen atoms are on the chemical chain. Often the more saturated a fat is, the harder it is. Compare the rind of fat on a beefsteak with liquid corn oil. The more saturated a fat is, for the most part, the more cholesterol-forming it will be in our bodies.

Many years ago, scientists learned that the ratio of saturated, monounsaturated and polyunsaturated fats, especially that of saturated and polyunsaturated fats, has a dramatic effect on cholesterol levels. The higher the ratio of polyunsaturated fat to saturated fat, the greater the cholesterol-lowering effect. The opposite, of course, is also true. Therefore medical authorities began advising us to consume more polyunsaturated fats and oils, and less of the saturated types. This made good sense and was proved effective in test after test.

The only problem that showed up was that a diet high in polyunsaturated fats, that is, one having a high P/S ratio, tends to also lower the level of the protective HDL. It was one of those damned if you do and damned if you don't situations.

Then along came some more research information from work headed up by Dr Scott Grundy at the University of Texas Health Science Center in Dallas.

For years it has been known that there was little or no heart disease in the Mediterranean countries and the cholesterol levels of Mediterranean people are traditionally low. The foods there are low in fat and cholesterol. The cooking oil used is primarily olive oil, a monounsaturated oil.

Interestingly, however, when one looks at the complete lipid profile of Mediterranean people, one finds that while the total cholesterol levels remain low, the HDL levels stay high. Therefore it appears that, by using olive oil instead of the polyunsaturated types such as corn oil, one can lower total cholesterol while preserving HDLs.

How does the lowering effect compare between the two oils? Dr Grundy studied 20 patients who were fed either monounsaturated oils or the polyunsaturated type. Both were equally effective in reducing total blood cholesterol levels. Importantly, the levels of protective HDL did not drop with diets high in monounsaturated fats as they did with high-polyunsaturated-fat diets. Most medical authorities are not ready, however, to recommend exclusive use of monounsaturated oils such as olive oil. They suggest using both the polyunsaturated and monounsaturated types.

Well, before sitting down to that meal of fish sautéed in olive oil, bean soup, and perhaps some oat-bran muffins or rolls, how about a cocktail?

For some time now, researchers have observed that moderate alcohol intake is associated with a lowered rate of heart disease. At first no one knew why this was the case, but a closer look demonstrated that a little daily drink raises the protective HDL level. Actually, to be precise, alcohol tends to raise the so-called apolipoprotein component of HDL.

How much is enough and how much is too much? Moderation is the key word. Moderate alcohol intake has been defined as about 1½ fl oz of the drink of choice. Having that martini before dinner, or a glass of wine or beer with dinner, or a nightcap snifter of brandy seems to be perfectly acceptable. But doctors hurry to say that they do *not* suggest that previous teetotalers start to tipple. These data merely indicate the safety of moderation in alcohol consumption for those who do choose to imbibe.

Bear in mind, however, that recent studies have been completed which show the toxic effects of immoderate alcohol usage. Cardiologists at the University of Chicago have shown that three drinks of 90-proof scotch at one sitting have a definite negative effect on heart function.

To my mind, it's nice to know that we have some very interesting choices to make when shopping in the supermarket. Scientists have provided the knowledge we need to avoid the foods that are harmful and to choose those with excellent nutrient contributions and cholesterol-lowering potentials.

And now a word about sodium . . .

Just as cholesterol has been positively associated with heart disease in as much as half the population, sodium is associated with hypertension, or high blood pressure. To explain briefly, sodium is essential in the diet in small quantities in order to preserve blood volume and pressure by attracting and holding water in the blood vessels. But for many individuals too much sodium brings the blood pressure too high. Actually, two things happen. First, the sodium results in the body's inability to excrete water properly. That's why doctors often prescribe diuretics for hypertensive patients. Second, there is a long physiological process by which the kidney produces chemical substances that directly elevate pressure in the arteries.

Six million men and women have frank hypertension, and millions more are 'borderline' hypertensives. The problem is that no one knows who will develop high blood pressure. Many people have the disease without even knowing it. That's why health authorities have recommended that all of us should reduce our sodium intake.

How much is too much? The COMA report claimed that the intake of salt in the UK diet was 'needlessly high' at an estimated 7-10 grams per day. The report recommended that the addition of salt in cooking or at the table should be 'decreased immediately'.

Salt is the principal source of sodium in our diets. But one must also consider the input of sodium from food preservatives and curatives such as sodium nitrite, sodium nitrate, and sodium benzoate. In addition, many Oriental foods contain a large amount of the flavour enhancer MSG, monosodium glutamate. Soy sauce is another source.

Some authorities estimate that as much as one-third of our sodium comes from salt added either during cooking or at the table. How significant is that shake of the salt shaker? Try this for yourself. Shake out some salt over an empty plate as though you were seasoning food. Then collect the salt and measure it. If you used about ⅛ teaspoon, that amounts to 250 milligrams of sodium.

You've probably heard this before, but it's worth repeating. Salt is an acquired taste and habit. Absolutely *no* added salt is needed in the diet. Sodium is naturally occurring in many, many foods throughout the diet, and levels consumed in normal eating habits provide more than enough. Many of us salt our food before even tasting it. Weaning ourselves from the shaker may be difficult at first, but after not too long a time our taste perceptions begin to change. Soon the natural flavours of foods predominate, and, at the very least, we need to add less salt. The first step is to take the salt shaker off the table. There are a wide variety of seasonings that can easily replace salt. Try some garlic powder, a pinch of pepper, or a squeeze of lemon.

Next, start to pay more attention to the labels on foods in the supermarket. And because so many of us are trying to limit the sodium in our diets, manufacturers are now offering low-sodium and reduced-sodium alternatives. One can even buy low-sodium soy sauce.

Cheese is a major source of sodium in many diets. One ounce of Cheddar cheese contains 173 milligrams. And that same slice of cheese also comes loaded with nearly 10 grams of fat, practically all saturated. The best advice about cheese is to avoid it completely.

As with cholesterol, knowledge of content levels is an important step in controlling sodium intake. Table 10 included in Chapter 3, 'Winning by the Numbers', also lists the sodium content of foods.

If you are already under a doctor's supervision for hypertension, by all means follow his or her advice and recommendations. If you don't know your blood pressure, make the small effort to find out.

High blood pressure has no symptoms. You cannot 'know' when the pressure inside your arteries rises. This is truly a silent killer, resulting in strokes and heart attacks often without warning.

Even if you find that your blood pressure is currently normal, it's wise to consider a sodium-limited diet. Simply enough, you cannot know whether you are prone to developing the disease later in life. Why take the chance for the sake of a seasoning?

While you're limiting your sodium, think about yet another bit of very interesting research data done by Dr David McCarron at the Oregon Health Sciences University. In studying patients with hypertension, he found that the disease correlated not only with high sodium intake but also with low calcium intake. Dr McCarron speculates that the two minerals may be involved in a balance; if one is out of balance, blood pressure can be affected. His suggestion is to increase the calcium intake in the diet.

Although this theory remains controversial, and certainly it should not be construed as a denial of the importance of sodium moderation, increasing calcium in the diet can do no harm but can do much good, for we all need calcium throughout our lives. Certainly there has been considerable publicity given to the problem of osteoporosis for women, whose bones slowly demineralize with the passage of time.

There are a number of calcium-rich dairy foods that are also low in fat and cholesterol. Two servings of nonfat milk or low-fat yogurt a day provide much of the calcium needed for good health. Women, especially, may also require a calcium supplement.

Ultimately, the most marvellous word in nutrition is moderation. We are blessed today with an abundance and variety of foods never before imagined. We can have strawberries in the winter and squash in the summer. Fish from oceans and streams across the country and around the world can be on our tables every night of the week if we choose. Many of those foods in our supermarkets can control and even improve our blood lipid profiles. Let's enjoy them all in moderation, with a toast to good health and well-being!

7. WINNING BY LOSING

Following the nutrition advice in this book will ensure that you can eat all you want of the right foods, with no feelings of hunger, and never gain a single pound. Simply enough, you'll be eating the foods that are lower in calories and, especially, lower in fat content. If you're a few pounds overweight now, that weight will slowly disappear. In our research, those who were compliant with the programme lost weight in just weeks—and while eating a wide variety of satisfying foods.

But, if you have a significant amount of weight to lose, more than fifteen pounds or so, it will be worth your while to pay special attention to your diet. Again, you can do this without ever feeling hungry or deprived. It's just a matter of tipping your eating patterns more in favour of those foods that will help you lose those pounds.

It's worth the effort. You'll see the immediate benefits in the mirror, and you'll love the compliments you'll get—not to speak of the added confidence you'll feel, and the increased vitality. But there are even more important reasons to attain and maintain your ideal weight.

First of all, just reducing down to the ideal weight for your size will automatically reduce your cholesterol level. How this happens is not fully known, but as weight falls, cholesterol levels fall. It may have something to do with the sequence of blood fat storage. Blood pressure is also greatly affected by weight. If you have diabetes, your need for drugs will decrease. And you'll vastly improve your shot at longevity.

These are not idle promises. They're backed up by the findings of the most recognized authorities in the medical and scientific communities. In an article published in the *Annals of Internal Medicine*, Drs Artemis Simopoulos and Theodore Van Itallie, writing for the Nutrition Coordinating Committee of the National Institutes of Health, concluded that the weight associated with the 'greatest longevity tends to be below the average weight of the population.' Speaking even more strongly, they say that 'overweight persons tend to die sooner than average-weight persons.'

The fourteen-member panel of the NIH concluded in 1985 that the 34 million Americans who are more than 20 per cent overweight should be treated for obesity. The panel chairman, Jules Hirsch, M.D., said that 'Fat is not just a cosmetic affair—a concern of especially vain Americans. At surprisingly low levels, it's a biologic hazard.' He estimated that half the medical problems seen in overweight patients in doctors' surgeries are obesity related.

The evidence has been building for a long time. The Provident Mutual Life Insurance Company studied male policyholders from 1947 to 1964. In every group, the mortality rate increased with weight. The more overweight, the more likely to die prematurely.

Investigators involved in the famous Framingham Heart Study showed a linear relationship between obesity and coronary heart disease. That study also demonstrated a direct link between obesity and total mortality.

Dr Hirsch went so far as to say that 'Obesity is a killer. It is a killer just as smoking is.' Another panel member, Dr Harriet P. Dustan, Professor of Medicine at the University of Alabama in Birmingham, said that about 40 per cent of new cases of hypertension in whites and 28 per cent in blacks could be prevented if weight were to be controlled.

The American Cancer Society concluded after a long-term study that the lowest mortality rates occurred in persons weighing 80 to 89 per cent of the average weight. And literally every national and international medical and health organization has stated again and again that overweight individuals are at the greatest health risk.

What is ideal weight? Certainly a man who is six feet tall can weigh around 13 stones without being overweight—and we've all heard the joke about the doctor who tells the patient that he or she isn't too heavy, just too short! Various tables and charts have been devised to determine and identify ideal or desirable weights. Table 12 lists weights according to body-frame type for men and women. But, if you're seriously overweight, you really don't need a table or chart to tell you.

There is no 'magic' about weight control. It's all a matter of proven, hard-nosed science. Weight gain is one of the laws of nature. You just can't break those laws. No matter how many times you drop an apple from a tree, it's going to fall to the ground. That's the law of gravity. You can't break it. And the same goes for weight gain. Or weight loss.

Here's a simple fact. Not much fun, but a good, solid example. If you watch every calorie you eat every single day, go through the ritual of dry toast and skimmed milk for breakfast, cottage cheese and tomatoes for lunch, and a nice nutritious, low-fat dinner for supper, you may be just fine.

But let's say you keep eating those good foods, exercising the same amount, sleeping the same hours, and keeping everything else equal. Only now you start having just one doughnut for your coffee break. Not a big one, just a medium-sized doughnut. Not covered with chocolate, just plain. That's 100 calories. In thirty-five days, about a month, you'll take in an extra 3500 calories. And you'll gain a pound. After a year you'll gain over ten pounds. Just because of that one little doughnut. That's the 'Doughnut Law'.

Actually, scientists have another name for it. They call this is law of thermodynamics. If you take in calories, a measure of energy, you will either expend them as energy or the body will store them as fat.

No matter how much we learn about nutrition, the basics still apply. All food can be measured in terms of the energy supplied. Protein and carbohydrates provide 4 calories per gram. Fat yields 9 calories per gram. Alcohol supplies 7 calories per gram. Obviously, then, those eating less fat and more complex carbohydrates—starches rather than sugars—will take in fewer calories.

For the average adult male, it takes 15 calories per day per pound of body weight to maintain the same weight. Let's say that hypothetical man weighs 150 pounds. That means he must consume 2250 calories daily in order not to lose or gain any weight. But let's take another hypothetical case of the man who wants to weigh 150 pounds, but currently tips the scales at 180. If he, too, eats at the 2250-calorie-per-day level, eventually he'll weigh 150. The food eaten still maintains the 150 pounds, and the rest gradually disappears. And he can speed up the process by cutting his calories back even further.

Of course, every situation differs. If one is far more active than the average person, more calories will be needed to maintain weight. Completely sedentary individuals need fewer calories. As one gets older, the need for caloric energy decreases. And, unfortunately, the needs for women are less than those for men. An average, moderately active adult woman needs not 15 but only 12 calories per pound of ideal body weight.

The sad truth is that most people who try to lose weight fail. And most people who do lose weight gain it back almost immediately. In one study done in 1983, 43 per cent of all Americans went on diets; 53 per cent of all women did so. Of those, 35 per cent started their diets six times or more that year alone.

Doctors often consider treating obesity one of the least rewarding efforts because of the high failure rate. Weight loss has become one of the biggest health-related industries.

In the long run, diets simply do not work. Going on a diet normally implies eventually going off that diet. In the meatime, nothing has happened to change the poor eating habits that led to obesity in the first place. The only way to lose weight permanently is to completely change one's attitudes and approaches toward food. Certainly that's not easy. Nor is it easy to quit smoking cigarettes. But both are necessary for anyone who really wants good health and long life.

The first step is to take a really close look at your current eating habits. Do this by starting today to keep a daily log of everything you eat and drink. Keep track for two weeks. I recommend carrying a little note pad in your pocket, wallet, or handbag. Don't trust your memory. Jot down even the tiniest nibble.

Then look at your diary with objective eyes. What foods can be completely eliminated? What foods can be replaced? What foods can you cut down on? Buy one of those little calories counters. What foods have the most calories?

At the same time, follow the recommendations in Chapter 3 to cut out much of the fat in your diet. Keeping the diet diary will also help you watch the fat and cholesterol.

For the next week or two, make the adjustments in your eating patterns. Continue to keep a diary. See how much you've improved. Ask yourself whether there are foods that really don't belong on your table anymore.

Don't delude yourself that for you it is completely impossible to lose weight. Cruel as it may sound, if you stopped eating completely you would eventually starve to death. But at some point between now and then you would be at your ideal weight.

That's not to say that fasting is the way to go. Although some doctors have used this approach under careful supervision, it can be dangerous. Moreover, the basic eating patterns do not change because, after all, eventually one must begin eating again. Ultimately, any type of calories-restricted diet will achieve weight loss. The fewer calories consumed, the faster the weight loss. Whenever you follow a highly restricted diet, it's best to take a complete vitamin/mineral supplement.

For a short period of time, not more than seven days, you can take a 'break' from normal eating. You may, for example, decide to limit your daily intake to just the three oat-bran muffins. Eat one for breakfast, lunch, and dinner. Wash each one down with a glass of skimmed milk. Drink lots and lots of water throughout the day.

Each muffin has about 150 calories when made with lots of fruit and sweetened with apple-juice concentrate. You can cut the calories down a bit by making them plainer. An eight-ounce glass of skimmed milk has about 100 calories. So the daily calorie intake on such a programme would be about 675 calories. At that rate, you would lose weight quickly.

If that sounds too difficult, try adding some fruit juice to the diet, and an apple for the mid-morning snack. And a big salad with a squeeze of lemon or lime juice in the evening. You'll still be at about 1000 calories.

Interestingly, if you take this approach you can gradually build your diet up from the basic three-muffin-a-day plan to the total calories you will eventually need to maintain your ideal weight. For the hypothetical 150-lb (10¾-stone) man we spoke of earlier, this means that he can add another 1250 calories to the 1000 calories above. Those 1250 calories can come from breads, cereals, fruits, vegetables, and, of course, some meats, poultry, and fish. All that food for a reasonable amount of caloric intake.

The best part of having oat-bran muffins as the basic foundation of your diet is that they are incredibly satisfying. The reason is that oat bran absorbs a lot of water in the digestive tract. As it soaks up the water, it expands, filling the stomach and giving one that satisfied 'full' feeling.

Because of this property of oat bran, it's best to drink a lot of water. Eight eight-ounce glasses a day would be best for everyone, regardless of other dietary considerations. The advice from your school nurse back in elementary school still holds today: you just can't drink too many fluids. If you don't like water, soda water with a squeeze of lemon also counts. As do coffee, tea, and all other beverages. Make your selections wisely. Pick decaffeinated coffee and tea. Limit the number of high-calorie beverages. A six-ounce serving of apple juice contains more than 90 calories. And while beer and other alcoholic beverages do contain water, they also provide a lot of calories.

Many people today take diuretics on their doctors' orders to help control blood pressure. Often those men and women make the mistake of thinking that, since the pills help drain water from the body, they shouldn't drink extra water because it would defeat the purpose of the pills. Not true at all. The pills control the amount of water stored in the tissues. The water taken daily as beverages will be naturally excreted in the urine by the kidneys. Ask your doctor if you have any doubts or questions. He or she will agree that more water in your diet is not only acceptable, it is advisable.

No matter what you weigh or how many calories you are consuming, it's important to keep the metabolic rate up. A frustrating physiological phenomenon that occurs when people try to diet is that the body compensates for reduced food intake by burning calories more slowly. Actually this is the body's natural way to deal with times of famine and starvation. When there is less food available, less energy is consumed and burned by the tissues.

To get around this, one must become more active, to reach the next level of calorie burning. For most people this can be done merely by taking a walk once a day. If you haven't already done so this would be a good time to begin a regular exercise programme as described in Chapter 8. 'Exercise Your Options for Long Life'.

In a study done at Stanford University, fourteen sedentary middle-aged men were asked to run as much as they could and to eat as much as they wanted. over a two-year period of time, they ran an average of twelve miles a week. That also happens to be just right for cardiovascular fitness. They increased their calorie intake by 15 per cent. In the process, however, their proportion of body fat fell from 21.6 per cent to 18 per cent. In addition, the levels of their blood lipids dropped significantly.

Take a good look at the foods you're eating. Go into the supermarket and look for good alternatives. Think of all the fruits and vegetables grown all over the world that you've never tried before. If you were on a luxurious holiday on some tropical island and went to a buffet dinner, the table wouldn't be laden with cakes, would it? You'd find fruits of all kinds, shapes, and colours and you'd think it was delicious. So go to that supermarket and pretend you're on a tropical island!

Another food that works well for those trying to lose weight is soup. First of all, soup is an excellent way to get more vegetables into your diet. It's a nice alternative to having salad all the time. Pick the types that are not loaded with cream and butter, of course. And soup takes time to eat—one spoonful at a time. You'll eat less that way, and set a slower pace for the other foods you'll eat at that meal.

A study done with soup eaters showed that they ate an average of 5 per cent fewer calories for the day. Now 5 per cent may not sound like much, but keep adding it up and it becomes significant. Just as having an extra doughnut a day puts the weight on, soup can help take it off.

While we're talking about how fast one eats food, remember that it takes about twenty minutes from the time you eat a morsel of food to the time the body absorbs it into the blood to give that satisfied feeling. So give yourself time before reaching for that second helping.

Speaking of timing, remember how your mother always told you never to eat before dinner because you'd spoil your appetite? Well, this is the time to disobey your mother, and get your daily dose of oat bran at the same time. Twenty minutes before each meal, eat an oat-bran muffin. You'll find that just one muffin, washed down with a glass of water or a cup of coffee (preferably the decaffeinated type) will effectively cut down your appetite and you'll eat less food during the meal to come.

If you prefer to eat your muffins at breakfast, try having a piece of bread or a small piece of fruit before meals. The same principle applies.

When it's time to sit down for that meal, think of the behaviour-modification techniques you've probably heard many times before. This time, actually start to practice these techniques. They really work.

Start by using a smaller plate to make your meals look larger. Eat at the same times each day. When you eat, concentrate on your food, not the TV or a magazine. Always sit down to eat; never nibble away at the counter. In general, these techniques help you focus on how much you actually are eating.

You'll find that you'll enjoy your foods more when you take the time to taste them rather than gulping them down. Take small pieces. Put down your fork between bites. Chew each mouthful fully before the next bite.

Many overweight individuals have no idea how many calories they take in each day while snacking. Keep that diet diary and see for yourself. Is the midnight snack your downfall? Do you destroy all your good intentions with a candy bar in the evening?

Here are a couple of ways to think about snacks. Instead of having an ordinary bar of chocolate, treat yourself royally: have strawberries skewered on fancy toothpicks. Or arrange orange slices on a nice platter with a maraschino cherry for colour. Now and then splurge on something special like raspberries, or melon out of season. You're saving money not buying fat foods, so you have the extra grocery money.

The experts refer to the next step in changing our behaviour and attitudes 'cognitive restructuring'. In simpler English that simply means learning to think positively rather than negatively about our diets—and everything else in our lives.

Interestingly, most of us at one time or another start to see things in a gloomy, negative way. Just by becoming aware of it we can change the way we think. How does this apply to eating habits and staying at ideal weight? Let's look at some examples.

NEGATIVE: It takes *forever* to lose weight.
POSITIVE: I *am* losing weight and I *will* be slender.

NEGATIVE: I've tried all sorts of things that failed.
POSITIVE: This is *the* answer I've been looking for.

NEGATIVE: I hate giving up snacking.

POSITIVE: I love these beautiful strawberries.

NEGATIVE: I keep thinking about chocolates and cheese.

POSITIVE: I keep thinking about my weight falling.

NEGATIVE: This is so hard for me to change.

POSITIVE: I'm so glad to be heading in the right direction!

If any of those negative statements sounds like something you might have thought, it's time to start some 'cognitive restructuring'. Think positive!

While you're thinking along positive lines, try a simple mental exercise. Each day spend a bit of time, perhaps five to ten minutes, completely alone in a darkened, quiet place. Close your eyes. Relax. Let your body loosen up. Concentrate on slow, regular, deep breathing. Then picture yourself when you've lost twenty, twenty-five, thirty pounds or whatever. Imagine how your friends and loved ones will react.

Each day picture yourself thin. What will you do? Will you buy some new clothes? How will you reward yourself with something other than food?

Start thinking also about your levels of cholesterol. Close your eyes and picture the blood actually becoming 'cleansed' of those dangerous lipids.

Those who succeed in any of life's ventures have a very positive outlook. They think of themselves as successes and never doubt that they'll succeed. Our research has proven without a doubt that cholesterol levels *can* be reduced to completely normal levels. And thousands of people have successfully lost weight and kept it off. You can too!

Table 12. Height and weight standards for adults

		Desirable Weights for Men of Ages 25 and Over Weight in Pounds According to Frame		
Feet	Inches	Small Frame	Medium Frame	Large Frame
5	1	112–120	118–129	126–141
5	2	115–123	121–133	129–144
5	3	118–126	124–136	132–148
5	4	121–129	127–139	135–152
5	5	124–133	130–143	138–156
5	6	128–137	134–147	142–161
5	7	132–141	138–152	147–166
5	8	136–145	142–156	151–170
5	9	140–150	146–160	155–174
5	10	144–154	150–165	159–179

Table 12. Height and weight standards for adults

		Small Frame	Medium Frame	Large Frame
	Desirable Weights for Men of Ages 25 and Over Weight in Pounds According to Frame			
Feet	Inches			
5	11	148–158	154–170	164–184
6	0	152–162	158–175	168–189
6	1	156–167	162–180	173–194
6	2	160–171	167–185	178–199
6	3	164–175	172–190	182–204
	Desirable Weights for Women of Ages 25 and Over Weight in Pounds According to Frame			
Feet	Inches	Small Frame	Medium Frame	Large Frame
4	8	92–98	96–107	104–119
4	9	94–101	98–110	106–122
4	10	96–104	101–113	109–125
4	11	99–107	104–116	112–128
5	0	102–110	108–119	115–131
5	1	105–113	110–122	118–134
5	2	108–116	113–126	121–138
5	3	111–119	116–130	125–142
5	4	114–123	120–135	129–146
5	5	118–127	124–139	133–150
5	6	122–131	128–143	137–154
5	7	126–135	132–147	141–158
5	8	130–140	136–151	145–163
5	9	134–144	140–155	149–168
5	10	138–148	144–159	153–173

Essential to any approach to weight loss and weight control is a moderate intake of calories equal to the expenditure of calories in your life. Moderation can be delicious when one considers all the marvellous foods available to us. This is one time when you lose you're the real winner!

8. EXERCISE YOUR OPTIONS FOR LONG LIFE

To exercise or not to exercise. For an ever-increasing number of people of all ages that is no longer the question. When the Gallup Organization did a survey they found 66 per cent in the 18-to-29 age group exercising regularly. A full 54 per cent of the entire population now does some kind of workout.

Those sweating masses appear to be on the right track. Dr Ralph Paffenbarger, speaking of his research published in the 6 March 1986, *New England Journal of Medicine*, said those who regularly exercise throughout their lives add from one to more than two years to their lives. Those are average numbers, with some individuals expected to tack on ten or even twenty years of living. Put another way, Dr Paffenbarger said that every hour spent exercising will be returned in added life, with an extra hour as a dividend. You just can't beat that kind of investment.

Three separate studies have now provided definitive proof that regular aerobic exercise improves the health of the heart. These research studies used animals rather than people for the very simple reason that animals could be sacrificed so their hearts could be examined.

One study at the University of California used pigs, whose hearts and circulatory systems are similar to ours. A coronary artery was artificially blocked in eighteen animals. Nine were then strenuously exercised on a treadmill for five months; the other nine did no exercise. At autopsy, the hearts of the exercised pigs showed twice the development of collateral vessels. That's important because, when an artery is blocked, no blood can get through. Collateral vessels can form a kind of natural bypass around the blockage, providing the needed blood flow. A good system of collateral vessels can sometimes prevent a heart attack and can lessen the likelihood of death should a heart attack occur.

For many years, advocates of regular exercise have cited the development of collateral circulation as a major benefit. Now we have the proof.

In a second study, physical exercise was shown to protect against sudden cardiac death. This work was conducted at the University of Oklahoma, using dogs that had had previous heart attacks. Some were given exercise and others were not. After just six weeks of training, all the dogs were put on the treadmill for testing. None of the exercising dogs showed any cardiac arrhythmia or ventricular fibrillation, signs of weakened or malfunctioning hearts, while seven of eight non-exercising dogs showed those signs.

A third study showed the benefits of exercise for those with high blood pressure. At Montefiore Hospital in New York ten rats were put on a programme of regular swimming while another ten remained sedentary. All had high blood pressure. Cardiac function returned to normal in all the rat swimmers.

For those of us concerned about the risk factor of cholesterol, there is more heartening news. It appears that strenuous exercise on a regular basis can elevate the protective levels of HDL. A study reported in the *Journal of the American Medical Association* indicates that's even true for older men and women. Participants in that study showed an HDL increase from 52 ± 5 to 58 ± 6, enough to strongly affect the total cholesterol/HDL ratio, indicating protection from coronary heart disease.

Documentation on the importance of exercise continues to build. One such report came from the US Centers for Disease Control. Researchers there said flaws in earlier studies kept authorities from making a firm connection between inactivity and heart disease.

The CDC did a comprehensive two-year analysis of all studies published in English dealing with exercise and heart disease. The conclusion they reached was that the least active people were almost twice as likely to have heart disease as those who were most active.

The importance of inactivity is becoming more apparent because so many men and women do not do enough aerobic exercise. Yes, smoking is probably a more significant risk factor. But only 18 per cent of the US population currently smokes cigarettes. Yes, hypertension is probably a more significant risk factor. But only 10 per cent of adults have a systolic blood pressure level above 150. The bottom line is that 80–90 per cent of our population still does not do sufficient cardiovascular exercise.

An interesting side effect of exercise is that those who get actively engaged in such activities as swimming and jogging tend to quit smoking cigarettes. This is true even for those who have smoked for years and who have tried to quit before.

Then, of course, there's weight loss. Exercise should be an integral part of any weight-loss programme. It appears that exercise speeds up the metabolism in such a way that calories are burned more efficiently for hours afterward. The result is pounds lost even when one is eating the same amount of food.

A final benefit also involves cholesterol, but in an indirect way. Stress raises cholesterol levels and has been considered a significant risk factor in heart disease. For more details, see Chapter 9, 'Defusing the Stress Bomb', in this book. Exercise, it turns out, can effectively reduce stress, and, in turn, cholesterol.

What kind of exercise is best? Basically any kind of strenuous workout—jogging, energetic walking, swimming, various sports—you may enjoy is fine. The important thing is to make a commitment to exercise regularly, three to five days each and every week.

If you haven't done any physical exercise in quite a while, be certain to start off slowly and gradually increase your tolerance. Especially if there has been any family history of heart disease or if you are over the age of 35 it's best to check with your physician before starting off on an exercise programme.

The consensus now is that regular exercise will have both long-term and short-term benefits for all. So exercise your options for a long and healthy life.

9. DEFUSING THE STRESS BOMB

Although it is only recently that stress has been given a great deal of attention, it is by no means a purely modern phenomenon. Back in time before history began, our ancestor the cavemen experienced stress; even they had their problems. Finding food. Fighting off a sabre-toothed tiger. Getting out of the way of a mastodon stampede. But, when measuring stress, the caveman had it a lot easier than we do today. After that battle with the tiger, he could sit back and rest for a while. Once the stampede passed by, he could contemplate his navel. Stress was an intermittent thing that came and went.

Today, on the other hand, for many people stress never lets up. Or at least people don't give it a chance to let up. It's one crisis on top of another, from traffic jams to irate customers to family arguments—all superimposed over our ongoing anxiety about money, careers, and any number of things.

It's enough to give one a headache. Even worse, it's enough to contribute to heart disease. That's why this chapter is in a book about cholesterol. So let's start at the beginning and see what stress is, how it affects our health, and what we can do about it.

Stress can be defined as any unpleasant emotion, be it anxiety, worry, anger, hostility, or pressures of many kinds. There's no way to eliminate all stress from our lives. Besides, we really wouldn't want to do so. A bit of stress has been shown to enhance performance, whether on an athletic field or during a college exam. Waiting for the winning ticket to be drawn in a lottery has its own excitement. But there's a point where the constructive stress gives way to a far more destructive form.

The first man to study this was the famous Canadian medical researcher Hans Selye. His detailed observations of both animals and humans led to dozens of articles and books on the subject. One of his classic studies involved a population of house mice allowed to grow to overcrowded conditions. As their numbers grew and interactions and confrontations increased, the mice developed a number of physical reactions. Hostility and aggression increased. Food intake was affected.

Even reproduction was decreased. Sadly, the conditions are those found today in our overcrowded, bustling cities.

For many years, medical authorities have felt that stress can be both counterproductive and destructive. In their book *Type A Behavior and Your Heart* Drs Meyer Friedman and Ray Rosenman discussed the time-conscious, driven individual whose lifestyle differs so much from that of his more laid-back Type B counterpart. The Type A person is always in a hurry, so much so that he often completes your sentences before you can do so. There's never enough time for him to finish his business, and no time at all for him to relax.

Invariably, the Type A considers the Type B as either flat-out lazy or at least not working at his fullest potential. But, as Drs Friedman and Rosenman point out, that's not at all the case. In fact, many Type A individuals are so flustered all the time that they are working inefficiently. And in some closer looks at success there seems to be no correlation to stress type. The Type B has just as much or even more chance to succeed. And he's much more likely to enjoy his success.

Stress takes its toll by contributing to a number of physical ailments including ulcers, headaches, stomach aches, colitis, and high blood pressure. It can make asthma and arthritis worse. Stress can even be traced to sexual dysfunction. And, it seems certain to say today, stress kills.

While many authorities have believed that for some time, today we have documented proof. We now have a physiologic explanation for what happens, and we can see the effects of stress on the heart with various modern diagnostic techniques.

For our friend the caveman, when those sabre-toothed tigers jumped out of the woods, his body's chemistry changed. The sympathetic nervous system produced chemical agents known as catecholamines. The best known of these is adrenalin, the so-called 'fight or flight' hormone. It served the caveman well for his encounters with dangerous animals.

Not only was Neanderthal man ready to do battle mentally, his body also reacted to protect him from any injuries. In case of cuts blood was drawn from the limbs. And the blood became enriched with platelets that facilitated the clotting process.

As man evolved, he kept those protective devices. Except today there are no sabre-toothed tigers. And for many of us there are no rests in between fights. But the stress encountered still causes the clotting process to accelerate. The problem with this is that those clots can lead to deposits in the arteries and can actually precipitate a heart attack.

And, unfortunately, there's even more. The coronary arteries, which supply the blood to the heart, have a muscular layer that gets its supply of nerves from the same sympathetic nervous system that produces those fight or flight hormones. Stress, it turns out, causes the nerves to react in such a way that the muscle tissue of the arteries constricts. Doctors call this a 'spasm'.

In an individual with no blockage in the arteries, the potential problems with spasm are great enough. But, when the arteries are occluded by deposits of plaque formed from cholesterol deposits, the spasm may completely shut down the flow of blood to the heart. The result is a heart attack. In less severe cases of spasm brought on by stress, an individual may experience the chest pain known as angina, signalling that the heart isn't getting enough blood supply. The pain felt is really very similar to that experienced when other muscles cramp or have a spasm, say, for example, after extensive exercise.

Interestingly, some people can take a stress test on a treadmill in a doctor's office and show no blockage whatever. Yet in times of stress they feel chest discomfort. Modern diagnostic techniques show why.

One such test is called Holter monitoring. The patient has electrodes attached to the chest, which lead into a kind of tape recorder worn at the waist. The machine runs for a full twenty-four hours, during which time the patient keeps a diary of what's happened and how he or she has felt. Then the doctor can compare the recorded tracings with the diary. Often the periods of discomfort as written down by the patient coincide with indications on the recording of insufficient blood supply to the heart.

Insufficient blood supply results in insufficient oxygen, given the term 'ischaemia'. When the person relaxes, and the blood flow increases with its supply of oxygen, the discomfort passes.

How much stress can cause such reactions? Of course it depends on the individual. *The Lancet* reported a study in which fourteen very sick patients were hooked up for ECG readings and asked to perform relatively simple arithmetic problems. Even though they experienced no pain, the ECGs showed the telltale signs of cardiac insufficiency. While a simple arithmetic problem may not be enough to precipitate stressful oxygen deprivation in healthy individuals, the frenetic pace of modern society may be just as destructive.

The case has often been cited of the accountants whose cholesterol levels were tested just before a tax deadline and two weeks afterward. There was a significant drop after the deadline. The same thing happened when medical students were tested before and after examinations.

There we have the stress-cholesterol link. As much as we try to control the amount of cholesterol in our blood through the dietary aspects of this programme, stress may be thwarting our good intentions.

The answer is to do something about reducing the effects of that stress.

There are three things to aim for in dealing with stress: (1) reduce the number of stressful incidents, (2) reduce the intensity of those episodes, and (3) find ways to rest and relax in between. While it may be difficult, taking those three steps is not impossible.

The first thing to do is to become aware of your own stressors, the things that lead to your personal feelings of pressure and stress. Just as it is a good idea to keep a diary of what you eat and drink when trying to modify the diet, it is very helpful to keep a log of daily stresses.

Let's say that you record stress while driving to an appointment for which you might be late. Perhaps a way to deal with that is to leave ten or fifteen minutes earlier the next time. Maybe you can make the drive more pleasant by bringing a long a cool drink and turning to a soothing music station on the car radio.

Your daily log may also show that you're going from one stressful episode right into another without having a chance to rest and recuperate in between. The body is a truly resilient machine, but such abuse can't go on for long without ill effect. If you think honestly about it, there must be a way to give yourself a 'breather' when one stress ends and before another begins.

The next step is more difficult for the vast majority of fast-paced people. Learn to relax during those breathing spaces between stresses. For most people, that time is spent simply stewing about what made them anxious or angry in the first place, making matters even worse as the mind allows the episode to gain even greater proportions.

There is no best prescription for relaxation. For some lucky men and women, it's enough to simply remind themselves to stop and smell the roses. For others, the old prescription of counting to ten really helps. But for most of us special efforts are needed.

Fortunately, professionals have come up with a number of techniques to help defuse the stress bomb. A number of self-help books and tapes are available. And, for those who need special assistance along these lines, professionals can help with such techniques as biofeedback training or group sessions of self-analysis.

There are tremendous relaxation benefits from regular exercise workouts. Ask runners or swimmers and they will tell you about the blissful feeling they get. Scientists explain that feeling as the result of a chemical substance called a beta-endorphin, which is released into the blood during heavy-duty exercise.

Even if you don't become a marathon runner, regular exercise pays off in a number of dividends. The late President Eisenhower's personal physician and famous cardiologist Paul Dudley White lived to a ripe old age, attributing much of his vim and vigour to regular exercise, including bicycle riding. For others a nice long walk at the end of the day is a veritable tonic.

Just as with the type of exercise you do, the trick is to find a relaxation technique that's right for you. It has to be something that fits your own lifestyle, and that you find actually enjoyable. Don't let your efforts to relax become yet another source of stress.

Diet and alcohol play important roles in terms of stress, since many people use both food and drink as ways of dealing with their emotions. That heavy meal or enormous snack at midnight eaten as consolation for a miserable day will only lead to a miserable, sleepless night. Ironically, the same thing applies to alcohol. While drink in moderation can be an enjoyable part of living, it's not meant to be used as a general anaesthetic. Instead of leading to a good night's sleep, excessive alcohol intake results in poor rest and a terrible feeling in the morning.

Drinking coffee with caffeine is like pouring petrol on a fire. The last thing one needs is jittery 'coffee nerves'. Try some of the new decaffeinated coffees.

A great way to cope with daily stress is to do something nice for yourself—like taking that long walk. We often don't treat ourselves well out of a misguided sense of guilt, living as we do in a society where hard work is praised and 'play' gets short shrift. For my own personal treat, about every two weeks or so, I indulge in a full hour of massage. The person I go to has arranged a room as a 'sanctuary' with plants growing, water trickling, and music playing. I lie down on that table and allow those fingers to whisk me away from daily pressures and gently ease away tensions and anxieties. Yet, as much as I enjoy those sessions, I frequently find myself coming up with excuses to cancel out for the day. Then I have to remind myself that this is just as important as exercise or even diet in terms of maintaining good health.

Think of something that would be equally enjoyable for you. Perhaps a facial. Or a manicure. Or a steambath or sauna. Maybe something as simple as a cup of decaffeinated coffee in a snackshop with the morning paper or a crossword puzzle. If you're not good to yourself, how can you expect the world to be any better?

Which brings up the next step in learning to deal with stress. The problem, of course, is in those six inches between the ears. The way we think about things is the way those things will be. The self-fulfilling prophecy, as it were—an old adage, but true nonetheless. One man looks at a glass of water as half full while another views it as half empty. The result is that the first man is happy and contented while the other is sad and disappointed. If you wake up in the morning thinking that everything bad will happen, it probably will. Instead, try getting up after a good night's rest and vow to think of something good in everything that you experience that day. Turn those lemons into lemonade. Someone's late for an appointment with you? Great: a good time to read a magazine! Your spouse is in a lousy mood in the evening and can't face up to fixing dinner? Terrific: a wonderful opportunity to try that new Japanese restaurant down the street. No parking place close to where you need to go? Marvellous: another chance to take a stroll down the sidewalk and do a little window shopping. Don't scoff: it can be done and you know it can. We all know someone who is virtually unflappable. Try to be more like that person.

This leads into the next step in the anti-stress programme. Drs Friedman and Rosenman have demonstrated that the Type A person can gradually turn into a Type B personality. And that can be done without any loss of ambition or chance at success. Take another look at that daily stress diary you've been keeping.

Compare your notes about your stressful episodes with those of a personality Type A. You're a Type A person if you overly stress certain words during conversations—driving the points home in case your listener doesn't catch them to your satisfaction. You do everything rapidly, both working and playing—never taking the time to savour the moment. You're impatient with how slowly everything takes place and you want to speed things along. You find it difficult to enjoy a conversation that doesn't have anything to do with your own interests or current lifestyle. You feel somewhat guilty about relaxing, thinking of work that could be done instead. You judge your own efforts in terms of numbers and you gauge progress by the clock and calendar, and somehow there's never enough time. You're more interested in things to have than enjoyable things to do. You find yourself doing or redoing the work of others because your standards so far exceed theirs. And you're certain that everything you've ever achieved is the result of your hard-driving personality. In short you're the kind of person the world needs more of to be a better place!

If you're nodding your head 'yes' to even a few of these traits, it's time to start thinking about how to reverse the process. Face the hard, cruel facts of life: if you died today, the world would go on without you. No man or woman is indispensable. *Yes* you have time to go on holiday. *Yes* that appointment can be postponed until later. *Yes* your children will love you if you don't bring home as much bacon. *Yes* it doesn't really matter if the appointment starts ten minutes late.

You're not a horse with blinkers. You're a thinking human being who is smart enough to realize that, if you don't come to grips with the stresses around you, those stresses will come to grip you—around the heart.

10. DINING OUT: TO YOUR HEALTH!

Salud! L'Chaim! Na Zdrowya! All over the world, diners raise their glasses to each other and toast 'To your health!' There couldn't be a better wish to make. And there isn't a better time or place to pursue a healthful diet than in a fine restaurant. 'To health!' 'To life!'

Some health writers have given eating out an unjustified bad name. Nathan Pritikin actually calls restaurants 'the enemy camp', and advises against going out to eat at all. When forced to do so, he advocates, order steamed vegetables and rice. That's rather a gloomy future for most of us who truly enjoy the pleasures of restaurant dining.

Now, by this time in your reading of this book, it must be perfectly clear that I don't recommend the fatty and cholesterol-laden foods that may be on the menu. Fast-food spots, for example, have little to offer anyone seeking a healthful meal. Just take a look at the calorie, fat, cholesterol, and sodium content of fast foods listed in Table 10 in Chapter 3, 'Winning by the Numbers', and you'll see what I mean.

On the other end of the spectrum, the old-fashioned cuisine of traditional French restaurants can be equally unhealthful. Interestingly, however, even some of the great French chefs have gravitated to a lighter version of cooking called *nouvelle cuisine*. Those dishes get away from rich butter-and-cream sauces and emphasize the fresh tastes of fish and vegetables prepared in novel and delicious ways.

Somewhere in between the fast-food restaurants and the traditional French restaurants, however, are a wide variety of dining experiences that are not only delicious but also healthful, and they can be found all over the world. In fact, a great way to decide on a place to eat out is to spin the globe, close your eyes, and point your finger. Ethnic cooking offers a never-ending variety of tastes and textures, from the sauces of Thailand to the ratatouille of the Mediterranean.

Like Marco Polo, you can explore the Orient. The cuisines of China as well as Korea, Japan, Thailand, and Vietnam can be a dieter's delight. Deciding on Chinese isn't specific enough. There are Cantonese restaurants, serving the traditional chop suey dishes as well as chow mein, won ton soup, mu shu, and moo goo gai pan; or, if you prefer, the spicy Szechwan cuisine, offering da-chien chicken made with hot peppers, yu-shong scallops, hot braised fish, and tongue-twisting listings with black mushrooms, ginger, and oyster sauce.

When I eat Chinese with friends, we always enjoy ordering a number of dishes. For four persons, for example, we'll get a fish dish, a chicken dish, a vegetable dish, and plenty of steaming rice. Those vegetable dishes are anything but boring. Try yu-shong eggplant, cooked with hot garlic, ginger root, and green onion. Or a dish called imperial jade with garden-fresh snow pea pods sautéed with crunchy and tasty water chestnuts. Or a medley of vegetables done in the inimitable manner of the stir-fry wok.

Fried? Yes, I did say fried. But notice some important differences. First, the Orientals use no butter. They prefer the very healthful (monounsaturated) peanut oil, which imparts a unique flavour. Second, the amount of oil used is very small indeed. Third, the wok, a large bowl-like cooking utensil, is heated so hot that foods are cooked before they have a chance to absorb much oil. To be even more cautious, as I am in unfamiliar restaurants, I request that the chef use very little oil, and no MSG—monosodium glutamate. Many restaurants, in fact, now advertise that they use no MSG at all, since so many people are becoming sodium conscious.

Can you eat anything at all on the Chinese menu? No, of course not. Avoid the typical appetizer dishes such as egg rolls and spring rolls. These are deep-fried and often contain eggs. Second, duck dishes are absolutely out. That delicacy Peking duck is primarily skin, and a 3½-ounce serving contains nearly 30 grams of fat. Choose chicken or seafood dishes over those containing either lamb or pork to avoid fat. The nice thing about Chinese restaurants is that the same dish can be ordered with any meat, so one need not be deprived of a specific flavour sensation just because it is listed on the menu as containing pork.

If you've had enough Chinese food for a while, it's time to turn the corner and try one of the many Thai or Vietnamese restaurants opening up all over the country. The dishes are flavoured in ways you may never have tried before. Salads, a great way to start, come with dressings made with peanut butter and cilantro. One local restaurant lists 'pla lard plick', which is a sweet white fish specially imported from the China Sea, prepared with a light red curry sauce with bamboo shoots. Or how about 'goong nai som', which turns out to be boiled prawns in a fresh orange shell with orange sauce. If there's something about the dish that you don't want, chopped egg yolks, for example, simply have them eliminated. Everything is made to order, so you get to design your own meals.

And don't forget the wonderful meals waiting at any Japanese restaurant. Many people have come to love the fresh tastes and textures of sashimi and sushi, specially prepared raw fish delicacies, sliced before your eyes by chefs wielding razor-sharp knives. Not ready for that yet? Then consider yosenabe, a Japanese-style bouillabaisse made with a variety of seafoods and vegetables. Then there are always the teriyaki chicken and sukiyaki. But don't forget to inform your waitress that you don't want eggs in your dishes. You'll never miss them in your sukiyaki. The only other advice is to avoid the soy-sauce container on the table. While the Japanese have almost no heart disease, thanks to their low-fat, low-cholesterol foods, they have a considerable amount of high blood pressure because of the high levels of sodium in their diet.

Moving west, we come to the foods of India. Again, practically every city has at least one Indian restaurant. And most offer that delicacy known as tandoori chicken, specially marinated and baked in an Indian clay oven. There is no way to precisely describe the flavour and texture—it's like nothing else. Other dishes worth mentioning are 'murg jalfraize', chicken flavoured with fresh spices and sautéed (ask for no butter) with tomatoes, onions, and bell peppers, and 'saag' chicken prepared with spinach and Indian spices. Then, of course, there are the traditional curries, as hot as you want them to be, washed down with lots of tea or cold beer.

The foods of other countries also offer taste treats. Consider the whole culinary experience of Mexico. While it's true that many of the dishes contain a great deal of cheese, which is high in fat and cholesterol, most can be ordered without it. And the sauces created to go with seafood are excellent.

The USA has contributed a large number of excellent, healthful dishes. This is the time to discover the large variety of American foods, including New England seafoods, New Orleans Creole, and Cajun gumbos and jambalayas. Then there's the Western-style mesquite broiling technique that's taken over like wildfire. Somehow foods seem to taste so much better when cooked over the coals in this manner.

Another particularly American phenonomen of late is the salad bar. We're not talking here about a few leaves of wilted lettuce and a limp piece or two of radish. Instead, experience a salad bar that extends over an entire wall of a restaurant, laden with twenty or thirty or more different ingredients to build your own creations.

One of the nicest parts about salad-bar eating, in my opinion, is the opportunity to go back again and again. And the sheer beauty of it is that you can do so without guilt, as long as you avoid the egg yolks, limit the avocado, and make wise decisions about the salad dressings.

Most people, speaking of salad dressings, think that the best bet in terms of calories and fat content is oil and vinegar. Wrong. Actually, some creamy dressings are lower in both fat and calories. Ask the waiter or manager about the ingredients used. And, of course, limit the dollops you lavish on your greens.

Notice that one or more times I've mentioned asking the waiter or waitress about the foods served in a restaurant. I find it almost incredible that people can be shy when it comes to speaking up about the foods they're about to order and eat and pay for. When you're in a restaurant, you're the boss!

If an item is listed as being sautéed, simply ask that the dish be prepared without butter. The chef can sauté in either a bit of broth or a dash of vegetable oil. If you're not sure of a certain offering, ask how it's prepared. Then, if there's an offending ingredient, request that it be substituted or eliminated. If you find yourself in a restaurant that balks at your requests, you're in the wrong restaurant. The best ones have no problem with such requests.

Often restaurants serve extra-large helpings of foods. There are a number of ways of getting around this. If you're with other people, why not consider ordering a number of appetizers, then splitting an entrée? Or try getting two entrées for three people. Or any combination you can think of. This not only cuts down on the amount of food eaten but also gives you a chance to taste more than one dish.

When your meal comes, mentally divide what you really need to and should eat. Then eat only that amount. If you've ordered a piece of meat and they give you, say, twelve ounces, cut it in half. Your waiter or waitress will know how many ounces are in every entrée—that's a major consideration for every restaurant.

What to do with the amount not eaten? Ask for a 'doggie bag' to take the leftover food home. This is accepted practice, and nothing to be ashamed of at all. Everyone does it, in even the very finest restaurants.

A word of explanation is in order. Restaurants today must keep their prices up in order to pay for the ever-escalating operating costs. To justify those costs, they offer much more food than you want. It's impossible for the restaurants to reduce costs by giving you less food. So simply take that extra food home. It'll make an excellent lunch or even another dinner.

Obviously, not everyone is concerned about limiting fat and cholesterol in his or her diet. My brother, as I've mentioned before, views the baked potato as a vehicle for butter and sour cream, and maintains a cholesterol level of just 4.4. But, if you're not that lucky, you'll want to order your baked potato plain.

Now that can be pretty dull and boring. So here are a few suggestions. Try some spicy salsa. Or ask the waitress if she has any sauces in the kitchen that would be appropriately low in fat and cholesterol.

Does that mean you can never have the sour cream? Or the butter? Or the dessert? Of course not. Remember the advice in Chapter 3, 'Winning by the Numbers'. The important thing is the total amount of fat and cholesterol you consume during the entire day.

So, if you order a low-fat broiled fish, it's perfectly OK to enjoy some sour cream on your potato. Or you may prefer to have a nice dessert. Remember that it's your choice and the only thing that counts is keeping the total number of grams of fat and milligrams of cholesterol under your own personal limit.

Personally, I have the greatest difficulty not with elaborate sauces and fancy desserts, but with junk foods. So, if I've watched my intake during the day, I permit myself some guacamole and tortilla chips, even though I know they're loaded with fat. After a day of salad for lunch, fish for dinner, and, of course, my oat-bran muffins, I feel no guilt about having that special ice-cream treat later in the evening.

It's important to realize that just because you've decided to lower your cholesterol levels you don't have to enter a monastery and give up all the taste treats in the world. In fact, those who try to follow such a spartan regimen typically fail in the long run.

Let's get back to the restaurants for a moment. If you've been used to a lifetime of eating in Italian places, it's ridiculous to think that you can simply stop going to them. Instead, compromise a bit. Order your veal dish with tomatoes and basil instead of a cheese sauce. Have linguine and clam sauce instead of fettunccine Alfredo.

The worst thing to have happen in a restaurant is to be surprised by a menu that offers nothing appealing that satisfies your needs. If you find yourself in a restaurant with nothing but fried foods, you're going to eat a lot of fat and there's practically nothing you can do about it. So be prepared by first knowing the restaurants you go to. If in doubt, call them and ask about the menu. You may have to suggest an alternative to your friends if you find that the menu doesn't permit you to order enjoyable food without a lot of fat.

One way to choose restaurants is by reading the restaurant review sections of newspapers and magazines. The reviewer typically describes the ingredients of a number of dishes in detail, so you'll know in advance what you're getting. Another way is to purchase a book of discount coupons. My wife and I frequently use these books to find restaurants that we would otherwise never consider. One book, *Entertainment '87* (or whatever year it happens to be), prints the menus from a large number of restaurants. With the coupon, one gets the lesser-priced entrée free along with one purchased at the regular price. We often plan our meals well in advance, and there are no unpleasant surprises.

But no discussion of dining out would be complete without considering the problems (if you want to think of them as such) of eating at friends' homes. Again, this is a simple matter of communication. First, remember that these are your friends. Friends care about each other. For you, eating a cheese omelette can actually be an unpleasant experience when thinking about what it's doing to the lining of your arteries. So talk to your friends about it.

The time to start, actually, is before a luncheon or dinner invitation. Let people know how excited you are that you've discovered a way to control your cholesterol and that you've cut the risk of coronary heart disease. Let them know that there are certain foods you prefer to avoid or at least limit. Then when it comes time to go to their homes, it'll be almost an afterthought to mention that you're still not eating butter or egg yolks, and that you keep the cheese intake low. No surprises.

You'll find—at least I've found—that most people who know you're watching what you eat will ask about the foods you'd rather have.

Today more people than ever before are aware of the impact food has on their health. In any given group of men and women, one will be cutting down on calories, another will have gone vegetarian, another will have found that he or she is allergic to certain foods, and still another will have developed intolerance over the years to, say, dairy foods. And almost everyone today knows the relationship between fat and heart disease and cancer.

That's why more and more restaurants are catering to health-conscious individuals. Occasionally you'll even find whole special sections on menus that feature particularly healthful dishes.

Restaurants not only can provide the kinds of foods you need to reduce your total intake of fats and cholesterol, but also offer ideas for cooking in your own home. Ask about certain recipes you find enjoyable. Or invest in a cookbook featuring the foods you relished.

But by all means don't limit the pleasures of dining out. Next time, just raise your glass in that worldwide and traditional toast: To your health!

11. PAINLESS PRIMER ON PROPER NUTRITION

The problem with most attempts to teach us an overview of nutrition, I believe, is that writers get carried away. People don't have to become nutritionists in order to select foods wisely for themselves and their families. What everyone does need, however, is an understanding of the basic principles that should affect food choices. This is particularly true when we make a concerted effort to alter the diet, in this case to reduce the amount of fat and cholesterol we plan to eat.

Ultimately the whole science of nutrition comes down to this: Nutrition is the process by which food and everything else we consume becomes a part of our bodies and affects our total health and growth. Food allows us to function. It's as simple as that.

The next concept to grasp is that food consists of various chemicals working together in interaction with the chemicals of our bodies. Certain foods have certain nutrients while other foods have other nutrients. By eating a wide variety of foods, as we'll see, we ensure that we get a full spectrum of those nutrients.

Everyone, regardless of age, sex, or other physical or medical characteristics, needs the same nutrients. Some need more and some require less food. But throughout our lives we continue to need the basic nutrients offered in the foods we eat.

Food plays important roles in life. The feast has long been a part of ceremony, whether on a jungle island or in a lavish Mayfair reception room. When guests arrive in our homes we offer food. Gatherings and celebrations of all sorts frequently involve meals, often on a grand scale. Yet, regardless of what, when, how, where, or why we eat, food supplies those basic nutrients. Those nutrients provide materials to build, repair, and maintain body tissues. They supply the chemicals we need for regulating our bodily functions. And they furnish fuel needed for energy.

As a broad classification, there are six classes of nutrients: protein, carbohydrates, fat, vitamins, minerals, and water. (Yes, water is a distinct nutrient we just can't live without.) Each nutrient has its own particular function, but many of them work together. For example, to build bones vitamin D, calcium, and phosophorus interact. In this case, bone will not form efficiently when one of those nutrients is inadequate or deficient. Within the broad classification of six classes of nutrients, there are about fifty specific nutrients.

Does that mean we have to be aware of fifty different nutrients in the foods we eat daily? That would take a lot of effort and calculation. Instead, nutritionists have designated just ten as what they call the 'leader' nutrients. Those ten are protein, carbohydrates, fat, vitamin A, vitamin C, thiamin, riboflavin, niacin, calcium, and iron. The generally accepted belief is that, if one consumes those nutrients in sufficient amounts, the foods containing them will also provide the other forty. With that in mind, let's look at those ten leader nutrients.

Protein

Throughout our lives we need protein to maintain and build body tissues, which are constantly being replaced; to make haemoglobin in the blood to carry oxygen to the body's cells; to form antibodies in the process of immunity, which protects our bodies from infection; and to produce enzymes and hormones that regulate bodily functions. Excess protein may also be used, though inefficiently, as an energy source. While we can store some nutrients, protein cannot be stockpiled for later use. That's why we need to eat protein on a regular basis. Happily, that's easy to do.

The fact of the matter is that most people consume far more protein than they actually need. There are a number of reasons for this. First, we live in a land of plenty. Second, protein is found in a wide variety of both animal and plant foods. Third, our tastes lead us to choose foods with high protein levels.

What we really need are the eight or nine indispensable or essential amino acids, which are the 'building blocks' of protein. When we get those eight, our bodies can construct complete molecules of the total twenty-two amino acids in our bodies. Protein from animal sources contains all the amino acids we need in one place. Proteins from a variety of plant sources can also provide that complete amino-acid profile. For example, beans and rice work together beautifully, and are part of many Latin diets. Unless one is a strict vegetarian, however, it's not terribly important to worry about balancing those amino acids. Again, we actually consume more—far more—protein than we require. Even following a strict vegetarian diet, it's not difficult to get all the protein one needs.

This is important to remember when reducing fat and cholesterol. Since the majority of that fat and cholesterol comes from meat and eggs, there's no need to worry that by cutting back on the amounts we eat we'll have protein deficiencies. Actually, cutting down on protein saves wear and tear on the kidneys, which metabolize the nitrogen byproducts.

If you wish to do so, you can very easily determine how much protein you're consuming on a daily basis. Keep a little diary for a few days. Look at the nutrient lables on various packaged foods and add up the grams of protein you're eating on a per-serving basis. Next count on 30 grams average per serving to calculate the protein you're getting from animal foods. You'll probably find you're far beyond the basic Recommended Dietary Allowances.

Vitamins

Most nutritionists feel that the foods we typically eat contain enough of the thirteen known vitamins. Many people, however, feel that swallowing a multivitamin tablet or pill daily provides extra insurance. I've never heard anyone say this could do any harm, and many authorities, especially in private, say it's probably a good idea.

There are basically two types of vitamins, the fat-soluble and the water-soluble kinds. Fat-soluble vitamins are stored in the body and include vitamins A, D, E, and K. Water-soluble vitamins are not stored in the body and include vitamin C and the whole series of B vitamins. Water-soluble vitamins are excreted in the urine when the body receives an excess amount, whether from foods or pills. The fat-soluble vitamins are stored, and toxicity can result if excess amounts are consumed.

Let's take a moment to very briefly review the thirteen known vitamins. RDAs for each are listed in Table 13 (see pages 135-7).

Vitamin A helps to build cells in the body, is necessary for seeing in dim light, and prevents certain eye diseases. We get this nutrient in vegetables, including carrots, sweet potatoes, and green, leafy vegetables as well as in enriched foods such as milk and cereals. Is it difficult to get enough? Just one-half cup of sweet potatoes contains 150 per cent of the RDA.

Vitamin D aids in building bone tissue and in absorbing calcium from the digestive tract. We get all we need from fish oils, fortified milk and other dairy foods, and sunshine. Vitamin D deficiencies are simply unknown in this day and age.

Vitamin E protects vitamin A and unsaturated fatty acids from destruction by oxidation. While deficiencies can lead to sexual dysfunction, excessive amounts cannot promote sexuality. Claims for the role of vitamin E in preventing heart disease have never been substantiated. Foods containing vitamin E include vegetable oils, green leafy vegetables, whole-grain cereals, wheat germ, butterfat, and egg yolks.

Vitamin K is the last of the fat-soluble vitamins and is essential in the clotting of blood. There is virtually no chance of deficiency here, since in addition to the vitamin K contained in vegetables and elsewhere, the body produces its own supply in the intestine.

Vitamin C forms the substances that literally hold the cells and body together, hastens the healing of wounds, and increases resistance to infection. Found in a variety of fruits and vegetables, vitamin C is also added to a number of foods and beverages. No one to date has been able to prove the benefits of *very* large doses.

Vitamin B_1 (thiamin) contributes to the functioning of the nervous system, promotes a normal appetite, and aids in the use of energy by the body. This nutrient is found in nuts, fortified cereal products, and lean pork. Just a little is all we need.

Vitamin B_2 (riboflavin) promotes healthy skin and eyes, and also aids in the utilization of energy. Milk, yogurt, and cottage cheese are excellent sources of this nutrient.

Niacin is also known as vitamin B_3. It promotes healthy skin, nerves, and digestive tract, and also is a part of energy utilization. Natural sources of niacin include meats, fish, and poultry as well as peanuts and fortified cereal products. In large doses niacin has the effect of lowering levels of LDL cholesterol and triglycerides while raising those of HDL cholesterol. The niacin metabolite, niacinamide, does not have this property although it does perform the functions listed above.

Vitamin B_6 assists in red-blood-cell regeneration and helps to regulate the use of protein, fat, and carbohydrates. It's found in various meats, soybeans, lima beans, bananas, and whole-grain cereals.

Vitamin B_{12} assists in the maintenance of nerve tissues and normal blood formation. Only animal foods supply this nutrient. Sources include fish, shellfish, milk, and other dairy foods. Vegetarians must take vitamin B_{12} supplements if they are strict practitioners.

Folic Acid/Folacin assists in maintaining nerve tissues and blood cells. it is mainly found in green leafy vegetables, nuts, and legumes. There has been some evidence that women taking the contraceptive pill need more than the RDA minimum.

Biotin is another B vitamin but does not have a specified RDA. Found in most fresh vegetables and in milk and meats, this nutrient helps regulate carbohydrate metabolism. There is no problem with deficiencies.

Pantothenic Acid is another vitamin without an RDA. Found in wholegrain cereals and legumes, this nutrient aids in general nutrient metabolism.

Minerals

Daily recommended allowances have been established for six minerals, including calcium, phosphorus, iodine, iron, magnesium, and zinc. In addition to these, there are nine other minerals that are needed in lesser amounts and that are considered to be supplied by the same foods offering the six major minerals. Minerals in general are required for body building and regulatory functions.

Calcium requirements continue throughout life to ensure sufficient amounts of this mineral for bone health and for regulatory functions in the blood serum. The major sources of calcium are milk and other dairy foods. While it is possible to get calcium from sardines and canned salmon by eating the bones, this is not a practical source on a daily basis for most people. Vegetable sources are also not practical both in terms of frequency of consumption and poorer availability of the nutrient. Dairy foods also provide the vitamin D and phosphorus necessary for formation of bone tissue.

Two eight-ounce servings of milk or their equivalent in other dairy foods provide most of the calcium needed for an adult according to the RDA. Happily, there is as much or more calcium in skimmed or low-fat milk as in whole milk. There is no dietary reason to consume whole milk. To get the amount of calcium found in an eight-ounce glass of milk from cheese, a one- or one-and-a-half-ounce serving will do. Cottage cheese is a poor choice for calcium. Imitation or so-called filled cheeses contain calcium without cholesterol in the large quantities found in real cheese. If one prefers yogurt, bear in mind that fat content varies greatly. Choose the low-fat or non-fat varieties. Other dietary sources of calcium, including sardines and various vegetables, add to the day's total but cannot efficiently replace dairy foods.

For women the need for calcium is particularly great. Pregnancy and nursing double the requirement for this nutrient. And during the ageing process women tend to lose calcium from the bone. This often results in the bone-demineralizing disease known as osteoporosis. For women, especially those past menopause, it's a good idea to take daily calcium supplements. Medical authorities recommend a daily total intake of 1000 milligrams or more. The best source of calcium in supplement form is calcium carbonate, since it provides the greatest percentage of actual calcium to the body.

Iron combines with protein to make haemoglobin, the red substance in red blood cells, which facilitates oxygen transport to all parts of the body. There is a continuous turnover of iron in the body, resulting in a regular need for this nutrient. This is particularly true for menstruating women, who may require supplements of iron to fulfil their requirements. Dietary sources of iron include beef and cereals, especially the fortified types.

Phosphorus combines with calcium to form bone tissue and assists in a number of regulatory functions. Sources include milk and other dairy foods, meat, fish, poultry, eggs, whole-grain cereals, and legumes. Soft drinks and other processed foods also provide a great deal of phosphorus in the diet. Some authorities have proposed that we consume too much phosphorus, causing an imbalance between calcium and phosphorus. They recommend cutting back on soft drinks and processed foods.

Iodine helps to regulate the rate at which the body uses energy and prevents the formation of goitre. Dietary sources include seafoods of all sorts and iodized salt. There is absolutely no problem with iodine deficiency, even for those who have totally eliminated the use of table salt. In addition to the normal sources of iodine, there is a considerable amount of the nutrient in all forms of milk, owing to current farming techniques.

Magnesium aids in metabolism and assists in the functioning of nerve and muscle fibres. Sources include legumes, whole-grain cereals, milk, meat, seafood, nuts, eggs, and green vegetables.

Zinc becomes part of a several enzymes and insulin. It is found in meat, eggs, oysters and other seafoods, and whole-grain cereals.

Copper is involved with iron storage and plays a role in the formation of red blood cells. This nutrient has no designated RDA but is found in a wide variety of foods, including seafood, meat, eggs, legumes, whole-grain cereals, nuts, and raisins.

Fat

While it's certainly true that the vast majority of Americans and others eating a Western-style diet consume far too much fat, a certain amount is essential for life and health. Fat supplies indispensable essential fatty acids, carries the fat-soluble vitamins, and is an integral aspect of the metabolism of all food. In the body it is a component of cell walls, cushions vital organs, and provides insulation.

Fats are found in both animal and vegetable foods as well as in all varieties of cereals. Based on the molecular structure of the fat, it is classified as saturated, monounsaturated, or polyunsaturated.

Saturated fats include those from animal sources as well as coconut oil, palm oil, and hydrogenated oil, cashews, and avocados contain sizable amounts of monounsaturated fats. Polyunsaturated oils include corn oil, safflower oil, and other vegetable oils. No food has one type of fat exclusively, but rather contains predominantly one type or another.

Most authorities recommend that the average consumption of fat be reduced from the typical level of 40 or even 50 per cent of calories to a maximum of 30 per cent of calories. This means a reduction in total fat—fats of all kinds. Typical recommendations call for 10 per cent of calories as saturated fat, 10 per cent as monounsaturated, and 10 per cent as polyunsaturated. For a normally active 150-pound adult male this translates to about 65 to 75 grams of fat daily, 20 to 25 grams of each of the three types. Those wishing to modify their diets further, say to 20 per cent of total calories as fat, would consume only 50 grams of fat, one-third from each of the three types.

Interestingly enough, while such reduction may at first seem dramatic, the most obvious modifications do a large part of the job. Fried foods, whether at home or away, provide a large amount of the fat we consume. Baked goods contain as much as 50 per cent of calories as fat. Fats added to foods, including butter, margarine, oils, and mayonnaise, contribute a great deal. When such foods are reduced, there is less need to be concerned about the more hidden forms of fats.

Cholesterol is found only in animal fats. There is no cholesterol at all in any foods of plant origin. Even if all cholesterol were eliminated from the diet by means of a strict vegetarian programme, the body would produce enough to meet its needs. For many individuals, in fact, the body produces too much and even dietary cholesterol restrictions are insufficient to completely normalize levels in the blood. Fat must also be reduced, since the body produces cholesterol from fat sources. And for certain individuals additional measures must be considered, such as the inclusion of oat bran and higher-than-RDA doses of niacin.

Carbohydrates

Sugars and starches are the two main types of carbohydrates in the diet. These are chemically related and are principally classified by molecular complexity. Hence the term 'complex carbohydrates', which are the preferred form of carbohydrates in the diet.

While it's true that most of us consume far too many 'simple sugars' we also have to remember that the body does not distinguish between sugar taken in as sucrose and that eaten, say, as fruit juices. All sugars provide the same number of calories and are ultimately converted by the body to glucose, the sugar found in the blood. Complex carbohydrates, the starches, are metabolized by the body more slowly than simple sugars, thus keeping a more stable, constant blood-sugar level. Those simple sugars are also more likely to elevate triglyceride levels. Finally, simple sugars contain no fibre.

Fibre is a form of carbohydrate we've heard a great deal about. There are two main types of fibre, soluble and insoluble. The insoluble types, such as wheat fibre, have a beneficial effect in the intestines by speeding along the process of faecal elimination. Many authorities believe that fibre has a protective effect against colon cancer. Such insoluble fibres are termed non-nutritive, since they are not absorbed by the body. Soluble fibres, on the other hand, do provide a valuable amount of nutrition.

Water

If asked to name the nutrients essential for health and life, few persons would include water. Yet this nutrient accounts for one-half to three-quarters of the body's entire weight. Water is used in the production of tissue, acts as a solvent, and regulates body temperature. It carries nutrients to cells and carries wastes away in the urine. Water is the principal component of blood. It aids in digestion and is required for a wide spectrum of chemical reactions.

We lose water every day in a number of ways. Of course a great deal is used to produce urine to flush out the body's wastes. Water loss also occurs through sweat, both perceptible and imperceptible. The faeces contain a large quantity of water. All this fluid must be replaced.

Remember the old advice to drink eight eight-ounce glasses of water each day? Well, the wisdom of that advice holds true today. This is particularly true for those consuming oat bran and other fibre foods; the water needs increase in order to form the faeces and prevent constipation.

Bear in mind that oat bran absorbs water readily. It takes a great deal of fluid to keep this fibre in a soft state as it passes through the digestive tract.

Water is the ideal thirst quencher, with no calories or added chemicals. Whether it's straight from the tap or out of an imported bottle, water hits the spot. But other fluids can be counted in the day's intake. Diet sodas, decaffeinated coffee and tea, juices, and milk all contribute to the total.

Nutrition supplements

Traditional nutritionists and dietitians state rather unequivocally that diet alone provides all the nutrients we need. They say supplementation simply results in expensive urine. On the other side of the argument are those who say supplementation is more important than the foods we eat. The truth probably lies somewhere in between.

As we have seen, large doses of the vitamin niacin can be very effective in controlling fats in the blood. The evidence is overwhelming.

But does evidence exist for supplementing other nutrients as well?

Calcium supplements can supply the bone-building mineral missing in so many diets. Reaching the one or one-and-a-half gram level recommended by many authorities to prevent osteoporosis may be difficult if not impossible with diet alone, though diet is the place to start. And calcium has also been shown to slow down the proliferation of epithelial cells in the colon, thereby protecting against cancer.

Survey after survey shows most women's diets are too low in iron. Again, diet alone cannot bring the level of this mineral up to the amounts needed for women during the years between puberty and menopause. Supplementation certainly would help.

Next, women taking oral contraceptives are very likely to be deficient in folic acid. The same applies to those who smoke cigarettes. Again, diet alone is unlikely to supply sufficient folic acid.

The controversy regarding vitamin C is unlikely to be resolved in the near future. Nutrition surveys show diets of many men and women to be low in this vitamin. Many dentists recommend vitamin C for patients with gingivitis (tender and bleeding gums). And, of course, Dr Linus Pauling and others maintain that large doses of vitamin C can both prevent and lessen the severity of the common cold. It's no surprise that many persons routinely take additional vitamin C.

What about vitamin E? Few people actually believe that supplementation with this vitamin can improve sexual performance unless an actual deficiency state exists. That was a claim frequently encountered a few years ago. But today there may be other reasons to consider adding vitamin E to the diet in amounts beyond those found in grains and other foods. Vitamin E is an antioxidant, and as such it may protect against the effects of pollution in the air and the rancidity of fats and oils in our foods. Absolute, unequivocal proof does not yet exist, but the logic behind the argument seems sound.

The same kind of logic applies to supplementation of trace nutrients, those found in only minute amounts in our foods. Do you know for certain the amount of copper, zinc, and other minerals in the foods you eat daily? Probably not. On the other hand, no harmful effects have ever been shown in terms of supplementation short of massive amounts.

There is, however, some potential harm in large doses of vitamin A. This is one of the fat-soluble vitamins; it is stored in the tissues of the body rather than being excreted in the urine. Long-term damage has been reported when individuals supplement their diets with megadoses.

Especially for those reducing the amount of red meats in the diet, there may be concern about vitamin B_{12}. This is particularly a consideration for vegetarians. Adding a small amount of vitamin B_{12} to the diet seems logical.

Similarly, other B-complex vitamins may come up short in the diets of those under stress either mentally or physically. Moreover, it may be wise to balance the B vitamins for those of us who take large doses of niacin.

Faced with all these considerations, I have made a personal decision to supplement my own diet. While I do not necessarily recommend following my own regimen for others, I do not hesitate to say what I take. In addition to niacin, I take a full-spectrum vitamin/mineral supplement which includes all the trace nutrients. I take a balanced B-complex tablet, a 500-milligram vitamin C tablet, and a 400-IU vitamin E capsule as well. I feel confident that this provides the safeguard or insurance I want.

When I began writing about health and medicine twenty years ago, nutrition supplementation was considered in the realm of faddism. Solid scientific research has shown the benefits of many aspects of supplementation. And I believe we will see additional proof of such benefits as research continues.

Food selection

It certainly would be inconvenient to go to the supermarket or restaurant with a list of the nutrients needed for the day. Most of us don't think in terms of milligrams of this or grams of that. So there must be a better way to select the day's foods.

As it turns out, one of the best ways is not new. The Daily Food Guide was first developed by the US Department of Agriculture back in the forties. It was and is a system by which nutrition scientists determined average nutrient intake achieved by eating a number of servings of various kinds of foods, often called the 'four food groups'.

Diabetic patients use a variation on this theme in the form of 'exchange groups'. Whatever form or name given, this approach specifies the number of servings of foods from the four basic food groups, which will provide the required nutrients to prevent deficiencies. Those four groups are the meat group, milk group, fruit-vegetable group, and bread-cereal or grain group. Today nutritionists and dietitians also refer to the 'extras' group or the 'others' group to talk about foods that offer insignificant nutrients but that contribute flavours and calories. Condiments, oils, butter, sugar, and alcohol are included in such 'others'.

While it is certainly true that many different foods offer a particular nutrient, the four groups are based on certain foods that are especially rich in particular nutrients.

The so-called 'meat' group should probably be termed the 'protein' group since that's the nutrient the foods in this classification contribute most. In addition to meats, this group includes fish, poultry, eggs, nuts, and dry beans, such as lentils or pinto beans.

Obviously some of the foods in this protein group also contain a great deal of fat and should be limited. Although nuts, for example, contain no cholesterol, they are very high in fat. Does this mean one should eliminate them? Not at all. Simply limit the total amount eaten. Moderation is the key word. The same applies to meats. Certainly they are much higher in fat content than fish, but when properly trimmed and broiled rather than fried, meats have a place in a fat-and-cholesterol-controlled diet. Even eggs make a wonderful contribution. But, for those of us watching cholesterol intake, the yolks go down the drain or into the dog's food dish. Egg whites are an excellent source of protein, have no cholesterol, and are very low in calories.

The ideal way to approach the selection of foods from the protein or meat group is to go for a wide variety. One day have fish, another day turkey, the next day a vegetarian bean-and-rice dish, then a veal entrée, and so on. By seeking such variety, one may eat a bit more fat and cholesterol on one day and make up for it by eating less on another. That way the fat and cholesterol intake over the long term remains reduced.

How much is enough? That question reflects the major problem with typical eating habits. For many men, a 24-ounce porterhouse steak is a 'serving' of meat. To a dietitian or nutritionist, however, a serving of meat is 3½ ounces or so. Two daily servings of meat, fish, or other foods from this group will satisfy one's protein requirements and provide a variety of other nutrients as well.

When choosing which of the great variety of foods to eat, spend a few moments with Table 10 included in Chapter 3, 'Winning by the Numbers' (see page 56). You'll see that the fat content of these foods varies tremendously. As a result, in our household turkey has replaced beef as the dominant meat. We still enjoy beef and veal, but only as an occasional treat rather than the practically daily routine of old.

Besides, when trying to vary the diet as widely as possible, there really isn't 'room' to have any one type of food too frequently. And, when we do have beef, we try to enjoy it in smaller quantities than in the past. An excellent example is skewered beef with vegetables (see recipe page 220). We use marinated chunks of filet mignon (four ounces raw per person) along with mushrooms, tomatoes, green peppers, and onions. Broiled over the charcoal, this is a sumptuous treat that looks as good as it tastes. Yet the meal has a very reasonable amount of fat and cholesterol. Served with a baked potato or rice and a fine bottle of red wine, it's a fabulous example of how delicious a low-cholesterol diet can be.

At first it may appear difficult to consider the serving size so carefully. But here's a very simple way of dealing with this: when you buy a pound of beef, simply divide it into four equal portions for storage. That way when it's time to cook you'll have a proper four-ounce serving for each person. The same applies to fish, poultry, or any other meat.

It's just as easy to determine your needs from the milk group. This group contributes calcium as its predominant nutrient. Included are milk, yogurt, and cheese. Adults need two or more servings each day. That means two eight-ounce glasses of milk, two cups of yogurt, two one-and-a-half-ounce servings of cheese, or any combination of these dairy foods. Needless to say, the best are the low-fat or nonfat varieties. Read the label to see just how much fat you're getting per serving.

The next group gives us no such problems with cholesterol. The fruit-vegetable group provides our vitamins A and C along with a substantial amount of fibre. Some authorities feel there should be separate fruit and vegetable groups, rather than combining them in one group. Each day an adult needs two servings of fruit and two servings of vegetables at a minimum. Here's the place to satisfy your appetite without guilt. Pile on that corn, squash, spinach, and salad! Enjoy all the seasonal fruits as well as splurging on important delicacies.

The same also applies to the bread-cereal or grain group. This includes all the breads, cereals, and grains, especially the whole grains. Here's the source of abundant fibre, thiamin (B_1), iron, niacin, and good complex carbohydrates. For many societies around the world, foods from this group comprise the staple diet: Rice in the Orient. Pasta in the Mediterranean. Hearty breads in Europe. Instead of thinking 'mince and spaghetti' think in terms of 'spaghetti with a little meat'. As an additional benefit, you'll be able to enjoy more food on your plate for fewer calories. Adults need a minimum of four servings daily from this group. This is where to balance off your calorific needs for the day. Eat all the grains, breads, and pastas you like without gaining weight.

Most of us were taught to believe that starchy foods are fattening and should, therefore, be limited by those watching their weight. Actually, it's the butter and sauces that add the calories. Breads, pasta, and a wide variety of whole-grain foods supply a lot of nutrition for the calories. Remember, too, that you'll be replacing fat calories with carbohydrate calories. Each gram of fat contains nine calories, while a gram of carbohydrate provides only four. You'll find that eating more carbohydrate-rich foods will give you a tremendous feeling of satisfaction. In fact, you'll be amazed at how much you'll eat while either maintaining or actually losing weight.

The only warning or caution flag that goes up here is in the bakery. Many or most of the commercially prepared baked goods have a high content of fat and cholesterol. Choose sourdough and rye bread and commercially baked breads that do not contain eggs and shortenings on the ingredients label. Unfortunately, this excludes virtually every biscuit, pie, and cake in the bakery. Your best bet for such baked goods is to prepare them at home from scratch, using low-fat milk and egg substitutes.

Read Chapter 12, 'Let's Go Shopping', for tips and hints about selecting the best foods for a cholesterol-controlled diet. You'll find that with a little thought you can enjoy practically all the dishes on your list of favourites. It simply takes a modification here and an adjustment there.

This book does not include any suggested menus for the day. In my opinion, based on a number of years of experience, no one pays any attention to such menus, or takes the time and effort to follow them faithfully. I do, however, show some examples of typical days' food intake to demonstrate how a wide variety of foods can be chosen while remaining within reasonable limits of fat and cholesterol. See pages 149–51.

Your best approach is to modify your existing eating habits, using your favourite recipes and favourite restaurants. It's ridiculous to expect that anyone is going to change a lifetime of eating patterns overnight— or ever. But it's not at all out of the question to make a few adjustments. If a recipe calls for heavy cream, use evaporated skimmed milk. If baking, replace butter with tub-type margarine—in half the quantity. Use two egg whites instead of one whole egg.

Table 13. Recommended daily amounts of nutrients for population groups (DHSS, 1979)

Age ranges	Energy		Protein	Calcium	Iron
years	MJ	kcal	g	mg	mg
Boys					
Under 1	3.25	780	19	600	6
1	5.0	1200	30	600	7
2	5.75	1400	35	600	7
3–4	6.5	1560	39	600	8
5–6	7.25	1740	43	600	10

Age ranges		Energy		Protein	Calcium	Iron
years		MJ	kcal	g	mg	mg
7–8		8.25	1980	49	600	10
9–11		9.5	2280	56	700	12
12–14		11.0	2640	66	700	12
15–17		12.0	2880	72	600	12
Girls						
Under 1		3.0	720	18	600	6
1		4.5	1100	27	600	7
2		5.5	1300	32	600	7
3–4		6.25	1500	37	600	8
5–6		7.0	1680	42	600	10
7–8		8.0	1900	48	600	10
9–11		8.5	2050	51	700	12[2]
12–14		9.0	2150	53	700	12[2]
15–17		9.0	2150	53	600	12[2]
Men						
	Sedentary	10.5	2510	62	500	10
18–34	Moderately active	12.0	2900	72	500	10
	Very active	14.0	3350	84	500	10
	Sedentary	10.0	2400	60	500	10
35–64	Moderately active	11.5	2750	69	500	10
	Very active	14.0	3350	84	500	10
65–74		10.0	2400	60	500	10
75 and over		9.0	2150	54	500	10
Women						
18–54	Most occupations	9.0	2150	54	500	12[2]
	Very active	10.5	2500	62	500	12[2]
55–74		8.0	1900	47	500	10
75 and over		7.0	1680	42	500	10
Pregnant		10.0	2400	60	1200	13
Lactating		11.5	2750	69	1200	15

[1] Most people who go out in the sun need no dietary source of vitamin D (p. 125), but children and adolescents in winter, and housebound adults, are recommended to take 10µg vitamin D daily.

[2] These iron recommendations may not cover heavy menstrual losses.

Vitamin A (retinol equivalent)	Thiamin	Riboflavin	Nicotinic acid equivalent	Vitamin C	Vitamin D[1]
µg	mg	mg	mg	mg	µg
300	0.6	0.7	8	20	10
300	0.6	0.8	9	20	10
300	0.7	0.9	10	20	—
400	0.8	1.0	11	20	—
575	0.9	1.2	14	25	—
725	1.1	1.4	16	25	—
750	1.2	1.7	19	30	—
450	0.3	0.4	5	20	7.5
300	0.4	0.6	7	20	10
300	0.5	0.7	8	20	10
300	0.6	0.8	9	20	10
300	0.7	0.9	10	20	—
400	0.8	1.0	11	20	—
575	0.8	1.2	14	25	—
725	0.9	1.4	16	25	—
750	0.9	1.7	19	30	—
750	1.0	1.6	18	30	—
750	1.2	1.6	18	30	—
750	1.3	1.6	18	30	—
750	1.0	1.6	18	30	—
750	1.1	1.6	18	30	—
750	1.3	1.6	18	30	—
750	1.0	1.6	18	30	—
750	0.9	1.6	18	30	—
750	0.9	1.3	15	30	—
750	1.0	1.3	15	30	—
750	0.8	1.3	15	30	—
750	0.7	1.3	15	30	—
750	1.0	1.6	18	60	10
1,200	1.1	1.8	21	60	10

Such recommendations apply to the entire population rather than only those with a particular need to reduce the cholesterol risk factor. A diet high in fibre and complex carbohydrates and low in fats and cholesterol has been generally regarded as best for all people, male and female, young and old alike. The same principles, with particular emphasis on simple sugars, apply directly to those trying to control diabetes. Such a diet is widely believed to offer protection against a number of cancers, especially colon and breast cancers. The low-fat diet is inherently lower in calories, benefiting those many people who are overweight. All necessary nutrients are provided in abundant quantities, ensuring proper growth and maintenance even for children. On the other hand, there are absolutely no contraindications for following this type of diet for the entirety of one's life. The nutrition plan described in this book assures one of a balanced diet, complete with sufficient protein, vitamins, and minerals.

Moreover, this approach to nutrition puts a high value on the pure enjoyment of food. Our abundance of food should be relished and cherished. The variety most authorities encourage allows one to savour all the many flavours and textures in our cornucopia of foods.

Bear in mind that those rich French sauces were originally developed to mask spoiled and rotten meats in the days prior to refrigeration. Remember that those fast-food nuggets of chicken are up to half chopped skin and gristle. Hot dogs contain ingredients that virtually no man or woman would eat if they were not disguised. Read the ingredients on some snack-food labels and ask yourself if you really miss nibbling at a chemical factory. Remember the times you overindulged and suffered with gastric upset and indigestion.

Instead of those 'delights' plunge into the wealth of natural, delicious flavours of foods as they were meant to be. Enjoy! That's all the nutrition you need to know for a healthful diet!

12. LET'S GO SHOPPING

The place to start improving your eating habits and those of your entire family is the supermarket. A bit of planning can make a huge difference in the way you eat, and in the success of lowering your cholesterol levels. And, in the process, you'll save time and money and you'll come to a whole new enjoyment of food.

For years home economists have urged cost-conscious homemakers to use a shopping list. Now that may not sound like an earthshaking idea, but the fact is that many or even most shoppers go into the market without much idea of what they'll buy. Purchases are based on impulse, and the bill at the checkout counter often is more than expected. Making a list and sticking with it helps to save money.

At the same time, calorie-conscious shoppers are warned not to venture into the aisles of the market while hungry. We've all done that, and the result is always the same. We buy more food than we really want or need—and the wrong kinds of food. And again, the foods are based on impulse decision making.

You've probably heard this advice before. But now it's time to put these suggestions into practice in order to purchase foods in a more logical manner for more healthful eating. And let me add one more suggestion, especially for your first few trips: Go to the market when you have plenty of time. Don't rush. Make shopping a learning experience.

Now let's get down to some details. First we'll consider a new approach to making the shopping list. Remember that the best way to select nutritious foods is on the basis of the four food groups. Each day we want to eat foods from the meat, milk, fruit-vegetable, and bread-cereal groups. By doing so, as we discussed in the chapter on nutrition, we'll get all the nutrients we need, without a lot of calories, and without a lot of fat and cholesterol.

The meat-group shopping list
The meat-group category includes a wide variety of protein-rich foods.

Some are better choices than others. Too often when we think of meat, the mental image is that of a rare cut of beef. But the word 'meat' includes veal, fish, chicken, turkey, and, in terms of protein contributions, eggs and dried beans.

Let's start with beef. There's no reason to completely eliminate red meat from the diet, especially if you really enjoy it. Select those cuts that are lowest in fat content, as shown in the charts in Chapter 3, 'Winning by the Numbers'. Notice also that those figures refer to a three-ounce cooked serving that has been well trimmed of visible fat. So when shopping count on four ounces per person.

But, if you haven't already started to do so, broaden your selections of meats. Veal, for example, is a delicious alternative that's considerably lower in fat content. Minced veal contains only about 10 per cent fat, while the leanest minced beef has about 15 per cent. It's also a good value when compared with lower-fat-content minced beef, and gives you a greater cooked yield. Try it as a substitute in any recipe calling for minced beef.

But for the lowest fat content of all, shop for poultry. Regular-grade minced beef contains 30 per cent fat. Lean minced beef has 15 per cent. Veal can bring that down to 10 per cent. But turkey breast has a mere trace of fat, less than 4 per cent. Note that I'm referring to turkey breast, not skin or dark meat. Skin contains more than 39 per cent fat. Dark meat has more than 8 per cent. These figures are on the average, with young birds having less fat, and mature birds having more.

When shopping, read the label on prepackaged turkey and you'll see that sometimes these products are made from the entire turkey, skin and all. This results in a fat content of about 15 per cent, no better than lean minced beef.

The solution is to ask the butcher to skin and bone a turkey breast and to mince it like hamburger. While he's at it, ask for some turkey cutlets, which you can keep in your freezer, packaged in convenient sizes.

Chicken is another excellent source of protein without a lot of fat and cholesterol. But again note that dark meat contains higher amounts of fat. Chicken breasts are best, and there are hundreds of ways to prepare them.

Other poultry is not as good a choice. Both duck and goose contain high levels of fat, and should be kept for special occasions if you really like those birds.

Next on your shopping list should be lots of fish. If you're not already an avid fish eater, there are a number of ways to start appreciating and enjoying this meat alternative. Most fish haters still like tuna fish in salads or sandwiches. Try using canned salmon in some recipes that call for tuna. This is even easier if you can find salmon canned without the skin and bones. You can use it straight out of the can, just like tuna.

Shellfish lovers learned in Chapter 6 that previous figures for cholesterol content were greatly exaggerated because of faulty testing methods. Shrimp and lobster contain a fair amount of cholesterol. But all shellfish have only traces of fat. And, for the most part, we tend to eat smaller amounts of shellfish at a time than meat, so having a few shrimp really won't hurt at all. The winner of the low-fat, low-cholesterol contest, though, goes to the popular and versatile scallop.

For those of us who also have to watch the price tags of the foods we buy, imitation shellfish made with surimi are getting better and better.

If you prefer your fish in the convenient frozen and breaded form you can still enjoy it, but start to read the labels carefully. Some of the batters are made with egg yolks and a lot of fat. Others contain no egg yolks and have a low fat content, considering that they are fried foods. Even so, limit fried foods of any kind.

When selecting fresh fish, let your taste buds be your guide. As more and more people have learned to enjoy fish, the variety and selection have grown. You don't have to live near the sea to get the freshest fillets.

Moving down the aisle of the meat section, we come to luncheon meats—the downfall of many of us. The unhappy fact is that such meats, even when made from turkey or chicken, contain an unhealthful amount of fat. Just one slice of salami has 9 to 12 grams of fat. And I've never known anyone who eats just one slice. Good choices are sliced turkey breast and ham. Surprised that ham is on the list? Read the labels on these foods and you'll see that some ham products contain as little as 2 per cent fat.

The hot dog, unfortunately, is another source of excessive fat in the diet, so we've virtually banned hot dogs from our house.

The same thing applies to breakfast meats. Bacon and sausage have far too much fat and contain a walloping amount of sodium as well. A good alternative is turkey breakfast sausage. This has 15 per cent fat. And, if you want the ultimate sausage, try your homemade variety using ground turkey breast and the recipes found at the end of this book.

Eggs—an excellent source of protein—have one of the highest contributions of cholesterol. The ultimate horror to the cholesterol-conscious individual would be the elegant dish Eggs Benedict. Between the egg yolks and the butter, each serving contains nearly 1500 milligrams of cholesterol. The alternatives are eating only the egg whites. The whites provide an excellent source of protein, with absolutely no cholesterol.

Because the meat group is comprised of those foods that offer a significant amount of protein, dried beans and peanut butter are also included. Dried beans include lentils, haricot beans, pinto beans, chick peas, kidney beans, and others; you can also buy them canned to avoid the process of cooking. Dried beans have also been shown to significantly reduce cholesterol levels. Try them in salads, soups, and a number of dishes such as dips.

Peanut butter poses somewhat of a problem. While it contains no cholesterol, it does have a large amount of fat. One tablespoon contains more than 7 grams. A sandwich typically will have two or even three tablespoonfuls. Keep this to a once-in-a-while treat.

The same applies to nuts of all sorts. One tablespoon of chopped walnuts contains 4.8 grams of fat. Peanuts have 7 grams. One ounce of almonds provides more than 16 grams in the roasted and salted variety.

A delicious alternative to those of us who love the crunch of nuts is chestnuts. These are not really nuts at all, but they're delicious when roasted in the shell. Just score and pop them into the oven at 350°F (180°C/Gas Mark 4) for an hour. Peel when cool and enjoy. Two large chestnuts contain only 0.2 grams of fat. So munch a handful! Be aware, however, that these are not free of calories. The carbohydrate content results in 29 calories for those two chestnuts. But, in the total picture of your entire day's foods, that's really not bad.

The milk-group shopping list

Dairy foods, as we've all learned from school days, provide the majority of calcium in the diet. While it's certainly true that we never outgrow our need for calcium, we don't need the fat and cholesterol. So selections from this group should be made accordingly.

Choose nonfat or low-fat milk rather than whole milk. The differences are enormous. Whole milk contains 9 grams of fat per 8-ounce serving. Low-fat milk has 4 grams. And nonfat milk has only a trace remaining. The cholesterol disappears right along with the fat. After a while, you'll actually prefer the lighter, fresher taste. Start weaning yourself away from whole milk. Go first to the low-fat and then on to nonfat types. The same applies to cheese.

One nice way to get the flavour of cheese in your foods without all the fat is to use grated Parmesan cheese. One tablespoon has only 1.5 grams of fat. But a one-ounce portion of hard Parmesan bounces the total up to 7.3 grams.

Bear in mind that cholesterol levels drop right along with the fat content. So there is, of course, a lot less cholesterol in the low-fat varieties than in the regular types.

Keep reading those labels when you come to the yogurt section. You'll find a big difference from one container to another. The most commonly found and eaten kind of yogurt is low-fat, which has about 3.4 grams of fat per cup. Nonfat brands have a mere 0.4 grams. Whole-milk types, on the other hand, have 7.7 grams per 8-ounce container. Calorie content varies widely in various kinds of yogurt, depending upon the amount of fat and sugar. Read the labels.

What about some other dairy products? Sour cream can easily be replaced with nonfat yogurt for a big saving in fat and cholesterol. Eggnog has 19 grams of fat and lots of cholesterol in every 8-ounce glass.

Cream contains a lot of fat and cholesterol. Non-dairy creamers cut out the cholesterol, but the fat content is just as high—and the fat they use is saturated. An alternative is low-fat or nonfat yogurt.

The fruit and vegetable shopping list

Spend some time in the produce section of your store. Go to some of the specialty shops. Stop at roadside stalls. Try all the different kinds of fruits and vegetables from all over the nation and around the world. Talk to the manager to find out how to prepare and cook some of the more exotic varieties.

Now that you're saving money by cutting down on the amounts of meat and cheese you're eating, you can spend some on fruits and vegetables you may have avoided before.

There's only one fruit that you should limit during your trips to the supermarket. Avocados have 16.4 grams of monounsaturated fat per 3½-ounce serving. Of course there's no cholesterol, since that's limited to animal foods. Though monounsaturated fat is better than saturated, that's still a lot of fat to consume. If you enjoy the special flavour and delicate texture of avocados, keep the servings small.

With that one exception, you can enjoy all the fruits and vegetables in the market-place. Canned and frozen vegetables contain all the nutrients in fresh varieties, at typically lower cost. But, if using the canned types, read the labels for sodium content or choose the salt-free brands.

Canned fruits can also be a welcome treat for dessert or as a snack. It's best to choose the types canned in plain water or the fruit's own juices rather than heavy syrup, which adds a lot of sugar.

The bread-cereal shopping list

This group includes all the foods made from grain. They're an important part of the diet, providing fibre, carbohydrates, and many of the B vitamins. But, again, read the labels to see exactly what you're eating.

Commercially baked goods frequently are made with egg yolks, fat, or both. Soft white bread, for example, has one gram of fat per slice. That adds up quickly. The same applies to many of the whole-wheat breads. Again, read the ingredient labels carefully to spot those 'partially hydrogenated fats'.

How about pasta and noodles? Most spaghetti and other pastas are made with only flour and water. But egg noodles contain, of course, eggs. This adds 50 milligrams of cholesterol per cooked cup of noodles. But you can find noodles made without eggs.

Another source of hidden cholesterol includes all the packaged cake and pancake mixes, which are made with egg yolks. Your best bet is to make your own pancake or cake mixes, using the recipes found at the end of this book, and keep them stored in the freezer.

When it comes to breakfast cereals, fat and cholesterol are not a problem, but sugar is. The old-fashioned cereals, free of added sugar, are still the best. And, of course, you'll want to increase your consumption of oat bran both in cereals and made into muffins. Some stores now carry oat bran in bulk, bringing the price down considerably.

Other foods shopping list

In addition to the basic foods we've discussed, most shopping lists include a wide variety of foods best listed as 'others'. In these category one can group the oils and fats, sugars, spices and herbs, and many condiments. These offer more enjoyment than nutrition, and selections should be carefully made.

When it comes to fats and oils, there are some items it's simply best to avoid completely. These are butter, lard, hard margarine, and foods described as containing 'partially hydrogenated vegetable oils'. In addition there are two vegetable oils that are as saturated as animal fat. Palm oil and coconut oil are often used in commercially fried or baked goods. Try at least to limit these in your shopping trolley.

The advertising on TV seems to make selection of vegetable oil difficult, but the facts make the choice a lot simpler. Regardless of what advertisers say about their particular products, the fact is that *no* vegetable oil contains cholesterol. As far as cholesterol is concerned, then, one oil is as good as another.

The next point in those advertisements regards how much polyunsaturated fat the oil contains. Yes, safflower oil has more than corn oil. But the difference is made up by monounsaturated fat, which is just as desirable. In fact, monounsaturated fats have more capability of maintaining the protective HDL levels than do polyunsaturated fats.

So, for general-purpose cooking oil, the choice is yours, to be made on the basis of personal preference and cost. Healthwise, one is as good as another.

But you may wish to buy two oils in addition to your routine vegetable oil. As discussed in Chapter 6, olive oil and peanut oil are primarily monounsaturated fats; their use in certain world populations has been correlated with reduced cholesterol levels with no reduction in protective HDLs. Both add their own flavours to certain kinds of cooking. We use all three—vegetable oil, olive oil, and peanut oil— in our house.

Regardless of the type of oil, though, it's best to limit the total amount you use.

Moving down the cooking-oils aisle we come to the salad-dressing section. Again, your best bet is to start reading labels. See how many grams of fat are to be found in each tablespoonful. This doesn't necessarily mean buying only those that have the lowest amount, regardless of personal taste. Rather, it may be a matter of using a bit less of one particular type. It's a trade-off.

You may be surprised to see that the traditional bottled oil-and-vinegar dressings contain more fat per serving than a similar amount of Thousand Island dressing. Make your shopping trips a learning experience by standing in the aisle and reading those labels before you buy the foods. Many products are available with no oil at all. As time goes on, you'll know the brands and types to select.

Tartar sauce, for example, varies enormously from product to product. Read the label. If the product's ingredient list includes egg yolks, move on to the next one. The same applies to salad dressings.

Many people already buy packets of salad dressing seasonings to mix together at home. The directions often call for mayonnaise. One suggestion would be to use low-fat mayonnaise. Another is to substitute nonfat yogurt. If directions call for oil, simply use half the amount listed and increase other liquids.

But what about mayonnaise? Again, read the labels. There are a number of reduced-fat brands on the market. I'm particularly fond of Weight Watchers'. And, while mayonnaise is made with egg yolks, the actual amount of cholesterol is so small in a single serving that it's almost insignificant. On the other hand, you may prefer the taste of salad dressing, which contains no cholesterol at all. Pick the reduced-fat brands.

The next big source of calories in the supermarket and in the diet is sugar. Brown sugar, granulated sugar, 'natural' turbinado sugar— they're all the same in terms of calories and the way your body digests them. Sucrose is sucrose, no matter where it comes from. And *all* sugars, including honey and fructose, eventually get broken down by the body into blood sugar, called glucose.

Your choice of the type and amount of sugar you want in your diet, then, depends only on personal taste and your waistline. While sugar does not directly elevate cholesterol levels, it may lead to overweight or raised triglycerides.

That brings us to the next category in the 'others' group. Desserts pose somewhat of a problem for those of us trying to limit fat and cholesterol. The same appllies to snacks. Ice cream, pies, cakes, cookies, and other treats are loaded with fat and cholesterol. And the richer and better tasting they are, the higher the levels of those offenders. In many cases it's a matter of complete avoidance.

Instead of ice cream, try some of the newly introduced sorbets. Read the labels and you'll see that the principal ingredient is fruit purée. They are truly delicious.

When it comes to cakes and biscuits, there are few acceptable types other than angel-food cake, which is made with only egg whites, no yolks. If you are a true cake and biscuit lover, it may be worth the effort to return to home-made baked goods from scratch.

While you're shopping you'll also want to pick up some packages of raisins and dried fruits. Arrange them attractively in bowls so they are available whenever you get the urge to munch. For a special treat, why not buy a gift platter of fancy fruits for yourself? You deserve it.

Finally we come to the category of beverages to wash down all those foods. There are few limitations here. People are really catching on to the idea of drinking bottled water, both fizzy and still, both imported and domestic. You can even find reduced-sodium waters. And today there are a spectrum of calorie-free soft drinks.

Here's a bit of personal preference and practice: I've cut out the sugar in soft drinks, and use it in my cooking and baking. Again, a nice trade-off. I can't tell much of a difference in a cola drink, but I appreciate the touch of sugar sweetness in my oat-bran muffins and in my home-baked biscuits.

The goal of your shopping list, then, is to select foods that will add up to your daily target of fat, cholesterol, and sugar without going over that target. And, of course, you'll also want to count the milligrams of sodium in tallying your lists.

There are two things that make the dietary-modification part of this programme work. First, knowing just how many grams of fat should be included throughout the day. Second, reading the labels on prepared foods and the charts listing fats and cholesterol in this book.

If, like me, you limit your fat to 50 grams per day, it's fairly easy to keep track of your intake. The three muffins I eat in the morning provide a total of 10.5 grams of fat. Using the oil-free recipe cuts out even this fat almost completely. Milk, coffee, juice, and other beverages have little or no fat. At lunch I may have a tuna-salad sandwich. The tuna has only 0.8 grams of fat for a 3½-ounce serving; that's half a can of water-packed tuna. I also use a tablespoon of Weight Watchers' reduced-fat mayonnaise, which adds 4 grams of fat. My drink, again, adds no fat. Nor does the fruit I nibble on throughout the afternoon as snacks.

So far I'm up to a total of 15 grams of fat. I've got 35 grams to go. For dinner I can have veal cutlets (9.0 grams per 3½ ounces), mixed green salad with blue-cheese dressing (7.3 grams per tablespoon), spaghetti with commercial sauce (1 gram for 3 tablespoons), a tablespoon of grated Parmesan cheese (1.5 grams), and tapioca pudding for dessert (3.1 grams per 3½ ounce serving). That comes to about 22 grams for dinner, still short of my allotted total. I remember that, and the next day I might be at a restaurant where I won't feel guilty about ordering the French-fried potatoes.

Try it for yourself. Think of a day's food. Make up some menus for yourself and start tallying up the grams of fat contained in each of the foods. You'll be absolutely amazed at how much food, and how many different kinds of food, you can eat and enjoy each and every day.

The only times you'll run into problems are when you want to eat foods you already know should be avoided. Like greasy fast-food meals. Or hollandaise sauce. Or a hot fudge sundae topped with whipped cream and chopped nuts.

After a while, you'll almost instinctively know when you're within your own permissible fat-intake level. You won't have to specifically count each food's fat content because you'll be selecting foods you know are within your set limits.

But be prepared for one frustration in the supermarkets. Not every food has a nicely spelled out nutrition label listing the content of fat, cholesterol, and sodium. The laws are not strict along these lines, but as time goes on, more and more foods will be labelled.

While making that shopping list, think also in terms of the meals you'll prepare. One nice and practical approach is to plan the meals for the entire week. That way you'll know what foods to purchase from each of the groups, and you'll see at a glance when you're choosing the widest variety of foods. Next comes the matter of cooking those foods.

To make them taste their best, you'll want to experiment with all kinds of herbs and spices. Every kitchen should be supplied with a broad assortment of dried herbs and spices. As you read through recipes, you may see some that you'll want to pick up. And, while you're at it, try some of the fresh herbs that are available in your produce section. There's nothing like fresh basil, for example, to put a zing into a tomato sauce. Or fresh garlic.

You'll also find that when you use herbs and spices there'll be less need for salt. A dash of this or a splash of that can replace the sodium very nicely.

The equipment you'll need

A lifetime of food enjoyment deserves a bit of financial investment. Some of the items that make low-fat and low-cholesterol cooking easier cost quite a few pounds. But they're worth it in the long run. Add to your kitchen as you're able.

A set of fine, sharp knives are a joy in the kitchen. There's nothing more frustrating than to try to chop and slice foods with a dull blade. A good set of cutlery is a lifelong investment. Add a cutting board and you'll be all set.

Two appliances that also greatly help are the mixer and the food processor. Both have come down in price considerably over the years, and are frequently in sales. Owning a food processor facilitates cooking so much that you'll be able to enjoy foods and dishes you'd otherwise pass by.

While you're slicing, dicing, and otherwise preparing your foods, you'll want to know exactly how much you'll be serving. That's why a food scale is an essential piece of equipment. As you use the scale, you'll start to develop an eye for measurements.

Then it's time to cook those foods. To do so, you'll want at least one nonstick pan for sautéing. This cuts considerably into the amount of oil needed. A good steamer, the kind placed in a pot with a cover, lets you prepare crisp, delicious vegetables. And a wok gives you access to the whole world of stir-fry Oriental cooking.

Whether a recipe is simple or complicated, it still takes some time to prepare. Why not double the recipe? Store the extra portions in the freezer for times when you simply don't have the time to cook.

It's often the hurried meal that's packed with the most fat and cholesterol. Think about it. It's been a long day at work, you're tired, it's late in the evening, and you don't feel like cooking. So you pick up a double cheeseburger on the way home—complete with French fries and a milkshake. Take a look at the numbers for such a meal in the charts to see just how much fat and cholesterol you're eating just because you don't have the time or energy to cook.

Instead, think how nice it would be to remember all the pre-prepared meals waiting for you in the freezer. Chilli made with minced turkey breast. A few Chinese entrées. Or perhaps one of the new low-fat entrées along with a salad.

As you put your shopping list together, plan on having some 'emergency meals' in your freezer. Plan the snacks you'll have when that midnight hunger strikes. Be ready for all the times when the choice comes down to healthful versus harmful food selections.

Each time you go shopping, read those labels. Try to find something different in the produce section. Soon your new eating patterns will become second nature, and you'll wonder why you didn't start doing this years ago.

Menu planning

Everyone's tastes and preferences are different, and trying to follow a specific, day-by-day diet is almost bound to fail, since those preferences are not taken into consideration. But, strictly for the sake of illustration, let's look at three 'typical' days' meals made from the foods we talked about buying in the market. All the recipes are listed in the book, and the listings of fat and cholesterol for each dish are based on the assumption that you'll be cooking with egg whites rather than yolks, and following the other ideas for reducing fat and cholesterol in your foods.

I've compiled these meal plans to fit my own needs as a 150 lb (10¾ stone) male, limiting fat intake to 50 grams and cholesterol to less than 250 milligrams. In order to calculate the values, I had to look up the numbers in the chart right here in the book. Why not try to add up some of your own favourites? If you near the end of the hypothetical day, and you've gone over your own limit, remember to cut back the next day. If you've got a few grams and milligrams to spare, that might be the day for a treat of some sort.

Certainly no one will calculate the exact figures for fat and cholesterol each and every day. That's just asking too much, even for the most dedicated person. But after a while, just a short while, you'll start mentally coming up with an average total and you'll be right on target.

Day One

	Fat (grams)	Cholesterol (milligrams)
Breakfast		
3 oat-bran pancakes with maple syrup	4.5	0
1 three-oz turkey-sausage patty	4.2	66
1 four-oz glass of orange juice	—	—
Decaffeinated coffee or tea	—	—
Lunch		
1 tunafish sandwich made with 3½ oz tuna and 1 tablespoon low-fat mayonnaise on sourdough bread	4.8	63

1 oat-bran muffin made with bananas and dates	4.5	—
1 eight-oz glass skimmed milk	0.4	5

Snack

1 medium apple	—	—

Dinner

Mixed green salad with 2 tablespoons green goddess or similar creamy dressing	5.0	—
5 oz roast chicken or turkey, white meat only, without skin	7.0	110
Mashed potatoes made with evaporated skimmed milk	—	—
Vegetable with 1 teaspoon margarine	4.0	—
Bread roll (wholewheat) with 1 teaspoon margarine	4.0	—
½ cup sorbet	4.0	—
Day's total:	**42.4**	**244**

NOTE: Vary total calories for personal needs by adding or subtracting amounts of nonfat foods such as potatoes.

Day Two

	Fat (grams)	Cholesterol (milligrams)
Breakfast		
⅔ cup (uncooked) oat-bran cereal with raisins	4.0	—
½ cup skimmed milk for cereal	0.2	5.0
½ cup tomato juice	—	—
Decaffeinated coffee or tea	—	—
Lunch		
Ham sandwich made with 3½ oz ham on sourdough or wholewheat bread with lettuce and tomatoes	5.0	50.0
1 tangerine	—	—
1 eight-oz glass skimmed milk	0.4	5.0
Dinner		
Green salad with creamy dressing	5.0	—
7 oz broiled salmon with lemon squeeze	14.8	94.0
Rice with 1 teaspoon margarine	4.0	—
Vegetable with 1 teaspoon margarine	4.0	—
Dinner roll with 1 teaspoon margarine	4.0	—
½ cup vanilla custard	0.3	3.0
Day's total:	**41.7**	**157**

Day Three

	Fat (grams)	Cholesterol (milligrams)
Breakfast		
3 oat-bran muffins made with blueberries	10.5	—
½ cup grapefruit juice	—	—
1 eight-oz glass skimmed milk	0.4	5
Decaffeinated coffee or tea	—	—
Lunch		
1 peanut-butter sandwich made with 2 tablespoons peanut butter and jam or jelly, on sourdough or wholewheat bread	14.4	—
1 eight-oz glass of skimmed milk	0.4	5
Grapes	—	—
Dinner		
Mixed green salad with creamy dressing	5.0	—
4-oz lean filet mignon, broiled	12.0	144
Baked potato	—	—
Vegetable	—	—
3½ oz tapioca pudding	3.1	53
Snack		
Raisins	—	—
Day's total:	***45.8***	***207***

NOTE: Here's an example of two fairly high-fat menu items, peanut butter and beef, both in the same day—possible when you watch the other foods eaten.

13. THE PROOF OF THE PUDDING

I'll never forget the day I heard about my own positive results with the diet-oat-bran-niacin programme. I was working out at the Santa Monica Medical Center Cardiac Rehabilitation Center. Specifically, I was sweating on the rowing machine when my blood-test data came through. When the nurse read those wonderful numbers, tears actually came to my eyes.

Remember that just a few months earlier I had had a total cholesterol level of 7.3 mmol/l. A highly restricted diet of absolutely no red meat, no eggs, and non-fat milk got it down only to a disappointing 7.0.

Then, after just eight weeks of eating my oat-bran muffins and taking my niacin tablets, I received the good news. My total cholesterol level had plummeted to 4.4. And my ratio of total cholesterol to HDL was a nice, healthy 3.4—far below risk.

A year later, subsequent blood testing came up with the same kinds of numbers time and time again. For me, I knew I had found the answer. And, being a writer, I wanted to share the news with others.

The fact of the matter is I probably had enough of a story to tell so that I could have published the book simply on the basis of my own spectacular results. But I also have scientific training and an ingrained scientific curiosity. Would the approach work for others as well?

Moreover, as a medical writer I've often been critical of books that make claims without very much documentation. I became determined that not only would I back up every statement in the scientific chapters with references from the most trustworthy scientific literature, but also I would tell how the programme can and has worked for many others.

We have the results now, and for many they are simply spectacular. Total cholesterol levels drop by 2½ points and more. Reductions total 30, 40, even 50 per cent. The protective HDL levels often double. Triglycerides are cut in half. And these cases are documented.

I began by approaching Dr Albert Kattus, the Director of the Cardiac Rehabilitation Center and a renowned cardiologist. We had developed a nice rapport during the time of my own treatment pre- and post-surgery. And I have enormous respect for his opinions.

Dr Kattus shared my enthusiasm and arranged for a meeting with the hospital's Medical Research Committee. After explaining our research proposal and pointing to its promise of success with little if any expectation of side effects, we received permission to go ahead with the study.

The idea was to recruit a number of people with elevated cholesterol levels. Potential subjects were told about the programme through a brief memo and signed an informed consent form. The programme lasted eight weeks, with weekly meetings every Monday evening. Those meetings gave participants an opportunity to talk about all the aspects of cholesterol now covered in this book, to ask questions, and to share experiences.

After a series of lectures, with handout materials and personal conferences, a total of twenty participating men and women were asked to follow a moderately restricted diet as discussed in Chapter 3, 'Winning by the Numbers', to consume fifty grams of oat bran daily either as cereal or muffins, and to gradually work up to three grams of niacin as described in Chapter 5, 'The Amazing Story of Niacin'.

In addition, three individuals, unable to take niacin owing to contraindications including diabetes and gout, came to the meetings, followed the diet, and took oat bran. Therefore we had a total of twenty-three persons coming to our Monday get-togethers. There were also two persons who followed the programme outside the hospital setting.

Of the twenty people beginning the full programme at the hospital, five failed to follow the modified diet, did not eat the suggested amounts of oat bran, forgot to take the niacin, or combinations of all three. Their results were predictably poor. But for the fifteen faithfully staying with the programme, the results were more than merely encouraging.

The average fall in total cholesterol was 22 per cent. Remember that authorities strongly believe that for every 1 per cent drop in cholesterol, the risk of coronary heart disease falls by 2 per cent. That means the subjects in our study had their risk of heart disease slashed by nearly half.

In addition, the two individuals who went on the programme outside the hospital setting were particularly motivated. One cut her total cholesterol from 6.7 to 4.3 in eight weeks. The other slashed his level from 6.5 to 3.7. In just eight weeks!

But that's just the beginning. For the participants at the hospital, the levels of the protective HDL (high-density lipoprotein) *rose* by an average of more than 22 per cent. Sometimes the numbers doubled or even tripled. That meant that the ratio of total cholesterol to HDL, a very important predictor of heart-disease risk, went to normal in every single individual who complied!

Simply stated, those results have never been seen in medical science before without the use of potent prescription drugs. Every single person who followed this programme eliminated totally the risk of heart disease from cholesterol. There is no reason to believe that others following the programme should have anything but success.

Two of the men on the programme during our study were physicians themselves. Both remained on the programme after the formal research came to an end, and both have demonstrated even greater improvements. Needless to say, they are now actively prescribing the programme for their own patients. Everyone who has an elevated cholesterol level learns about miracle muffins and niacin.

The results for each of the participants in the study at Santa Monica Hospital Medical Center are listed in the tables beginning on page 160. I've also commented on their compliance. And the three persons listed at the end of the tables took only the oat bran, without the niacin.

Oat bran, when combined with a modified diet as discussed in Chapter 4, 'Getting the Scoop on Oat Bran', can lower LDL cholesterol. HDL levels are not affected. Of the three persons taking oat bran without the niacin, cholesterol levels fell by 15, 10, and 5 per cent. Compliance with the dietary modifications probably determined their levels of success.

How can we tell about compliance? Niacin compliance is the easiest to detect. Those subjects taking niacin experienced a considerable decline in levels of triglycerides, often by 50 per cent or more. The average drop was 44 per cent. Typically triglycerides will come down when one takes niacin whether one follows other aspects of the programme or not.

Compliance with oat bran was a matter of simply asking the participants. Practically everyone enjoyed this part and compliance was good.

Dietary compliance was more difficult. We asked all the participants to keep a dietary diary for two weeks during the programme. They listed all the foods and beverages taken during each day. This served two purposes. First, we had a better idea of what people were actually eating. Second, the exercise was very educational. Often we don't realize what we're eating unless we actually list all those foods, step back, and take a look. After doing so, many were able to see where they were consuming fats and cholesterol they easily could reduce or replace.

Some individuals, however, were simply unable or unwilling to modify their diets even moderately. While this is the most practical and effective programme for reducing cholesterol and improving ratios described anywhere, it will not work if one continues disastrous eating habits. Most people in the study found that suggested modifications made reducing their fat and cholesterol levels of intake relatively easy.

Easy, yes, but totally effortless, no. As one of the men said in response to a complaint about missing fatty cuts of beef and cheese, 'You have to bite the bullet.' It's kind of like quitting the cigarette habit. The first few weeks are particularly difficult, and it gets easier as time goes on. After a while, the craving is gone completely. Sure it's tough, but it's more than worth it.

While every one of the compliant individuals left the study with completely normalized cholesterol ratios, some did better than others in terms of total cholesterol levels. Some who were content to make very few alterations in their diets achieved lowering of 10, 12, 15 per cent or so. Others who made a greater effort brought their levels down by 30, 35, and even 55 per cent.

In my own case, I limit my daily intake of animal meat of all types to six ounces. I rather carefully look at food labels, avoiding or at least limiting the amount of saturated fats. I enjoy cheese only rarely. And butter and eggs are completely out. But that still means I can enjoy a hamburger, an occasional steak, desserts, and a cornucopia of other foods. A year later and I'm still compliant, with few if any real cravings. The result? My cholesterol level remains around 4 every time I have it tested. From my original level of 7.3 mmol/l, that represents a 40 per cent reduction. Yet most people I have dinner or lunch with for business or pleasure never know I'm modifying my diet in the least.

It also appears that the three aspects of the programme have to come together. One man who dropped his level under the 5.2 mark later stopped taking niacin. His cholesterol level rose quickly.

Unfortunately, it also is true that not all people can tolerate the niacin. Most are willing to put up with the flushing sensation that occurs at the start of therapy but which diminishes once the three-gram level is achieved. A certain number of individuals, however, develop a rash that forces them to stop taking the tablets. One of our participants developed such a rash.

Bear in mind that *any* substance, even foods, can cause reactions in some people. Many are allergic to strawberries. Others are intolerant of dairy products. And a large number experience gastric upset from plain old aspirin. Some get an upset stomach from a single multiple vitamin-mineral supplement. There's no way to predict who might have an adverse reaction. But even if one does occur, cessation of the vitamin reverses the condition within just a few days. There are no long-term ill effects.

As indicated earlier, niacin appears to be safe even in long-term use. The vast majority of people will experience no difficulties whatever. In our study, we excluded from niacin those persons with either diabetes or gout or pre-existing liver malfunctions. Those with ulcers should also see their physicians before starting on niacin.

Out of both personal and professional curiosity, I decided to have a complete panel of blood studies done on myself a year after starting niacin. Every indicator came back completely normal after that year.

Upon completion of the study, I conducted a survey of everyone who had participated. Most agreed that the programme was easy to follow and that they intended to stay with it.

Meet the participants

B.R. was the first person I met. She was early for the first weekly meeting and we chatted as I set up my slides and other presentation materials. B.R. made it clear that she really didn't think the programme would work, since she had tried to lower her cholesterol levels many times in the past. But she figured she'd give it a try. B.R. gave it her best effort, followed the dietary modifications, ate the oat bran regularly, and took the niacin without any problems. Sceptical to the point of cynicism throughout the study, she was happy to learn that after just eight weeks her cholesterol level had dropped by 27 per cent and her ratio had gone from 12.3 to 3.1. A real success story, B.R. is now telling everyone about the programme.

C.O. had tried desperately to lower her dangerously high levels. Even drugs had been ineffective. But on this programme her total cholesterol level dropped by 4 points, for a 35 per cent reduction, and brought her ratio down to 3.4.

B.H. is retired and she and her husband travel extensively. Even for a vacation in Europe, B.H. took along a supply of oat bran and her bottle of niacin tablets. She was well rewarded with a 19 per cent dip in cholesterol and a safe ratio of only 2.3.

A.J. attended every meeting without fail. He was bound and determined to make the programme work for him. His perseverance paid off: his cholesterol fell from 6.3 to 4.2 in just eight weeks, with a doubling of HDL levels, resulting in a very healthy ratio of 2.6.

Similarly, the two physicians, R.G. and C.K., took the programme very seriously and followed it faithfully. Both achieved results they knew were important but were unable to reach with what medicine had to offer before. R.G. went from 7.5 to 5.3. C.K. watched his level fall from 6.6 to 4.8.

Even those who complied poorly achieved notable success. L.S. had a difficult time with diet, admitting that he didn't try as hard as he should have. Yet he saw his cholesterol level fall by 14 per cent and his ratio improve from 6.6 to 5.2. J.C. also was unable to control his diet, but with a 45 per cent rise in HDL, his ratio fell to a normal 4.1. The same applied to E.P., whose protective HDL level rose by 20 per cent.

There is still a great deal medical science must learn about cholesterol and how the body deals with it. In the meantime, however, we do know that total cholesterol should be under 5.2. The ratio of total cholesterol to HDL should be no higher than 4.4 for females and 5.2 for males. Achieving those numbers virtually eliminates this important risk factor of coronary heart disease.

'Do-it-yourself programmes'

The participants in our hospital study had the distinct advantage of those eight Monday-night meetings. They learned just about everything there is to know about cholesterol, how oat bran and niacin work, and how to painlessly improve their diets. Plus they had the reinforcement of meeting every seven days to ask questions, get support from the group, and perhaps to get back on the wagon after falling off for a while. An advantage, yes. But not a requirement for success.

A medical colleague of Dr Kattus referred to me a 28-year-old nurse who had just learned her cholesterol was a disturbingly high 6.7. Trained in the value of preventive medicine, she knew that if her level wasn't changed, she would be certain to develop coronary heart disease.

When I met her in Dr Kattus's office S.B. told me she was very health conscious. She ran twenty to thirty miles weekly, and her diet could best be described as 'California healthy'. S.B. ate meat only occasionally, and preferred fish and poultry. Her diet was loaded with fresh fruits and vegetables. Only the cheese had to be reduced in her otherwise perfect diet. (And, of course, those rich desserts she had always tried to limit because of the calories anyway.)

S.B. had no problem in getting to the therapeutic three-gram level of niacin. She enjoyed the oat bran. And in just eight weeks her blood chemistry was totally turned around.

From 6.7, S.B.'s cholesterol level dropped to 4.3. Her HDL rose from 1.1 to 2.5. The destructive LDL levels dropped from 5.3 to 1.6. The result was a change in ratio from 6.1 to 1.7. At the same time, her triglycerides went down from 67 to 33. To say that she was happy with the results is an understatement.

The same goes for my printer. R.R. runs the local Kwik Kopy Printing Shop, and has done all my printing for many years. One day, coincidentally, he asked me if I knew anything about cholesterol. R.R. didn't know about the book or the research study at that time, but he was aware that I wrote about medicine.

This is a guy who holds a black belt in karate, works out five days a week, and frequently runs in 10K races. In general, he's highly fitness conscious, also eating a 'California healthy' diet. That's why he was so surprised—and appalled—when his doctor told him his cholesterol level was at 6.5. For this 37-year-old man, coronary heart disease was ready to knock on the door if he didn't do something about that dangerous level.

Here's a good example of someone for whom a healthful diet wasn't enough. R.R.'s diet was already fine-tuned. He needed more.

I felt that R.R. would be splendid proof of the programme. The only modifications his diet required were cutting back on butter and cheese. The butter was used moderately, but cheese was a frequent part of the diet. He still eats it, but far less often.

R.R. enjoys three oat-bran muffins each day. He finds they fit perfectly into his busy life, and he brings them to the shop for breakfast and snacks.

At the beginning, I'd come into the shop and ask how the programme was going. R.R. said all was well but that the flushing from the niacin was uncomfortable. Later, the flushing persisted and kept him from going any higher than two grams daily.

One afternoon I came in with some printing to be done and noticed that R.R.'s face was a bright red. I asked whether he'd been out in the sun that weekend, surprised since he wasn't a typical California sun worshipper. R.R. said that was his usual niacin flush.

I suggested that he switch to Nicobid, the time-release capsules of niacin produced by USV Pharmaceutical. Nicobid comes in 100- and 500-milligram capsules, which slowly release the niacin into the system. For most people this completely eliminates the flushing. It worked beautifully for R.R. as it had for others during our hospital study.

At the end of R.R.'s 'test' period of eight weeks, I asked him what numbers he'd be happy with—how much of a cholesterol reduction he was expecting. He didn't know that I had just come back from the hospital laboratory with his test results. R.R. said he'd be pleased with anything under 5.2, the danger point for cholesterol levels. He was ecstatic when he learned that he had achieved a drop to 3.7!

R.R.'s complete 'lipid profile' was a joy to behold: from 6.5 to 3.7, a more than 2.5 mmol/l drop in total cholesterol. His level of destructive LDL had gone down to just 2. His protective HDL was up to 1.7. Triglycerides fell to 0.5. And the predictive ratio had improved to a very, very healthy 2.2—less than half the normal risk level.

'No excuses acceptable'

Even with R.R.'s flushing, he continued to take the niacin. Fortunately, the Nicobid was able to solve his problem completely. But the important thing was that R.R. stuck with it. He could have quit early on, and we'd never have known how well he could succeed.

When S.B. started the programme, she knew that she'd had to watch her diet, especially when out on dates. But she knew the importance of getting that cholesterol level down to normal. She stuck with it then, and stays with it now.

B.H. can afford all the finest foods at expensive restaurants throughout Europe as she travels with her husband. And it's also quite a problem to stay with the oat bran during their many lengthy trips. Yet she has decided that her health is more important than a fancy sauce Béarnaise. So B.H. selects broiled chicken and fish whenever she can. And her suitcase is never packed without a supply of oat bran to take along.

On the other hand, one of the study participants, who will remain not only unnamed but without even initials, gave in to excuses easily. A bachelor, he got his girlfriend to make muffins for him at the beginning. After an argument she stopped baking and he stopped eating the oat bran. It was too difficult to prepare them himself, so he simply stopped.

Can a bachelor or anyone else living alone be expected to bake muffins? Why not? The recipes are easy to follow and require just a bit of time each week. After my surgery, I prepared my own muffins just two weeks after the doctors had repaired my clogged arteries. Even though my energy reserves were low, I put a high priority on baking those muffins. There's no excuse for not doing it yourself.

Some have asked whether muffins will become boring after a while. Remember the French who eat their daily croissant for their entire lives. Actually the muffins are less tiresome, since they can be prepared in an almost infinite variety. Moreover, one day one can enjoy muffins and another day hot cereal.

There's also no excuse for forgetting even one dose of niacin. Many individuals, myself included, find that the best bet is to have a supply wherever they go. I keep a bottle in my bathroom for the morning and evening, one in the kitchen for lunch, another in the glove compartment of the car for when I'm out on the road, still another in my office, and a final container in my travel kit. No excuse to miss.

For most individuals, the diet is the toughest part, yet it remains crucial for total success. Yes, you can improve significantly without much change in diet, just by including oat bran and niacin. Yet for best results, the fat and the cholesterol intake must be modified. Sticking with the diet sometimes can be difficult.

I'm reminded of the business outing I was on some time back. In an unfamiliar neighbourhood, the only restaurant I could find was a Straw Hat Pizza place. There was not time to find an alternative, and I was starving. So in I went and ordered a pizza with green peppers, mushrooms, onions, sliced tomatoes, and, please, hold the cheese. It was delicious! And the person taking my order wasn't even surprised—it turns out that many strict vegetarians do the same thing. Now I can go into such pizza restaurants with family or friends, enjoy the environment, and relish the crispy crust and the fresh ingredients without concern or guilt. At home I frequently make pizzas with pre-formed crusts, pizza sauce, fresh vegetables, and a sprinkling of low-cholesterol low-fat cheese. Even my kids think they're great.

There are lots of other suggestions for enjoying restaurants while complying with cholesterol modifications in Chapter 10, 'Dining Out: To Your Health!' In many ways it's even easier to follow the diet when eating out than when preparing foods in one's own home. Even airlines provide a low-fat low-cholesterol menu for travellers. You just have to ask for it in advance.

What are some other excuses? How about 'My family shouldn't have to "suffer" because of my special diet.' First of all, the word 'suffer' doesn't apply. The foods best for this programme are best for everyone. Second, with a few simple modifications, practically every favourite family recipe can still be enjoyed.

There simply are no good excuses, no valid excuses, for not following the programme and reducing one's cholesterol to healthy levels. Any more than there are good excuses to continue smoking cigarettes. In both cases, the choice is completely yours and the rewards so totally outweigh the efforts that the decision should be immediate and final.

The programme has been clinically proven to be safe and effective. Followed properly, it can dramatically reduce cholesterol levels to completely healthy in just eight weeks. The risk of coronary heart disease will be greatly diminished. The chances of living a longer, healthier life are tremendously improved.

Table 14. Average results with the 8-week cholesterol cure programme

	Total cholesterol reductions (%)	Triglyceride decrease (%)	LDL decrease (%)	HDL increase (%)
Participants with good compliance	31.67	42.08	47.45	60.58
All participants	22.05	41.10	32.61	43.85

Personal notes

Charles E. Keenan, M.D. General Practice, Santa Monica, California

I appreciated being a part of the study just completed. It was quite revealing. I had a good deal of personal interest as my cholesterol has been slightly elevated throughout the years. I'd used the things available to me, other than drugs, but to no avail.

I must confess to a bit of initial scepticism and pessimism regarding the results of such a simple change of dietary habits. Many large drug firms are spending millions of dollars trying to find a medicine to counteract the cholesterol disease. Medically, it has been very frustrating to prescribe medications and have a limited amount of success, occasionally with significant side effects. Patients on these medications are on them for life. This makes one very hesitant to prescribe medications that have any significant side effects. Another concern is that medications either have to be given too frequently or cause significant diarrhoea and so forth, making it difficult to keep patients on them. They are also, in my experience, quite expensive.

I had tried and recommended yogurt, garlic, exercise, and a few other environmental changes, again, with rather questionable results.

I decided to try this approach to see how difficult it would be for my own compliance. It seemed too good to be true, just a mild dietary change and additional vitamin pills. I must admit to have been buoyed up by testing my cholesterol very early in the programme. I was astounded to find it down by 33 per cent. This made my enthusiasm and excitement for the experiment much greater.

Some of the interesting things that were by-products of my becoming a part of it were uncovering the talent for being a cook (baking bran muffins), enjoying the weekly lectures, and having a unique approach to tell my earlier hypercholesterol patients who had failed on other regimes. I was so encouraged that I told other patients to contact the programme for possible admittance to the study. I've subsequently been encouraging all my patients to make this dietary adjustment as it seems to be a painless change with dramatic results.

My results, I think, were as exciting and as successful as one could hope for. My initial cholesterol was 6.4 and the subsequent level was 4.8. It really makes me an apostle for the programme and I hope I can spread this simple, inexpensive, and drugless approach to health and longevity.

Exercise certainly is a valuable tool, but I doubt if it has anywhere near the effectiveness of this. I was amazed at the relatively little change in my lifestyle and the significant results I had with just the oat bran and niacin. If a person tries this approach and it is successful, there is no need to go on costly medications with significant side-effects.

If my initial enthusiasm proves accurate, this could be the greatest boon to longevity since penicillin. As with any other form of therapy, this may not be the panacea for everyone, but for many this will be a very significant factor in their future health.

I can recommend this wholeheartedly to everyone for their initial use and have them individually check their pre- and post-cholesterol levels. This could well be their passport to longevity.

In closing, I might raise my glass and toast saying 'long live oat bran and its users'.

Dr R.G., Santa Monica, California
Having discovered my serum cholesterol and serum triglycerides to be at the upper limit of normal (7.5 mmol/l and 5.4 mmol/l, respectively) several years ago, I was interested in a method of lowering these values.

Approximately three years ago I modified my diet by eliminating all eggs and significantly decreasing the amount of red meat, cheese, and other dairy products. This dietary change did not alter the serum cholesterol or serum triglycerides to any significant degree.

In January of 1985, I learned of the niacin-oat-bran study at Santa Monica Hospital and became a participant in that study. The study required the daily intake of niacin (three grams) and one-half cup of oat bran. Some initial flushing symptoms from the niacin (which can be almost completely ameliorated with one aspirin tablet) are no longer present. Since I had already modified my diet three years ago, there was no additional alteration in my diet during the course of this study.

I was pleasantly surprised to find that my serum cholesterol levels decreased by approximately 30 per cent (below 5.2) and my serum triglycerides decreased by 50 per cent over a three-month period of time. In addition, the ratio of total cholesterol to HDL changed from 6.15 to 3.4 over a similar period of time.

Because of this success and the paucity of side effects. I fully intend to maintain this programme indefinitely.

Sigrid Broderson, R.N., Private Duty Nurse, Los Angeles, California
Since I was young, I've always been very physically active. I've enjoyed sports, and have spent a lot of time snow skiing, even to the point of teaching others. I also enjoy windsurfing, tennis, racquetball, swimming, you name it. Last year I took up running and have done a few 10K races, and in 1986 I'm planning to do my first marathon. The point of all this is that I'm in good physical condition, and I'm interested in maintaining good health in general.

My health interests, of course, are both personal and professional.

As a registered nurse, since 1979 I've been involved with intensive care.

My own health, I've thought, has always been good. My heart rate has been in the forties, and my blood pressure has also been in the low-normal range. I've watched my diet carefully.

In April, after I had an accident, I decided to have my cholesterol checked. I'd been working closely with a patient who had a cholesterol problem, and I'd been giving nutrition counselling and helping him with his diet. So I became curious as to what my own cholesterol level was. To my surprise, the cholesterol was extremely elevated. I found this hard to believe. In fact, I had the test repeated the next week, this time a complete lipid panel to see not only my total cholesterol but also the levels of the protective HDL and the harmful LDL. Again the results were disappointing, with a high total cholesterol of 6.7 and high LDL of 5.3, along with a fairly low HDL of only 1.1.

I couldn't believe that one of the major aspects of health was so threatening since I'd been taking such good care of myself in terms of exercise and diet. It was particularly alarming to me since I'd spent so much time with coronary patients, those who had had heart attacks and open-heart surgery. I was very much aware of the risk factors of heart disease, and I knew that I was at risk. I had inherited the condition from my mother, whose cholesterol level was also high and who had developed heart disease.

I returned to my cardiologist, and he referred me to Mr Kowalski and his research study. After our first meeting I was more than eager to begin the new programme.

Taking the niacin, for me, was not much of a problem. I only remember a couple of days, as I was increasing my intake, that I experienced any flushing. It was mild, went away quickly, and wasn't really a problem. If I'm a bit late with my niacin dosage now, I occasionally get a little tingly feeling, but that only reminds me that I'm on the road to good health.

Another positive aspect of taking the niacin is that it gives me a schedule, a routine, that reminds me to take my other vitamins. It also reminds me regularly to watch my diet, since I take my niacin near mealtimes.

At first I started with oat bran as hot cereal, but after a month I tired of that and switched to the muffins from the recipes Mr Kowalski developed. Now I find myself often eating more than the three muffins a day, since I think they're so delicious. I actually have to limit myself, only because of my total calories.

Dietary changes weren't difficult at all, since my diet was pretty good to begin with. I've always enjoyed fruits and vegetables, and never had much fat in my diet. I did eliminate egg yolks and cut back

Table 15. Lipid profile records of study participants: baseline and after two months

Subject Number	Total cholesterol	Improvement %	Triglycerides	Improvement %	HDL	Improvement %	LDL	Improvement %	Ratio	Sex	Comments
1	6.5	43	0.9	50	1.0	65	4.6	60	6.5	M	Good compliance outside hospital
	3.7		0.5		1.7		1.8		2.2		
2	6.7	36	0.8	50	1.1	114	5.3	70	6.1	F	Good compliance outside hospital
	4.3		0.4		2.5		1.6		1.7		
3	6.6	27	—	—	1.9	0	—	—	—	M	Good compliance
	4.8		1.1		1.7		2.6		2.8		
4	6.3	33	4.1	88	0.8	100	3.6	35	7.8	M	Good compliance
	4.2		0.5		1.6		2.4		2.6		
5	7.5	29	2.4	40	1.2	0	5.2	33	6.2	M	Good compliance
	5.3		1.3		1.2		3.5		4.4		
6	6.0	36	0.7	0	1.4	33	4.3	52	4.3	M	Good compliance
	4.5		0.7		1.9		2.3		2.4		
7	8.4	27	2.6	76	0.7	200	6.4	40	12.0	F	Good compliance
	6.3		0.9		2.0		3.9		3.1		
8	11.8	35	1.2	34	1.9	20	9.4	46	6.2	F	Good compliance
	7.7		0.8		2.2		5.1		3.5		
9	7.0	19	2.2	69	1.4	81	4.6	39	5.0	F	Good compliance
	5.6		0.7		2.5		2.8		2.3		
10	5.7	55	0.8	05	0.9	0	4.4	65	6.3	F	Good compliance
	2.5		0.8		0.6		1.6		4.1		
11	7.8	30	2.6	40	1.1	24	5.6	39	7.1	F	Good compliance
	5.5		1.5		1.3		3.4		4.2		
12	6.4	10	2.2	53	1.7	90	3.7	43	3.7	F	Good compliance
	5.8		1.0		3.3		2.1		1.8		

No.										Sex	Compliance
13	8.4 / 7.5	15	1.2 / 0.8	30	2.3 / 3.2	36	5.6 / 3.9	30	3.6 / 2.3	F	Fair compliance
14	6.0 / 5.1	16	1.4 / 1.0	28	1.4 / 1.3	0	4.0 / 3.3	19	4.3 / 3.9	M	Fair compliance
15	7.5 / 6.5	14	1.9 / 1.3	30	1.1 / 1.2	09	5.5 / 4.6	16	6.8 / 5.4	M	Poor dietary compliance
16	6.6 / 6.9	0	4.3 / 1.6	64	0.9 / 1.7	80	3.8 / 4.5	0	7.3 / 4.1	M	Poor dietary compliance
17	6.8 / 7.1	0	1.7 / 1.3	24	1.5 / 1.8	25	4.6 / 4.7	0	4.5 / 3.9	M	Poor dietary compliance
18	6.5 / 5.7	13	1.5 / 0.7	55	2.6 / 2.5	0	— / 2.9	—	2.5 / 2.3	F	Poor dietary compliance
19	6.4 / 6.0	06	2.4 / 1.7	30	1.1 / 1.0	0	4.2 / 4.2	0	5.8 / 6.0	M	Poor dietary compliance
20	6.1 / 5.7	06	1.9 / 0.9	50	— / 0.8	—	— / 4.5	—	— / 7.1	M	Poor dietary compliance
21	5.8 / 5.4	07	3.0 / 1.6	47	0.9 / 0.7	0	3.5 / 3.9	0	6.4 / 7.7	M	Total noncompliance
22	8.0 / 6.8	15	2.4 / 2.3	0	1.2 / 1.1	0	5.7 / 4.6	20	6.7 / 6.2	F	Oat bran only niacin contraindicated
23	6.3 / 5.7	10	1.2 / 2.0	0	0.9 / 0.7	0	4.9 / 4.1	17	7.0 / 8.1	M	Oat bran only niacin contraindicated
24	5.8 / 5.5	05	0.5 / 0.5	13	2.0 / 2.2	09	3.5 / 3.1	12	2.9 / 2.5	F	Oat bran only

— Data not available

a bit on red meats. But I still enjoy eating out, and now I don't really think of this as a 'restricted' diet since there are so many foods to choose from.

It was all so easy during the first two months that I was actually scared when it was time to take my blood test again. Surely the results couldn't be very good when the programme was so painless. To my surprise, the results came out extremely well. What a terrific motivation to keep it up. My total cholesterol dropped from 6.7 to 4.3. My harmful LDL level went from 5.3 to 1.6. My protective HDL rose from 1.1 to 2.5. And the important ratio of total cholesterol to HDL dropped from 6 to 1.7.

Now I know I'm doing everything I possibly can to reduce the risk of heart disease. My health is my own responsibility, and it's up to me to protect my life.

On a professional level, this programme has motivated me to a new commitment to health counselling on a preventive basis. And I'm proud that I practise what I preach.

14. MIRACLE MUFFINS AND BREADS

Since discovering the vital role oat bran can play in living a healthful life, I've worked on a number of ways to incorporate oat bran into my own diet. Personally, I don't care much for hot cereal, which is the principal way oat bran is normally served. For me, the best way has been using oat bran in baking muffins.

Before you start saying to yourself that you don't have time to do any baking, consider the fact that in just 10 minutes of preparation time and 17 minutes of baking time you can have a week's supply. And you'll more than save that time when it comes to eating. Muffins are the ideal 'fast' food for someone on the run all the time as I am. Just gobble down two or three muffins along with a glass of skimmed milk or a fruit milkshake and you're set for hours.

I try to get one-half cup of oat bran into my diet each and every day. Three muffins supply that whole amount. And with the variety of muffins and other baked goods I've suggested here, plus others you may come up with on your own, you'll never get tired of them— anymore than people get tired of bread.

To get started, you'll need one or two metal muffin pans and a supply of paper baking cups to line the cups with. All the ingredients you'll need are listed in the Shopping List chapter, except for any fresh fruit you may wish to add for variety.

A few words about muffin making

While all the muffin recipes you're about to read have been extensively tested, a few words of explanation are in order. First of all, let me say that all these ideas were developed in my own kitchen, based upon an original recipe on the oat-bran packet in America. But I've made changes and additions.

For example, I have omitted salt entirely. I find that this makes no perceptible difference in flavour, and I'd rather not have the sodium in my food. The two tablespoons of cooking oil provide only one-half teaspoon of oil per muffin. You'll find that most muffin and biscuit recipes call for much more oil. You can also substitute corn syrup for oil.

Next, I have experimented with sugar content. I tried eliminating sugar entirely, relying instead on all-fruit sweetening. Both the flavour and texture of the product suffered. So now I routinely use one-quarter cup of brown sugar for a 12-muffin recipe. Again, note that this is just four tablespoons per batch, or one teaspoonful per muffin.

Don't forget that these oat-bran muffins have become a staple part of my daily diet, and hopefully they will be part of yours also. With this in mind, the amount of oil and sugar in the muffins, as part of your total diet, is really quite small.

If you prefer, however, you certainly may experiment on your own, trying less sugar or replacing some of it with additional fruit. But just for your interest and information, don't forget that the body metabolizes all sugars in the same way. Whether it's sucrose in brown sugar, glucose in honey, or fructose in fruit and juices, the chemical formula is similar and the effects the same. That doesn't mean you should go hog-wild and double the recipe's sugar content. Just keep the word 'moderation' in mind.

As I mentioned earlier, I did the first muffins in my own kitchen. I used a standard electric oven, and recommend an oven thermometer to be sure of the temperature: 425°F/220°C.

To have these muffins come out as perfect as possible, time is critical. For all recipes, use a timer and note that you set the time at *exactly* 17 minutes. When the timer rings, use a toothpick to test doneness. The toothpick should come out of the muffin just slightly tacky to the touch, not wet or dry.

If you overbake by even a minute or two, you'll have dry muffins. Other recipes are not as critical since they have more sugar and oil to retain moisture. It's better to return the muffins to the oven for an additional minute than to regret the extra minute if they are already overbaked. Depending on the particular recipe or the amount of fruit you're using, the batter will take up more or less time. The pineapple muffin recipe, for example, is quite moist and probably will require an extra two minutes.

By all means, experiment. Each time you try a recipe or a variation, jot down the temperature of the oven and the exact amount of time it took to bake the muffins. Also make a note as to just how juicy the fruit was that you used. These things make a big difference.

A word of caution so you don't make the same mistake I did at the beginning of my own muffin experience. These muffins do *not* get browned easily. At first you may think they don't look done. Use that toothpick. If you bake them until they're as brown as a typical flour-based cake would be, the muffins will be dry.

Unlike commercially prepared baked goods, these muffins do not contain any preservatives. If you don't expect to eat them within two or three days, by all means keep the muffins in the freezer or refrigerator. A large plastic storage bag is best to retain moisture. If you have a microwave oven, pop cold or frozen muffins in for a moment to warm them beautifully. Standard ovens have a tendency to dry out the muffins, if you leave them in too long.

Don't be discouraged if all this seems like a lot of trouble. Baking with oat bran is simply different from baking with wheat flour and butter- and sugar-laden recipes. You'll be comfortable with the procedures after just two or three batches, even if you've never baked before in your life. And the rewards you'll reap are simply spectacular!

If you own a food processor . . .

After trying a few of the muffin recipes, you'll find that they come out a bit on the crumbly side, rather like cornbread. Some people really like that texture. And I enjoy it too. But there's a way I discovered to give your muffins, breads, and brownies a more cakelike structure.

Take the whole box of oat bran and just empty it right into your food processor with the large blade set to grind. Let the machine run during the full time it takes to get all your other ingredients out and measured. When it's time to add the oat bran and mix the batter, you'll find that you've milled the oat bran down to a flourlike, powdery consistency. It makes a *huge* difference in the way your muffins turn out.

Basic Muffins

2 ¼ cups oat-bran cereal
¼ cup chopped nuts (walnuts,
  pecans, or even peanuts)
¼ cup raisins (or dates, currants,
  or whatever)
1 tablespoon baking powder (not
  baking soda)
¼ cup brown sugar or
¼ cup honey or molasses
1 ¼ cups skimmed milk
2 egg whites
2 tablespoons vegetable oil

This is a modified version of a standard muffin recipe. Start off with this one. Later you may wish to cut down on the amount of sweetenings added. Some of the other recipes for muffins offer excellent alternative sweeteners, such as frozen apple-juice concentrate.

Preheat the oven to 425°F (220°C/Gas Mark 7). In a large bowl combine the oat-bran cereal, nuts, raisins and baking powder. Stir in the brown sugar *or* liquid sweetening. Mix the milk, egg whites, and oil together and blend in with the oat-bran mixture. Line muffin pans with paper baking cups, and fill with batter. Bake 15 to 17 minutes. Test for doneness with a toothpick; it should come out moist but not wet. *Makes 12 muffins.*

Store in a plastic bag to retain moisture. Keep the muffins in the refrigerator if they will not be consumed within 3 days, as they contain no preservatives.

Oil-Free Muffins

2 ¼ cups oat-bran cereal
1 tablespoon baking powder
¼ cup brown sugar
½ cup dry fruits (raisins, dates,
  prunes)
1 ¼ cups skimmed milk or
  evaporated skimmed milk
2 egg whites
2 tablespoons syrup

One can also make muffins without any oil at all by substituting syrup for the oil. You can also make this substitution in any of the other muffin recipes in this section. Try substituting syrup for oil in other baking recipes as well.

Preheat the oven to 425°F (220°C/Gas Mark 7). Mix the dry

ingredients in a large bowl. Mix the milk, egg whites, and syrup together and blend with dry ingredients. Line muffin pans with paper baking cups, and fill with batter divided equally. Bake 13 to 15 minutes. Test for doneness with a toothpick. *Makes 12 muffins.*

NOTE This oil-free recipe requires a bit less baking time than the recipe for basic muffins.

Apple Cinnamon Muffins

2 ¼ cups oat-bran cereal
¼ cup brown sugar
1 ¼ teaspoons cinnamon
1 tablespoon baking powder
¼ cup chopped walnuts
¼ cup raisins
½ cup skimmed milk
¾ cup frozen apple-juice
　concentrate
2 egg whites
2 tablespoons vegetable oil
1 medium apple, cored and
　chopped

Mix the dry ingredients in a large bowl. Mix the milk, apple-juice concentrate, egg whites, and oil in a bowl or blender. Add to the dry ingredients and mix. Add the chopped apple. Line the muffin pans with paper baking cups and fill with batter. Bake in a 425°F (220°C/Gas Mark 7) oven for 17 minutes. *Makes 12 muffins.*

After cooling, store in a large plastic bag to retain moisture and softness.

TIP Serve with apple sauce or spread with butter.

Banana Nut Muffins

2 ¼ cups oat-bran cereal
1 tablespoon baking powder
¼ cup brown sugar
¼ cup chopped walnuts or
    pecans
1 ¼ cups skimmed milk
2 very ripe bananas (the riper
    the better)
2 egg whites
2 tablespoons vegetable oil

Preheat the oven to 425°F
(220°C/Gas Mark 7). Mix the dry
ingredients in a large bowl. Mix
the milk, bananas, egg whites, and
oil in a bowl or blender. Add to
the dry ingredients and mix. Line
the muffin pan with paper baking
cups and fill them with batter.
Bake for 17 minutes. *Makes 12
muffins.*

TIP Serve with a banana
milkshake.

Canned-Fruit Muffins

2 ¼ cups oat-bran cereal
1 tablespoon baking powder
¼ cup raisins
2 tablespoons vegetable oil
1 cup skimmed milk
2 egg whites
1 16-oz can pears (drained)

Preheat the oven to 425°F
(220°C/Gas Mark 7). Mix the dry
ingredients in a bowl. Mix
together all other ingredients
except the pears. Add the liquid
mixture to the dry ingredients and
mix. Chop the canned pears fine
and add to the batter. If the batter
seems dry, add a bit of the fluid
drained from the pears. Line the
muffin pan with paper baking
cups and fill with batter. Bake for
17 minutes or until a toothpick
comes out dry.

NOTE Always look for canned
pears without any added sugar.
Not only are they lower in
calories, but they also taste better.
And don't stop with pears. Look
for all the other canned fruits you
can store and use when you don't
have any fresh fruit and it's time
to make muffins. Peaches are
good. Or, for something really
colourful and delicious, try fruit

cocktail. Save the cherries to put on top. Even the kids will love these.

Strawberry Muffins

2 ¼ cups oat-bran cereal
¼ cup brown sugar
1 tablespoon baking powder
½ cup skimmed milk
¾ cup canned strawberry nectar
or strawberry juice
¾ cup fresh or frozen
strawberries
2 egg whites
2 tablespoons vegetable oil

Preheat the oven to 425°F (220°C/Gas Mark 7). Mix the dry ingredients in a large bowl. Mix the milk, strawberry nectar, strawberries, egg whites, and oil in a bowl or blender. (Reserve 12 pieces of fresh strawberry to place on top of the muffins.) Combine with the dry ingredients and mix. Line muffin cups with paper baking cups and fill with batter. Place a piece of strawberry on each. Bake for 17 minutes. *Makes 12 muffins.*

TIP Serve as strawberry 'shortcake'. Place each in a bowl and cover with chilled straw-berries. Top with whipped chilled evaporated skimmed milk.

Pineapple Muffins

2 ¼ cups oat-bran cereal
¼ cup brown sugar
1 tablespoon baking powder
½ cup skimmed milk
2 cans (8 oz) crushed pineapple
in its own juice (unsweetened)
2 egg whites
2 tablespoons vegetable oil

Preheat the oven to 425°F (220°C/Gas Mark 7). Mix the dry ingredients in a large bowl. Mix the milk, 1 can of crushed pineapple with juice, egg whites, and oil in a bowl or blender. Combine the ingredients and mix. Drain the second can of pineapple and add to the mixture. Line the muffin pans with paper baking cups, and fill with batter. Bake for 17 minutes. *Makes 12 muffins.*

TIP Serve with a pineapple milkshake.

Pineapple Upside-Down Muffins

Make these for a special treat.

Prepare the recipe as for pineapple muffins (see page 173). Before filling the muffin cups, place a slice of pineapple and a maraschino cherry in each. Pour in the batter. Bake for 19 minutes.

Another alternative is to use a cake pan instead of the muffin pan. Lightly grease and line it with pineapple rings with a maraschino cherry in each. Bake for 19 minutes. Turn out of the pan and serve as an upside-down cake.

Pear-fection Muffins

2 ¼ cups oat-bran cereal
3 tablespoons brown sugar
1 tablespoon baking powder
½ teaspoon cinnamon
¼ teaspoon vanilla
2 egg whites
2 tablespoons vegetable oil
¾ cup skimmed milk
1 large ripe pear (or 2 small pears), peeled and cored

Preheat the oven to 425°F (220°C/Gas Mark 7). Mix the dry ingredients in a large bowl. Mix all the other ingredients, including the pear, in a blender at low speed. Combine with the dry ingredients and mix. Line the muffin pan with paper baking cups. Fill the baking cups with batter. Bake 17 minutes or until a toothpick comes out dry.

TIP This is a good example of what to do with fruit that gets a little too ripe. The riper the better for muffins. Following the muffin programme, you'll never throw soft fruit away again.

Pumpkin Muffins

2 ¼ cups oat-bran cereal
3 tablespoons brown sugar
1 tablespoon baking powder
½ teaspoon nutmeg
½ teaspoon cinnamon
¼ cup raisins
½ cup canned pumpkin
½ cup frozen pineapple-juice
   concentrate
¾ cup skimmed milk
2 tablespoons vegetable oil
2 egg whites

Preheat the oven to 425°F (220°C/Gas Mark 7). Mix the dry ingredients in a large bowl. Mix all other ingredients in a blender. Combine with the dry ingredients and stir just to mix. Line the muffin pans with paper baking cups. Fill the cups with batter and bake for 17 minutes or until a wooden toothpick comes out dry. *Makes 12 muffins.*

TIP The pumpkin in these muffins is a fine source of both vitamin A and vitamin C. Serve them with turkey and cranberry sauce.

Dinner Muffins

1 ¼ cups oat-bran cereal
1 cup self-raising flour
1 ½ cups skimmed milk
2 egg whites
2 tablespoons honey
3 tablespoons vegetable oil

If you'd like to have some of your daily oat bran as dinner muffins, you'll probably prefer this less sweet variation.

Preheat the oven to 425°F (220°C/Gas Mark 7). Mix the dry ingredients in a large bowl. Mix the milk and the remaining ingredients in a blender at low speed, then add to the dry ingredients and stir until just mixed. Line a muffin pan with paper baking cups, and fill with batter. Bake 15 minutes or till a toothpick comes out dry.

TIP Experiment a bit with your dinner muffins. Some people prefer to add a few raisins. Or try using other fluids to replace part of the milk.

Molasses Muffins

2 ½ cups oat-bran cereal
1 tablespoon baking powder
¼ cup raisins
¼ cup chopped nuts
1 ¼ cups evaporated skimmed
   milk
2 tablespoons vegetable oil
2 egg whites
¼ cup molasses

Preheat the oven to 425°F
(220°C/Gas Mark 7). Mix the dry
ingredients in a bowl. Blend all
other ingredients in a mixer and
add to the dry ingredients. Stir
just to mix. Line the muffin pan
with paper baking cups and fill
with the batter. Bake for 16
minutes or until a toothpick comes
out dry.

NOTE This is a nice variation
from other muffins made with
brown sugar. The molasses gives
the muffins an entirely different
flavour. If you prefer, you can cut
down the amount of molasses to
reduce calories. And don't forget
that you can also substitute the
molasses for sugar in any of the
other muffin recipes to mix and
match flavours.

Dinner Rolls

¾ cup oat-bran cereal
½ cup self-raising flour
¾ cup skimmed milk
2 tablespoons honey
3 tablespoons vegetable oil

Notice that these are not *muffins! Yes, you
can make rolls and breads with oat bran.
This is a very simple recipe that can be
made at a moment's notice to have with
dinner. It's a variation on a pretty standard
recipe.*

To get these rolls to come out well,
first put the oat-bran cereal
through a food processor or
blender. This will further mill the
cereal to a more flourlike
consistency. Then blend in the
self-raising flour. Note that you'll
need no baking powder. Blend in
the other ingredients and drop the
batter onto a lightly greased

baking tray. *This will make about 12 rolls.* Bake them at 375°F (190°C/Gas Mark 5) for 8 to 10 minutes or until just barely browned, and serve them hot from the oven.

Cran-Bran Bread

2 cups whole cranberries
1½ cups oat-bran cereal
1 teaspoon grated orange peel
1 cup granulated sugar (reduce amount if you prefer)
⅓ cup brown sugar
2½ cups all-purpose flour
3 teaspoons baking powder
½ teaspoon ground allspice
¼ cup vegetable oil
4 egg whites
½ cup skimmed milk
½ cup chopped walnuts

My wife found this recipe in our local newspaper and we modified it to suit the programme by making a few healthful substitutions. It's really delicious, especially around the holidays. This recipe makes three small loaves; you'll want to wrap them in plastic and store in the refrigerator so they don't dry out.

Preheat the oven to 350°F(180°C/Gas Mark 4). Chop the cranberries and add to the oat-bran cereal along with the orange peel and sugars. Next, stir together the flour baking powder and allspice. Add the oil, egg whites and milk. Blend in the cranberry mixture and walnuts. Divide the batter between the pans, and bake for 40 to 50 minutes, or until a toothpick comes out dry.

Oatmeal Bread

¾ cup boiling water
½ cup old-fashioned rolled oats
3 tablespoons margarine
¼ cup honey
1 teaspoon sea salt
1 sachet active dry yeast
¼ cup very warm water
½ teaspoon sugar
2 cups plain bread flour
¾ cup oat-bran cereal, milled to
   flour in blender

Here's another delicious way to get oats into your diet. Even if you've never baked a loaf of bread before, it's a lot of fun and almost fool-proof.

Stir together the boiling water, rolled oats, margarine, honey, and salt in a large bowl until well mixed. Let cool to warm. Sprinkle the packet of yeast over the very warm water in a 1-cup container; add the ½ teaspoon sugar. Stir to dissolve the yeast, and let it stand for about 10 minutes or until the mixture bubbles. Next add the yeast mixture, 1½ cups of flour, and the oat bran to the oatmeal mixture. Beat with an electric mixer at low speed for 2 minutes while gradually adding the rest of the flour. Put the dough into a 9-by-5-by-3-inch. Cover with waxed paper and a towel and put the pan in a warm place away from draughts. (A turned-off oven with a pilot is a good place.) Let the dough double in bulk, about 45 minutes.

Bake in a preheated oven at 375°F (190°C/Gas Mark 5) for about 1 hour. The bread is done when it feels and sounds hollow when you tap it. Remove the bread from the pan and let it cool.

Next, beam with pride. Finally, serve and enjoy.

Bran Brownies

3 tablespoons cocoa powder
1 tablespoon instant coffee
1 tablespoon water
2 very ripe bananas
2 cups sugar (less if you prefer)
6 egg whites
1 teaspoon vanilla extract
1 cup oat-bran cereal
¼ teaspoon sea salt (optional)
1 cup chopped nuts (or substitute
  raisins to cut fat further)

Here's the way to satisfy that chocolate craving and get some of your day's oat bran at the same time.

Combine the cocoa, coffee, water, bananas, and mix in a blender or a large bowl with a hand mixer. Add the sugar, egg whites, vanilla, and mix well. Sift together the oat-bran cereal and salt, then add to the mixture. Fold in the nuts or raisins. Pour into a 9-inch baking pan. Bake at 350°F (180°C/Gas Mark 4) for 45 minutes. Cut into individual squares, cool, and serve.

These brownies are fudgy, gooey, and delicious. Your family and friends won't believe they're free of fat and cholesterol!

15. TASTE-TEMPTING TURKEY

Everyone truly interested in eating a more healthful diet owes that great bird the turkey a big thanks. Get rid of the idea that turkey belongs on the table only at Christmas. There are dozens of ways to prepare and enjoy this low-fat, low-cholesterol source of high-quality protein. In fact, just about any dish you'd want to cook that calls for high-fat meat can be done to perfection with turkey.

In addition to the savings in fat and cholesterol, you'll enjoy the savings in your shopping budget. Turkey is a real pound stretcher. And the food industry helps out by offering not only whole birds but also selected pieces and a variety of ground-turkey and turkey-sausage products. But you must realize that the portion with the least amount of fat and cholesterol is the breast. So here's what I do: go to the market and purchase a large turkey breast and have the butcher skin, bone, and grind it or prepare cutlets. When you get home, you can portion out the meat and store it in the freezer in convenient-sized packages. Figure four ounces per serving.

All the recipes you love that call for hamburger can be made with ground turkey breast. And those dishes you treasure that include cutlets or chops are delicious made with turkey cutlets. Experiment a bit. Soon you'll be savouring a wide variety of turkey alternatives.

Terrific Turkey Meatloaf

1 lb minced turkey breast
1 egg white
½ cup oat bran
3 tablespoons ketchup
1 tablespoon Worcestershire sauce
½ teaspoon Dijon mustard

When I started to cut back on high-fat foods, I mourned the loss of meatloaf, a favourite since childhood. But, with a few modifications, this recipe turns out extremely well.

Mix all ingredients together and

½ *green pepper, minced*
3 *slices onion, minced*
2 *tablespoons chopped green olives*
1 *large garlic clove, crushed (more if preferred)*
¼ *teaspoon each: sage, black pepper, marjoram, celery salt*

form into a loaf. Bake for 1¼ hours at 350°F (180°C/Gas Mark 4). Use a meat thermometer (170°F/77°C) to be sure of doneness. Don't overcook. Serve with mashed potatoes and gravy made the low-fat, low-cholesterol way. *Serves 4.*

TIP Make more of this turkey meatloaf than you'll need, and double the amount of gravy if you prefer. Both freeze beautifully for a fast dinner the next time. And the meatloaf makes a sensational sandwich on sourdough bread with lettuce and tomatoes.

Potatoes

Peel potatoes; cook at a low boil for 20 minutes or till tender to a fork. Mash with skimmed milk, and white ground pepper.

Italian Pizzaburgers

1 lb minced turkey breast
¼ cup oat-bran cereal
¼ teaspoon parsley, finely
   minced
¼ teaspoon oregano
¼ teaspoon marjoram
¼ cup chopped onions
Grated low-cholesterol cheese
4 tablespoons tomato sauce or
   Pizzaiola Sauce (page 188)
2 English muffins, split

Mix turkey, cereal, herbs, and
onions and form into four patties.
On a non-stick pan fry until
browned. Sprinkle on the cheese.
Cover and cook until the cheese is
melted.

While the burgers are cooking,
spread 1 tablespoon tomato sauce
over each English-muffin half.
Place the cooked burgers on the
muffins. Place in the preheated
350°F (180°C/Gas Mark 4) oven
and bake for 3 minutes. *Serves 4.*

TIP Serve these delicious
pizzaburgers with a crisp salad of
greens, tomatoes, and onions,
with an Italian dressing.

Turkey meatballs

I have no idea how many dishes in the world include some kind of
meatballs. Probably hundreds. There are meatballs and spaghetti,
Swedish meatballs, cocktail meatballs, and meatballs eaten all by
themselves. Whatever your favourite kind, they can all be made
deliciously with ground turkey breast. Just cut down on the amount
of fluid normally called for in the recipe, since turkey is more moist
than beef. Here are a few recipes to get you going.

Italian Meatballs

¼ cup oat-bran cereal
¼ teaspoon oregano
¼ teaspoon black pepper
¼ teaspoon thyme
1 tablespoon grated Parmesan
   cheese
1 large clove garlic, crushed
¼ cup chopped onion
¼ cup chopped green pepper
1 lb minced turkey breast

Mix the dry ingredients in a
large bowl. Add all the remaining
ingredients except turkey. Then
blend in the minced turkey and
form into 12-16 balls. Fry the
balls uncovered until browned.
Serve with spaghetti and meatless
tomato sauce. *Makes 12-16 meatballs.*

Gravy

¾ cup cold skimmed milk
¼ cup flour
1 cup hot turkey broth
1 egg white
½ cup skimmed milk
Mushrooms, lightly sautéed or
  canned
Sea salt and black pepper

Blend the cold skimmed milk into the flour until smooth. Blend in the broth. Bring to boil and cook 1 minute. Set aside. Blend the egg white and skimmed milk in an electric blender. Dribble hot milk-broth-flour mixture slowly into the blender set at low speed. Add the mushrooms, salt and pepper to taste, and your favourite seasonings.

The All-American (Turkey) Burger

1 lb minced turkey breast
¼ cup oat-bran cereal
1 large garlic clove, crushed
¼ cup finely chopped onion
⅛ cup finely chopped green
  pepper
1 teaspoon sea salt or sodium-
  alternative seasoning

It's one thing to cut down on caviar and pâté de fois gras. It's quite another to forget that favourite the hamburger. Just thinking of a patty grilled over the coals, smothered with onions, and nestled in a toasted bun is enough to set anyone's mouth watering. Here's a delicious, satisfying turkey alternative.

Mix all the ingredients and form into four patties; grill indoors or out on the barbecue. Serve on the proverbial toasted bun or choose sourdough bread for less fat and cholesterol. Pile high with lettuce, tomato slices, and onion rings grilled on a non-stick pan. *Serves 4.*

TIP While you're at it, why not make double the recipe and store the extra patties in the freezer for the next time?

Oriental Turkeyburgers

1 lb minced turkey breast
¼ cup oat-bran cereal
1 tablespoon low-sodium soya
sauce
½ teaspoon powdered ginger (or
try freshly grated ginger)
½ teaspoon powdered coriander
¼ cup chopped water chestnuts

Mix all ingredients in a large
bowl. Shape into 4 patties. In a
non-stick pan fry the patties until
browned on both sides and cooked
to preferred doneness.

Serve with rice and stir-fried
vegetables. Don't forget that you
can stir-fry the vegetables in a bit
of chicken broth rather than oil.
Stir in some freshly grated ginger
and just a touch of brown sugar
for a taste treat. *Serves 4.*

Meatballs in Creamy Paprika Sauce

1 lb minced turkey breast
¼ cut oat-bran cereal
1 tablespoon ketchup
¼ teaspoon black pepper
1 garlic clove, finely minced
1 cup chicken bouillon (made
from bouillon cubes)
1 ½ cups finely sliced onions
½ cup skimmed milk
¼ cup flour
1 tablespoon paprika
2 tablespoons minced parsley

Mix together the turkey, oat bran,
ketchup, pepper, and garlic. Shape
into small balls. Fry in a non-stick
pan. Remove the balls when
browned.

Add the chicken bouillon to the
pan along with the sliced onions.
Bring to a boil and simmer till the
onions are tender.

In a separate bowl, slowly blend
the skimmed milk into the ¼ cup
of flour until smooth. Then slowly
drizzle in the chicken bouillon and
onions and blend. Cook over
medium heat, stirring, until thick.
Add paprika to the finished sauce.
Pour over the meatballs. Garnish
with sprinkles of parsley.

Serve with mashed potatoes.
Use skimmed milk for the
potatoes. You'd never know you
were eating a low-fat dish. *Serves 4.*

Turkey cutlets

If you like veal or pork cutlets, try these turkey cutlets. Just tell your butcher to slice the breast meat appropriately. Again, plan on 4 oz per person. Then, when you see a recipe that calls for medallions or cutlets, just switch to turkey. Of course you'll also want to find substitutes for the high-fat and high-cholesterol ingredients in such recipes. Whenever you see 'cream' think low-fat yogurt. Whole eggs convert to egg whites. Butter, of course, is now synonymous with margarine—and then cut the amount in half. Here's an example:

Basic Cutlets

¼ cup flour
¼ cup oat-bran cereal
1 lb turkey cutlets (pound on
  board with hand to flatten)
2 egg whites

Mix the flour and oat-bran cereal in a large bowl. Dip the turkey cutlets into the egg whites. Place the cutlets, one at a time, into the flour-bran mixture until well coated. In a non-stick pan fry the cutlets until golden brown.

Serve either alone or with any of a variety of sauces.

They are delicious with mashed potatoes and apple sauce. Add a crisp salad. *Serves 4.*

Turkey sandwiches

A Christmas favourite has always been the turkey sandwich. Think of how you looked forward to having leftover turkey for sandwiches. Instead of just once a year or so, now start enjoying this low-fat, low-calorie, low-cholesterol sandwich throughout the year.

Whether it's a leftover piece of turkey meatloaf, turkey cutlet, or cold turkey breast from a roasted bird, this is a treat.

Select either sourdough bread or whole-wheat. Watch labels on bread. You'll want to avoid those with eggs or saturated fats listed. Sourdough bread is baked with no fat or eggs at all.

Next pile on the extras: crisp lettuce, tomatoes, sliced onions, perhaps a bit of avocado, a touch of mustard or ketchup or a dab of mayonnaise. Great!

Sauce for the turkey

Whether your menu for the evening calls for minced turkey meatballs or turkey cutlets or cold turkey, you can achieve wonderful variety with a number of sauces. Remember that the finest cuisines in the world are based on the sauce, not necessarily what the sauce covers. Here are a few sauces that go particularly well with turkey.

Mustard Sauce

2 tablespoons prepared mustard
¼ teaspoon curry powder (more
   if you prefer)
1-2 dashes Tabasco
¼ cup mayonnaise
¼ cup plain low-fat yogurt

Mix all ingredients together to form a smooth yellow sauce. You may wish to further cut down on fat by reducing the amount of mayonnaise. Serve with cold turkey or seafood.

Béchamel Sauce

2 tablespoons margarine
3 tablespoons flour
1½ cups skimmed milk
½ cup fresh lemon juice
2 egg whites

Mix the margarine with the flour over low heat. Gradually stir in the milk. Bring to boil, stirring constantly. Remove from the heat and add the lemon juice. Place the egg whites in a blender at low speed. Slowly dribble in the cooked mixture and blend until smooth.

This is a basic white sauce. You can also add a number of seasonings for a variety of tastes. Try some tarragon to make a béarnaise sauce. Or add a tablespoon or so of horseradish. Experiment with your favourite herbs.

Cumberland Sauce

2 tablespoons prepared
   horseradish
½ cup fresh-squeezed orange
   juice
⅛ cup grated orange rind
2 tablespoons currant jelly
1 teaspoon mustard
¼ cup red wine

Mix all ingredients and serve with cold or hot turkey.

Dill Sauce

1 cup chicken bouillon
3 tablespoons flour
2½ tablespoons dill weed (or
   snipped fresh dill)
½ cup skimmed milk

Stir the cold bouillon into the flour gradually. Bring to boil, stirring constantly, then reduce to a simmer. Add the dill. Remove from the heat and blend in the milk. Serve over turkey or seafood.

TIP This sauce is also delicious with meatballs and noodles.

Onion Sauce

2 onions, thinly sliced and
   chopped
½ cup water
¼ cup chicken bouillon
2 tablespoons flour
¼ cup skimmed milk
¼ teaspoon sugar

Cook the onions in ¼ cup water until tender, about 10 minutes. Stir the bouillon cube into the remaining ¼ cup water, and slowly blend into the flour until smooth. Dribble into the onions and hot water and stir in the sugar. Add the milk, and heat. Cook on medium heat, stirring, until thick.

Pizzaiola Sauce

½ cup chopped onion
2 large garlic cloves, minced fine
1 tablespoon vegetable oil
1 can salt-free Indian-style
   tomatoes, drained and
   chopped
1 teaspoon dry basil (fresh is
   even better if you can get it;
   use 1 tablespoon finely
   chopped)
1 teaspoon leaf oregano
4 teaspoons drained capers

This Italian-style sauce is equally good with turkey cutlets or fish fillets. You'll see this listed frequently in Italian restaurants. Enjoy it with a nice little bottle of Chianti and a side dish of fidellini (very thin spaghetti). Buon appetito!

Sauté the onion and garlic in oil until transparent. Stir in the tomatoes, basil, and oregano. Bring to a boil. Lower the heat and simmer uncovered while stirring frequently for 15 minutes, or until the sauce thickens a bit. Add the capers at the last moment before serving.

NOTE This is a very flavourful sauce that you'll come to rely on for frequent meals. Remember that you can make double or triple batches and keep the sauce in the refrigerator or freezer.

See also:
TURKEY CHILLI, page 193
TURKEY-VEGETABLE MEDLEY, page 193
GARLICKY TURKEY SAUSAGE, page 211
FAVOURITE BREAKFAST SAUSAGE, page 212
TOOTHPICK MEATBALLS, page 214
GALUMKI (Polish Stuffed Cabbage), page 226

16. YOU CALL THIS DEPRIVATION?

For most of us, food is an important aspect of life if not one of the major pleasures and rewards. The idea of giving up all those culinary delights would, at least for me, be difficult if not impossible. A few people can remain on diets of steamed vegetables and rice for years without much complaint. But most couldn't comply for very long with a programme of such deprivation.

That's why it was important for me to develop reasonable alternatives or modifications for the foods I enjoy so much. Whether in my own home or in a number of restaurants, I frequently point to the foods I'm eating and comment that this is far from deprivation.

Let me tell you a true story that, to me, puts it all into perspective.

One evening my accountant was over for dinner. Needless to say, he was given a meal straight out of this programme. On the menu for the evening were turkey cutlets, thin spaghetti with pizzaiola sauce, peas, and garlic bread. Everyone enjoyed it immensely.

The next evening there was some turkey left over, and I decided to repeat the meal for my wife and me. Since there wasn't quite enough to go around, I also prepared a veal cutlet for her. I might point out that the veal was the very finest, brought out fresh from Chicago and selling at a premium price. I didn't tell my wife she was getting veal instead of the turkey. Her comment? 'This doesn't taste as good as it did last night.' That's the absolute truth.

Our house is always filled with delicious aromas of baking muffins and simmering sauces. It's an adventure to discover more and more ways of preparing foods that are both delicious and healthful.

This chapter contains just a sampling of the many ways to prepare foods of all sorts without eggs, butter, or excessive amounts of fats and cholesterol. By all means, expand your recipe files with other books and newspapers and magazines.

It may take a period of adjustment, but soon you'll echo my sentiments, 'You call this deprivation?'

Scrumptious milkshakes: without guilt

Ever since the days when my father owned a drugstore with a soda
fountain, milkshakes have been a special favourite. And for a long time
I relied on Instant Breakfast in the mornings to supply some quick
nourishment. But the cholesterol and fat in the milkshakes, and the sugar
and chemical additives in the Instant Breakfast made me back off from
both. Instead, today I enjoy a variety of special, no-guilt shakes for
breakfast or at any other time of day.

Variety is limited only by your own imagination and the types of fruits
available at the time. Basically, you throw all the ingredients into a
blender, turn it on for a few seconds, and you have a delicious shake.
If you want a thicker, richer shake, use low-fat or no-fat yogurt. For a
lighter, cooler drink, use fresh skimmed milk. And, for a summer cooler,
add a handful of crushed ice. Here are a few ideas to start with.

Apple-Banana Shake

8 oz skimmed milk
1 ripe banana (the riper the
   better)
2 oz frozen apple-juice
   concentrate
1 egg white, uncooked

Strawberry Shake

8 oz skimmed milk
1 egg white, uncooked
½ cup fresh or frozen
   strawberries

Pineapple Shake

8 oz skimmed milk
1 egg white, uncooked
2 oz frozen pineapple-juice
   concentrate
¼ cup crushed pineapple
   (unsweetened)

Fresh Apple Shake

8 oz skimmed milk
1 apple, cored and chopped into
    small pieces before blending
2 oz frozen apple-juice
    concentrate
1 egg white, uncooked

Banana-Carob Shake

8 oz skimmed milk
1 ripe banana
1 egg white, uncooked
1 teaspoon carob powder

Use your imagination. Think about your favourite fruits. Combine
the fruit with the same flavour or low-fat or no-fat yogurt instead of
milk. Or mix different combinations of fruit together.

Low-Calorie Eggnog

1 quart skimmed milk
2 egg whites
1 tablespoon rum extract
Sugar substitute equal to ¼ cup
    sugar
Nutmeg to taste

Blend and serve. *Makes 10 four-ounce
servings.*

Meal in a Mixer

¾ cup skimmed milk
1 ripe banana
½ cup non-fat strawberry yogurt
¼ cup orange juice

Think about the nutrition packed into this shake: you get calcium from the milk and yogurt, potassium from the banana, and vitamin C from the orange juice. Drink it with a muffin or two and you'll be set for hours. A great way to start the day.

VARIATIONS Keeping the milk and banana the same, vary this recipe by using a variety of flavours of non-fat yogurt and different kinds of juice.

NOTE Whenever possible, do try to use non-fat yogurt. It's available in practically all stores. Why consume even the small amount of cholesterol and fat in the low-fat versions when the flavour is just as good without them?

One-pot meals

Although times have changed, our needs to fix foods that are quick and easy remain the same. Today we tend to rely on fast-food and convenience food. Yesterday our mothers and grandmothers (men didn't cook much back then) fixed one-pot meals that were really quite simple yet satisfying.

Today we can combine some of our newer food ideas with traditional, tasty one-pot meals that can be prepared in advance and enjoyed with a chunk of sourdough bread. The basic difference will be substituting low-fat and low-cholesterol alternative ingredients. Here are a couple of dishes to start with. Look in your own cookbooks and collections of favourite recipes to find ideas that can easily be altered to fit the more modern healthful way of thinking.

Turkey Chilli

1 lb minced turkey breast
1 medium green pepper, chopped
1 medium onion, chopped
1 can kidney beans or chilli
  beans
1 large can tomatoes (28 oz)
1 package commercial chilli mix

Brown the turkey in a large pan until broken apart and browned. Add the green pepper and onion, reduce the heat, and cover. Cook over medium heat until the peppers are tender. Add the beans, tomatoes and chilli mix. Simmer for 10 minutes and serve.

NOTE Here's a meal that freezes beautifully. Store in individual-serving-sized containers.

Turkey-Vegetable Medley

1 lb minced turkey breast
1 can cooked beans
1 green pepper, chopped
1 onion, chopped
2 celery stalks, chopped
2 carrots, chopped
1 tomato, peeled and chopped
1 can small peas
1 packet Knorr dried vegetable
  soup (or other brand)

In a large pan cook the turkey until broken apart and browned. Add all other ingredients, including some fluid from the canned vegetables to make a sauce. Cover and simmer just 10 minutes.

NOTE This is the easy way, but not necessarily the best. To do an even better job and have the vegetables come out better, first add the fresh vegetables; then, just a few minutes before serving, add the canned vegetables.

Vegetables

Most kids hate vegetables, and too many adults never acquire a taste for them. Maybe that's because they rebel against their parents' telling them that they can't have dessert until they finish every last soggy pea or overdone carrot. The problem for most people is that they never learned how terrific vegetables can taste.

The place to begin is at your supermarket or fresh fruit and vegetable store. Look for roadside stands during the summer and autumn. Go to some ethnic shops and ask about the exotic vegetables you never even knew about before. Make it an adventure in good taste and good nutrition.

The food charts call for at least two servings of vegetables daily. The green ones and the yellow or orange types. But view that as an absolute *minimum*. Shoot for four servings daily. Impossible? Not at all. Vegetable juices, potatoes, salads, finger-sized nibbles with dip—all these add up to lots of vitamins and minerals. And good eating!

Potatoes are a much-maligned vegetable. Unless you smother them with butter and sour cream, they're *not* at all fattening. You can enjoy potatoes several times each week. They're high in fibre and vitamins, tasty, and versatile.

Here are a few recipes to start with. Look through other cookbooks for more.

Gazpacho

1 large (48 oz) can tomato juice
1 medium onion, chopped fine
1 green pepper, chopped fine
1 jalapeno pepper, chopped fine
   (without seeds)
½ cup chopped fresh coriander
3 large garlic cloves, crushed
2 large tomatoes, peeled, seeded,
   and chopped (or canned
   tomatoes)
⅓ cup fresh lime juice
¼ cup red wine vinegar
½ teaspoon freshly ground black
   pepper

This one's so simple to prepare you won't believe it. Combine all the ingredients in a large bowl or jar, but not an aluminium pot, and store in the refrigerator overnight. Serve cold with sprigs of fresh coriander.

NOTE This is a favourite California recipe and a frequent noontime meal, especially during the summer. Serve with sourdough bread. What a marvellous way to eat your vegetables!

Oriental Carrots and Green Peppers

1 tablespoon soft margarine
1 tablespoon vegetable oil
1 tablespoon grated fresh ginger
   (powdered if you must)
1 tablespoon brown sugar
1 teaspoon mild soy sauce (added
   at end of sauté time)

Cut carrots and green peppers into strips about 3 inches long and ½ inch wide. In a medium-size saucepan sauté other ingredients briefly. Next add the carrots and green peppers to the mixture and simmer covered for 10 minutes or until the vegetables are tender. *Serves four.*
   Serve with grilled chicken and some steamed rice.

NOTE Obviously, if you have just enough vegetables for one or two, you'll need less margarine and oil. Use only as much of these fats as necessary.

Basic Baked Potatoes

You can bake both white and sweet potatoes. Both are delicious. Both use the same techniques equally well. First, if you have a microwave oven you're in luck. A snap to wash the potatoes, pierce them with a fork, and bake for 12 to 16 minutes. In the conventional oven or over the coals, first wrap the potatoes with aluminium foil after washing and piercing. This keeps them moist. Bake at 425°F (220°C/Gas Mark 7) for about 45 minutes or until they 'give' to the touch.

But what about that butter or sour cream? Here are a few suggestions. Try dry vegetable seasonings. How about some salsa or pizzaiola sauce (see page 188)? Or some non-fat yogurt flavoured with lemon juice and pepper? Finally, try being really adventurous and taste the potatoes without anything at all to see what they really taste like.

If you still miss sour cream, well, now you can enjoy all you like with either of these mock sour creams. You can also use these sour creams as bases for making excellent salad dressings.

Mock Sour Cream 1

¾ cup low-fat cottage cheese
¼ cup non-fat plain yogurt
½ teaspoon lemon juice
1 packet artificial sweetener

My personal favourite.

Mock Sour Cream 2

1 cup low-fat cottage cheese
1 tablespoon lemon juice
¼ cup skimmed milk

With either variation, simply put all the ingredients together in a blender and whirl them till smooth. Make enough to store in

the refrigerator for use throughout
the week. Enjoy all you want with
no guilt at all.

Mashed, Smashed, and Whipped Potatoes

Peel one white potato per person.
Bring to a boil in an uncovered
pot of water. Reduce the heat to a
simmer and cook for 20 minutes.
Drain off the water. Mash the
potatoes with skimmed milk,
added just a few drops at a time
until they are whipped perfectly.
Season with white pepper.

Roasted Potatoes

Boil unpeeled potatoes for about
15 minutes, or until you can pierce
them with a fork without too
much resistance. Drain them and
cut into chunks, still with the peel
intact. Preheat the oven to 375°F
(180°C/Gas Mark 4). Bake the
potatoes for 15 minutes, till they're
nice and crisp and browned. As to
salt, follow your own conscience
and health needs.

Chicory and New Potatoes

1 ½ lb new potatoes (the smaller
    the better)
½ cup chopped onion
2 large garlic cloves, chopped fine
2 tablespoons vegetable oil
1 pound chicory leaves
1 cup chicken broth
Pepper to taste

Boil the potatoes unpeeled for
about 20 minutes, then drain off
the water and cover (off the heat).
While the potatoes are cooking, in
a large skillet sauté the onion and
garlic in oil until transparent. Tear
the chicory leaves by hand into
pieces about 2 inches across. Put
the leaves into the pan with the
onions, cover, and toss to wilt the
leaves and cover them with the
onion-garlic oil. Slice the potatoes
into chunks and add them to the
pan. Stir in the chicken broth,
bring to boil, add pepper, and
serve. *Serves four.*

NOTE The liquid (pot liquor, it's
called) is so tasty that you'll want
to sop it up with big chunks of
sourdough bread. Serve with a
piece of broiled chicken or fish. (A
nice bottle of white wine wouldn't
hurt.)

French-'Fried' Potatoes

Boil potatoes, either peeled or not,
for 10 minutes. Drain them and
let cool. Cut them into strips,
crinkles, or however you like them
best. Preheat the oven to 375°F
(190°C/Gas Mark 5). Place the
potatoes on a baking sheet so
they're not touching. Bake for 30
minutes. Ketchup anyone?

Flavourful Rice Pilaf

4 cups water
1 teaspoon ground coriander
1 tablespoon vegetable oil
2½ cups uncooked white rice
½ cup dried apples, chopped
fine
¼ cup raisins (the golden type
are best)
¼ cup apple juice
¼ teaspoon cinnamon (optional)
4 chopped spring onions

Put the water into a saucepan with the coriander and bring to boil. At the same time, heat the oil in a flameproof casserole. Add the rice to the oil till grains are just coated, then add the water to the casserole. Cover and bake in a preheated 375°F (190°C/Gas Mark 5) oven for 25 minutes. By then, the water should all be absorbed into the rice. During the baking, put the apple slices and cinnamon into the apple juice to soak. When the rice is done, drain the apples and blend them into the rice. Add the chopped spring onion at the very end.

NOTE Once again, let your imagination go wild. After you've tried this recipe once and you've seen how easy and foolproof it is, you'll want to try a few variations. Instead of apples, next time use apricots and pineapple juice, or prunes with orange juice. Serve with baked chicken or fish.

Salad dressings

With the tremendous variety available, everyone should try to eat a
salad every day. Whether you prefer it as your noontime meal or as
an accompaniment to the evening dinner, a salad can supply much
of your daily vegetable needs.

Don't limit yourself to plain iceberg lettuce day after day. Any
vegetable or fruit can be fare for the salad of your dreams; the best
salad bars around are those with the most variety.

Go for colour with kernels of corn, shavings of carrot, and a spoonful
or two of red cabbage. Use last night's leftover vegetables. Add some
fresh pears or apples. Try all the different types of lettuce. Mix two
or three types together.

Then think about the dressings to top it all off. Ah, but there's the
rub. Most commercially prepared salad dressings are prepared with
whole eggs, saturated fats, and often a lot of sugar. Either look at the
labels carefully before you buy, or start preparing your own. Try some
of the new oil-free dressings. They have really improved and are
delicious.

Yogurt Dressing

1 cup non-fat plain yogurt
1 tablespoon fresh lemon or lime
   juice
1 ½ teaspoons fresh basil (½
   teaspoon if dry)
1 large garlic clove, crushed
1 tablespoon honey

Combine all the ingredients in a
storage container and let stand in
the refrigerator for at least 2 hours
before serving to develop the full
flavour.

Honey-Lime Dressing

¼ cup fresh lime juice
⅛ cup honey
¼ teaspoon Dijon mustard

Combine all ingredients and serve
cold. Delicious over a salad of
romaine and honeydew melon.

Tomato Dressing

1 cup salt-free tomato juice
½ cup peeled and chopped fresh
  tomatoes
1 tablespoon fresh lemon juice
1 tablespoon fresh chopped
  parsley
1 tablespoon fresh chopped
  coriander
Pepper to taste

Combine all ingredients in a
storage container and let the
mixture stand overnight to fully
develop the flavour. This has just a
few calories in the whole batch.

Thousand Island Dressing

1 cup low-fat mayonnaise
2 tablespoons tomato ketchup
1 tablespoon sweet pickle relish

Combine all ingredients in
advance. Store and use as needed
over all sorts of salads.

Herb Dressing

1 cup non-fat plain yogurt
1 tablespoon fresh lemon juice
1 ½ teaspoons fresh basil
1 ½ teaspoons tarragon
1 ½ teaspoons fresh chervil
1 large clove garlic, crushed
1 teaspoon ground red pepper
(optional)

Combine all ingredients in
advance. Store and use as desired
over salads. Use 2 tablespoons per
serving.

Desserts to your heart's content

There's no reason to think that just because you're trying to reduce
fats and cholesterol you can never have anything but a piece of fruit
for dessert. You'll just have to be a bit more careful than most people,
and a bit more creative.

For openers, start looking more selectively for items in the supermarket. Read labels before you buy to avoid not only eggs but also
'partially hydrogenated oils' and palm oil and coconut oil, which are
just as saturated as animal fats and butter. The more you shop the
more you'll realize how many acceptable products there are on the
market. And as more and more people become diet and health
conscious you can expect even more delicious food alternatives to come
along.

Frozen yogurt is an excellent example. Available in a wide variety
of flavours, these products are even better tasting than when they were
first introduced in the 1970s. And there are new desserts based on
yogurt that have practically no fat or cholesterol at all.

Also keep an eye out for shops and restaurants with desserts your
heart and waistline will love you for. Such places and products are
clearly on the increase as the business world recognizes the pent-up
demand. A while back I took my children out for the evening and
as a special treat decided to get them ice-cream cones. Naturally I
expected to watch them eat while I lived with memories of the gooey
sundaes I've sworn off. Surprise! As we walked into our local 31
Flavours Ice Cream shop, there was a sign for specially formulated,
Special Diet, ice-cream treats with a negligible amount of fat and
practically no cholesterol. As I'm writing this, there are four flavours
available: my favourite is coffee. I can eat this with no guilt and lots
of pleasure.

Angel-food cake is made with egg whites, not the yolks. Most of
those cakes, pies, and biscuits, though, are loaded with eggs and butter.

The solution is to start getting into dessert making yourself. Believe
me, it's really easy. Before going onto this programme myself I never
baked a biscuit in my life. The recipes I've listed here are simple to
follow and practically foolproof. It's fun to make biscuits, and if you've
got kids, it's a great way to keep them entertained helping you.

Apple-Oatmeal Treats

4 medium-sized apples
4 teaspoons cinnamon
1 tablespoon honey
1 tablespoon lemon juice
2 egg whites
¼ cup oat-bran cereal
¼ cup oatmeal
½ cup powdered skimmed milk
  (dry, non-fat)

First halve, core, and chop the apples. Put them in a steamer, sprinkle with cinnamon, and steam until tender, usually about 10 minutes. (If you don't have a steamer, try placing a strainer in a pot with about two inches of water and cover.)

Next, combine all the other ingredients. By the time you're done, the apples will be tender and aromatic from the cinnamon. Put them into a blender and liquefy. Combine all ingredients and plop the batter by teaspoonfuls onto a nonstick baking sheet.

Bake in a preheated 350°F (180°C/Gas Mark 4) oven for 20 minutes. This will make 2 to 3 dozen biscuits, depending on how big you make them.

Traditional Oatmeal Biscuits

¾ cup flour
¼ teaspoon baking soda
2 teaspoons vanilla
2 oz vegetable oil
½ cup granulated sugar
½ cup brown sugar
2 egg whites
1½ cups 1-minute oatmeal
¼ cup chopped walnuts or
    pecans

Here's a traditional recipe for delicious oatmeal biscuits, minus the cholesterol and much of the fat. It comes from the pages of one of my wife's magazines, with a few substitutions that make it fit for the programme.

First, sift the flour and baking soda together. Next blend vanilla, oil, and sugars, then add the egg whites. Finally stir in the flour, oatmeal, and nuts. Preheat your oven to 350°F (180°C/Gas Mark 4). Drop the dough onto a baking sheet with a teaspoon. Bake for 8 minutes.

NOTE Yes, there are sugar and fat in the recipe. But remember that you're making 72 biscuits in this batch. A little quick division shows that you can afford to have a biscuit or two once in a while without any guilt at all. You can store these biscuits in the freezer; one batch will last a long time.

Untraditional Oatmeal Biscuits

2 very ripe bananas
½ cup brown sugar
3 teaspoons vanilla
2 egg whites
2 cups all-purpose flour
1½ cups 1-minute oatmeal
1 teaspoon baking powder
½ teaspoon baking soda
½ cup skimmed milk
½ cup chopped nuts

This is the recipe for those who either don't want to have just one or two biscuits or don't want any fat at all. They're almost as tasty as the slightly more sinful traditional variety. These are chewy, tasty little treats you'll enjoy when that urge for a nibble strikes.

First mash the bananas with a fork or blend in a blender to a liquid. Place in a large bowl and mix the sugar, vanilla, and egg whites with the bananas. Mix together the flour, oatmeal, baking powder, and soda. Alternately add the flour mixture and the milk to the banana mixture, and finally add the nuts.

Preheat the oven to 375°F (190°C/Gas Mark 5). Lightly grease a baking sheet with a mixture of oil and flour. Plop the batter 1 teaspoonful at a time onto the sheet and bake for 10 minutes, till the biscuits are just barely browned at the edges.

Sweet Potato and Apple Cobbler

2 large apples, cored and cut in
  1-inch chunks
2 large sweet potatoes, peeled
  and cut in 1-inch chunks
½ cup brown sugar
½ cup oat-bran cereal, milled to
  flour in blender or food
  processor
½ cup 1-minute oatmeal
½ teaspoon cinnamon
⅓ cup unsalted soft margarine

This definitely isn't for someone trying to lose weight. It's got all the delicious calories with none of the cholesterol and little of the fat normally found in such a scrumptious treat. For those of us following a low-fat diet, this is a nice reward.

Mix the chunks of apples and potatoes in a 9-inch pie pan, and sprinkle with 2 tablespoons of the sugar. Mix the remaining sugar, oat bran, oatmeal, and cinnamon in a bowl. Work the margarine in a bit at a time until the mixture is crumbly. Sprinkle the crumbs over the apples and potatoes. Preheat the oven to 350°F (180°C/Gas Mark 4). Bake about 50 minutes, or until the potatoes are tender and the topping is browned. Serve when still warm.

For a special treat, beat chilled evaporated skimmed milk with a teaspoonful of vanilla to form a 'whipped-cream' topping.

Prune Bars

⅓ **cup brown sugar**
⅓ **cup vegetable oil**
¼ **cup apple-juice concentrate**
1 **cup whole-wheat flour**
½ **cup oat-bran cereal**
1½ **cups oatmeal**
1 **cup diced prunes**
1 **cup raisins**

Here's a yummy way to get a lot of nutrition into a dessert.

Mix the sugar, oil, and apple juice. Separately mix the dry ingredients. To them, gradually add all other ingredients, mixing just until crumbly. Put the mixture into a 9-inch baking pan. Bake in a preheated 375°F (190°C/Gas Mark 5) oven for 20 minutes or until resilient to the touch. *Cut into 12 bars.*

VARIATIONS Let your imagination run wild: For the prunes substitute apricots or other dried fruits, or try other frozen fruit-juice concentrates.

Pie Crusts

1 **cup sifted plain flour**
¾ **teaspoon salt (optional)**
⅓ **cup light syrup**
2 **tablespoons skimmed milk**

I happen to be a real pie lover, but the crusts can be loaded with lard. Just take a look at the ingredient labels of pre-made pie crusts, or at the recipes found in any cookbook. Here's a recipe for a traditional pie crust without saturated fat.

Preheat the oven to 475°F (240°C/Gas Mark 9). Mix the flour and salt in a bowl. Combine the syrup and milk and add all at once to the flour mixture. Stir with a fork until thoroughly mixed. Shape the mixture into a ball and place it between two squares of wax paper lightly dusted with flour. Roll the pastry into a circle large enough to fit a 9-inch pie pan. Arrange pastry in the pan. Cut off the edges with a

knife and press with a fork. Prick
the bottom all over with a fork.
Bake about 10 minutes or until
golden brown. Cool before adding
filling.

Fruit

While there are a number of low-fat, non-cholesterol desserts you can
choose from, don't forget to include lots of fresh fruits in your diet.
Fruit is packed with vitamins and fibre for a terrific nutrition mix;
it is convenient, easy to prepare, and a fast picker-upper. Best of all,
fruit is delicious.

A long time ago, when I was still eating rich foods, I took a series
of Provincial French cooking lessons. Needless to say, most of the recipes
I learned then are off-limits today. But I clearly remember how the
chef regarded fruit highly for dessert. As a challenge, I asked how
the lowly orange could be made into a culinary treat.

The teacher, Josie, smiled. She peeled a large navel orange, and
cut it into sections. Then she put the fruit into a bowl and poured
an ounce or two of dark Jamaican rum over it. Sound simple? It's
fantastic! Try the same thing with other fruits and liquors. Here are
a few to get you started:

● Banana slices and Grand Marnier

● Apple slices and calvados

● Raspberries and chocolate liqueur

● Pineapple and crème de menthe

● Strawberries and Cointreau

● Cherries and rum

● Peaches and brandy

Every nutrition book you pick up, going back years and years, lists
the need for two servings of fruit each day as part of the four-food-
group approach to eating. What most people don't read, however,
is that those two servings are the *minimum*. Try to have three, four,
five, even six servings of fruit each day, depending on your calorie needs.

It's really not hard to do. Start your day with one of the shakes
listed in this book. That'll give you a banana, let's say, and a serving
of fruit juice. Next, have a big glass of fresh fruit juice at mid-morning.
Then an apple or a pear for lunch. And some fruit for dessert at dinner.
That's five servings right off the bat.

Your body will love you for it, and you'll love your body when you
see the pounds disappear. Replace the fats and refined sugars in your
diet and you cant go wrong.

Bountiful breakfasts

No question about it, the most artery-clogging meal is the traditional English Breakfast. For many years mums prepared those bacon-and-egg meals thinking they were doing their families a favour on Sunday mornings. Even today restaurants tout their breakfast specials including eggs, bacon, sausage, and mushrooms dripping with melted butter.

When eating out, one should limit himself or herself to such staples as oatmeal or other hot or cold cereals, English muffins with honey instead of butter, and a variety of fruits and juices. But at home some of the ever-popular treats can be prepared in a safe and sane manner. It's a simple matter of substitution for the most part, and such meals also provide an opportunity to get even more oat bran into the diet.

Buttermilk Pancakes

6 egg whites
3 cups one-percent-fat
   buttermilk
6 tablespoons vegetable oil
1 cup self-raising flour
2 cups oat-bran cereal
1 tablespoon baking powder
3 tablespoons sugar

This recipe will make a lot of pancakes— enough for your family's breakfast and plenty to store in the freezer for those occasions when you don't have time to cook. The pancakes freeze well. Just pop them into the microwave. Or, if you don't have a microwave oven, let thaw at room temperature and warm for three minutes in a standard oven at 350°F (180°C/Gas Mark 4).

Simply mix the ingredients together and bake on a lightly greased griddle.

Serve the pancakes with fruit compotes, purées, or syrups. Remember that the commercial syrups have a lot of sugar—fresh fruits put through the blender taste even better, without the extra calories.

German Apple Pancakes

FRUIT MIXTURE
1 large green apple, halved, cored, and sliced
¼ cup sugar
¼ cup apple sauce
⅛ teaspoon nutmeg
½ teaspoon cinnamon

BATTER INGREDIENTS
8 egg whites
¼ cup self-raising flour
½ cup oat-bran cereal
1 teaspoon baking powder
1 tablespoon sugar
1 cup non-fat milk
1 teaspoon vanilla extract
1 tablespoon vegetable oil
⅛ teaspoon nutmeg

This recipe is incredibly delicious. You'll want to share it with all your friends and relatives on special occasions. These pancakes are just as good as you'd get in a pancake restaurant, without the fat and cholesterol.

Grease lightly an ovenproof glass casserole dish. Mix the apples, sugar, apple sauce, and spices and spread in the dish. Bake at 425°F (220°C/Gas Mark 7) for 10 minutes to partially cook the apples. In a large bowl, mix liquid ingredients for the batter, then add dry ingredients. Stir only until ingredients are mixed. Then pour the batter over the fruit and bake at 375°F (190°C/Gas Mark 5) for another 20 minutes.

Recipe as stated serves two substantial appetites. Increase ingredients as needed for more people.

French Toast

1 slice sourdough bread (nice and
   big and thick)
2 egg whites
1 oz (2 tablespoons) non-fat milk
1 dash of vanilla extract, orange
   extract, or almond extract

No cholesterol-conscious person would ever order French toast in a restaurant, but this recipe is both delicious and nutritious. The amount given is for one serving.

Mix the egg whites, milk, and flavouring in a bowl and dip in the bread to soak up the mixture. Grill on a griddle.

Serve with syrup, a fruit mixture, or, for something different, sprinkle with powdered sugar.

Waffles

4 egg whites
2 cups non-fat milk
1 cup oat-bran cereal
1 cup self-raising flour
1 teaspoon baking powder
3 tablespoons vegetable oil

If you have a waffle iron, here's a recipe that's sure to please your entire family. The first one always sticks to the iron, so plan accordingly.

Preheat the iron. Mix all ingredients in a container with a spout, and pour onto the waffle iron. Bake each waffle for about 5 minutes or until the steam stops. Enjoy while hot. *Makes 6 large waffles.*

Hot Oat-Bran Cereal

1 cup water (or any of various
   fruit juices)
1 cup skimmed milk
1 teaspoon honey or molasses
½ cup oat-bran cereal
¼ cup raisins (or dates, or
   prunes, or dried apricots)

There are many ways to make hot oat-bran cereal by using different combinations of the ingredient options in this recipe. Try a number of combinations and you'll never get tired of it.

Bring water and milk to boil. Stir in the remaining ingredients and cook gently for 10 minutes.

Breakfast meats

I haven't had a slice of bacon in years. What with the fat, cholesterol, and chemical additives, it's something I can do without. And if you read the ingredient labels, even the bacon substitutes don't sound too healthful. So for a meat side-dish at breakfast, you can't beat ham. That may sound surprising, but depending on the brand, a slice of low-fat ham contains only one gram of fat. And when you get a craving for breakfast sausage, these next two recipes fill the bill with ground turkey breast substituting for fat-laden pork. Note that these recipes call for ground turkey breast from your butcher, not packaged ground turkey.

Garlicky Turkey Sausage

1 lb minced turkey breast
¾ teaspoon ground coriander
½ teaspoon salt
½ teaspoon pepper
1 clove garlic, crushed

Mix all ingredients in a bowl and form into 8 patties. Refrigerate. Grease a frying pan and fry for about 12 minutes.

NOTE These sausages can be frozen either raw or cooked for later use. And you may also enjoy them for lunch with a salad and bread.

Favourite Breakfast Sausage

1 lb minced turkey breast
¼ teaspoon each cumin,
**   marjoram, pepper, oregano,**
**   cayenne pepper**
½ teaspoon each basil, thyme,
**   sage**
⅛ teaspoon each garlic powder,
**   nutmeg, ginger**
1 tablespoon oat-bran cereal (just
**   enough to 'bind' the sausage)**

This one comes really close to tasting like commercial pork breakfast sausage. Again, you can prepare a large quantity in advance and freeze it either raw or cooked. The flavour comes from the large number of spices and herbs used. Vary the amount of seasonings to match your own preferences. I like mine spicy.

Mix the minced turkey with the seasonings and refrigerate for a few hours. Form patties and bake in a 400°F (200°C/Gas Mark 6) oven.

Eggs

Although some cholesterol watchers will eat egg yolks in moderation, I prefer to avoid them entirely. Using the whites, I can make omelettes, scrambled eggs, or just about anything else—even 'sunny side up' style without the sunny side.

Appetizers and hors d'oeuvres

A while back I attended a presidential reception at a medical meeting and I was absolutely shocked at the foods served on the buffet table. Here were health professionals filling their plates with fat-laden goodies such as rumaki (chicken liver wrapped with bacon), fried chicken wings, greasy meatballs, and plates of cheese. That's the kind of occasion when you just have to munch on the fresh vegetables, and wait for dinner. But, when you have the opportunity to prepare your own buffet, there's no limit to the treats you can come up with for your guests and yourself. These are just a few examples.

Marinated Scallops

1 lb scallops
Juice of 1 lemon or 2 limes
2 tablespoons vegetable oil
1 onion, finely sliced
2 tablespoons capers
½ tablespoon celery seed
1 teaspoon Worcestershire sauce
2 or 3 drops Tabasco

Marinate the scallops overnight in the remaining ingredients and serve with crackers or toast points.

Pickled Mushrooms

MARINADE
¼ cup each olive oil, lemon juice, water
1 large garlic clove, crushed
¼ teaspoon pepper (white pepper is best)

1 lb fresh mushrooms
1 red or green pepper, sliced

Mix the marinade ingredients and pour over the mushrooms and pepper slices. Store in the refrigerator at least 3 hours. Drain and serve with parsley sprigs as garnish.

Marinated Vegetables

MARINADE
1 cup olive oil
½ cup white wine vinegar
½ cup water
1 teaspoon each sugar, thyme, marjoram, basil, pepper
1 large garlic clove, crushed
1 large bay leaf

VEGETABLES
Carrot slices
Courgette slices
Cherry tomatoes
Broccoli flowerets
Cauliflower
Celery chunks
Baby sweetcorn ears
Mushrooms

Mix the marinade, add the vegetables, and store in the refrigerator for several hours. Drain the vegetables thoroughly and place in a bowl to serve.

Chicken Teriyaki Sticks

MARINADE
⅔ cup soya sauce
¼ cup sweet sherry
1 tablespoon brown sugar
½ teaspoon freshly grated ginger
  root
1 large clove garlic, crushed
Juice of 1 lemon

1 lb boneless, skinless chicken
  breasts in chunks
Pineapple chunks

Mix together the marinade ingredients. Add the chicken and marinate in the refrigerator overnight. Skewer on bamboo sticks or chopsticks, alternating with chunks of pineapple. Grill about 10 minutes until done. Prepare in individual-sized portions.

Salmon Spread

1 large (15 ½ -oz) can salmon
½ cup low-fat cottage cheese
2 tablespoons finely chopped
  onion
1 tablespoon lemon juice
1 teaspoon prepared white
horseradish
½ teaspoon salt
¼ teaspoon white pepper

Clean the salmon of all bones and skin. On the other hand, you may wish to mash the bones in with the salmon for the calcium they provide. Place the cottage cheese in a strainer and place under running water to clean off all milk. Pat the cottage-cheese curds dry with a paper towel. Combine all ingredients in a bowl and mash until smooth and creamy. Chill in the serving bowl. Serve with crackers, toast 'fingers', or slices of cucumber and other fresh vegetables.

Toothpick Meatballs

1 small bottle ketchup
10 oz grape jelly
Juice of 1 lemon
1 lb minced turkey breast
¼ cut oat-bran cereal

Here's an example of substitution working beautifully. The original recipe called for ground beef, but ground turkey breast actually works better, forming firm meatballs that don't fall off the serving toothpicks. This is a simple yet festive buffet treat.

Mix the ketchup, jelly, and lemon juice in a medium-sized saucepan or flameproof casserole dish. Heat until bubbling. Meanwhile, mix the turkey with the oat bran, adding the oat bran a little at a time until the mixture is firm enough to form into walnut-sized balls. Drop the balls into the bubbling mixture to cook for about 30 minutes. Serve hot, with toothpicks to spear the meatballs.

This dish is even better when prepared the night before your party and stored overnight in the refrigerator to bring out all the flavours. Reheat at serving time. Don't let the weird combinations of flavours fool you—your guests will go wild over this one and they'll be amazed when you give them the recipe.

Hummus (Chick Pea Dip)

⅓ cup sesame tahini
¼ cup lemon juice
5 cloves garlic, crushed
5 drops Tabasco
¼ cup water
½ teaspoon cumin
2 15-oz cans chick peas, drained

This dish increases the soluble fibre content of the diet, a good way to control cholesterol levels. It can be served to company or kept in the refrigerator for quick snacks along with wedges of toasted pitta bread.

Simply combine all ingredients and blend until smooth. The easiest way to do this is in a food processor. If you do not have one, place ingredients in a large bowl and blend with an electric mixer.

Oriental cuisine

One of the earliest observations during the study of cholesterol and heart disease was that Oriental populations consuming little animal fat and cholesterol had virtually no heart disease. As Orientals migrated to the United States, their food habits changed and they began developing the same problems of clogged arteries. Many health authorities therefore recommend leaning heavily toward Oriental delicacies. And, since there's so much diversity, it's really easy to have Chinese, Japanese, Thai, and Korean foods frequently.

If you've never done any cooking of this sort, it may at first appear formidable. Yes, you'll have to buy a wok and a few utensils not now in your kitchen. And yes, you'll need some ingredients you don't have. But they're all easy to find in almost any supermarket.

You'll also want to get a cookbook or two that will show you in a step-by-step manner how to create some fabulous dishes in your own kitchen. There are a number on the market.

Chinese Chicken and Vegetables

1 cup chicken broth
1 lb skinless chicken breasts cut as strips
4 medium carrots cut either as strips or circles
1 small bunch broccoli cut as small flowerets
1 cup bean sprouts
1 green or red bell pepper cut in strips
1 tin straw mushrooms, drained
1 tablespoon reduced-sodium soya sauce
2 tablespoons oyster-flavoured sauce
1 tablespoon dry sherry
1 teaspoon or more ground red pepper (cayenne)
1 tablespoon grated fresh ginger
2 large cloves garlic, chopped fine

One of the nicest things about Chinese wok cooking is that you can use all the ingredients you love and cut out those you don't. In this recipe, for example, our kids prefer to have only carrots and broccoli along with the chicken. So my wife makes a separate batch that way. She and I prefer a variety of things in ours. And we think we've got the sauce perfected—spicy but not too spicy. To make it even better, we now use only chicken broth in the wok instead of oil to further reduce our fat intake. Mix and match vegetables to your own taste.

Heat two ounces of chicken broth in wok. Add chicken strips and stir-fry until tender. Remove chicken and put aside. Add remaining broth to wok, heat, and add vegetables. Cook till tender. Mix sauces and flavourings. Add chicken to wok. Pour in sauce mixture. Stir-fry till entire dish is

heated through. Serve with lots of
steamed rice.

When you look at a menu in a Chinese or other Oriental restaurant,
you'll find that a number of the dishes are strictly vegetables. But these
dishes are far from bland and boring. The sauces make them a meal
in themselves. Here's a recipe for a vegetable dish we love to have
over and over again.

Straw Mushrooms and Baby Corn

1 clove garlic, crushed
½ teaspoon grated fresh ginger
1 tablespoon peanut oil
1 15-oz can baby sweetcorn,
   drained
2 tablespoons oyster sauce
   (essential to bring out the
   flavour)
4 tablespoons chicken broth
⅛ teaspoon sugar
1 15-oz tin straw mushrooms,
   drained

*Make sure you use straw mushrooms, not
any other kind. These are found in tins in
supermarkets. For a complete meal, you
can also add some pieces of chicken or fish
or scallops.*

In a hot wok (375°F/190°C/Gas
Mark 5 in an electric wok or when
a drop of water sizzles), stir-fry the
garlic and ginger in the oil for a
minute or two. Add the sweetcorn,
and stir-fry until hot. Add the
oyster sauce, chicken broth, and
sugar. Stir and toss. When the
mixture is hot, add the
mushrooms and stir gently until
all the food is heated through. *This
recipe serves 3 or 4.*

Be sure to make plenty of steaming-hot rice to go along with this and
all Oriental dishes. You'll be amazed at how much rice you'll want
to eat. And don't forget you can enjoy a large quantity of this low-fat,
low-cholesterol, and low-calorie food.

Tori No Sanmi Yaki

3 tablespoons sesame seeds
2 large garlic cloves, crushed
½ small dried red pepper,
  without seeds
1 teaspoon fresh ginger (¼
  teaspoon ground ginger)
¼ cup sake (or you can use dry
  sherry)
⅓ cup soya sauce
¼ cup honey
2 boneless, skinless chicken
  breasts
1 large green bell pepper, cut in
  strips
1 tablespoon vegetable oil
  (peanut oil is best)
6 thin lemon slices without seeds
2 cups hot cooked rice

Here's a Japanese recipe for three-flavoured chicken. It's baked, not fried.

Toast the sesame seeds in a little pan for about 5 minutes. Mash the seeds along with the garlic, pepper, and ginger. Add sake, soya sauce, and honey. Coat the chicken breasts with the mixture and place in a glass casserole dish. Marinate the chicken at least 4 hours, or make it the night before and keep it in the refrigerator. Bake in a 325°F (170°C/Gas Mark 3) oven for 15 minutes, turn chicken breasts, bake 10 minutes more. Grill just a few minutes to crisp the chicken. Meanwhile, sauté the green-pepper strips until tender. Arrange chicken, peppers, and lemon slices on a platter. Serve with lots and lots of steaming-hot rice.

Italian cookery

The same scientists who studied the Oriental populations also found that people living in Mediterranean regions such as southern Italy have low rates of heart disease. Again, the cuisine of southern Italy is low in animal fat and cholesterol, and high in carbohydrates. These Italians use a lot of olive oil in their cooking, another monounsaturated fat that's been shown to reduce cholesterol levels while retaining the beneficial HDL levels. Note that were not talking about northern Italian food, which is rich and fatty.

Italian cookbooks abound, each with variations on pasta and vegetable themes. The sauces are fresh and bubbly and delicious. Remember that any dish that calls for veal can be made just as tender and delicious by substituting turkey breast.

But you don't have to get fancy to enjoy Italian cookery. Sure, you can prepare those multi-ingredient dishes when you have the time and the inclination. But, when it's just a matter of getting some hot food on the table fast, Italian food can come out of cans and jars.

Pasta is the mainstay of Italian cooking. Keep your pantry well stocked with pasta of all shapes and sizes. If you haven't already discovered this, pasta tastes much different when it's thin like vermicelli rather than thick like linguine. Try them all.

Just get the biggest pot you have in the kitchen, fill it halfway with water, bring to a boil, and add the pasta a little at a time so the water keeps boiling. Cook for about 7 or 8 minutes, or until *al dente*, or just a bit chewy to the bite.

Put together a simple salad with a nice Italian dressing, slice a loaf of bread, and you're ready to sit down and eat within 20 to 30 minutes. A nice glass of Chianti wouldn't hurt.

If you have just a few minutes more, try adding some seafood to the sauce. Nothing fancy; just sauté a quarter of a pound of scallops, for example, and toss them into the sauce. You can do the same, without even cooking, with the imitation crab and lobster products. If sodium is a problem, you may wish to soak the pieces in some lemon water before serving to remove some of the salt.

To get over the pizza craving that's bound to set in when you start reducing the fat and cholesterol in your diet, here's a perfectly satisfying and delicious alternative. Just go to the store and buy the following ingredients:

- Chilled prepared pizza crusts
- Commercially prepared pizza sauce
- Green pepper
- Onion
- Fresh mushrooms
- Tomatoes
- Olives

Preheat your oven to 375°F (190°C/Gas Mark 5) while you prepare the toppings. Ladle out the sauce over the crusts and top with sliced pepper, onion, and mushrooms, cut-up tomatoes and olives. Pop the pizza into the oven for 10 minutes or less.

What about the cheese, you say? Well, the pizza tastes delicious without any cheese at all.

The crust, by the way, is made without any eggs or animal fat, so you're perfectly safe in enjoying it. Again, if sodium is a problem, you may wish to make your own sauce rather than using the kinds that come out of jars. Just mix some low-sodium tomato sauce with ¼ teaspoon each of Italian seasoning, oregano, and garlic powder. You may also wish to add just a teaspoonful of olive oil to the sauce.

Another word about beef . . .

I want to make it perfectly clear that I do not advocate completely eliminating beef or other red meats from the diet. Yes, the recipes in this book call for chicken, turkey, and seafood. Simply enough, they are much lower in fat per serving size. Make your own comparisons in the charts included in Chapter 2, 'Winning by the Numbers'. But once in a while you and I will want to enjoy the flavour of a good piece of beef.

When you decide that you'd like to have a beef dish, just follow two simple rules. First, remember that a serving size is 4 ounces uncooked. If that sounds like a small amount, think of it as a quarter of a pound, as the burger advertizers tell us. Second, select those cuts of meat that are lowest in fat. Happily, at least in my opinion, one of those cuts is fillet mignon cut from the tenderloin. And here's one of my favourite beef recipes that's fit for a king.

Beef en Brochette

MARINADE
½ *cup red wine*
¼ *cup vegetable oil*
1 *teaspoon* each *Worcestershire
   sauce and sugar*
1 *tablespoon vinegar*
2 *tablespoons ketchup*
1 *clove garlic, minced*
½ *teaspoon* each *marjoram and
   rosemary*

1 *lb beef tenderloin (filet
   mignon) cut in cubes*
16 *large fresh mushrooms*
2 *green bell peppers*
2 *onions*
2 *tomatoes*

Mix the marinade ingredients together in a large plastic food-storage bag. Cut the meat and vegetables into chunks suitable for skewering. Marinate in the bag for 2 to 3 hours. Skewer the meat and vegetables and grill until the meat is at the doneness you prefer. Serve with wild rice or rice pilaf. They are beautiful on the plate, and delicious and tender.

This recipe serves four good-sized appetites. No one ever complains about wanting more meat. It is a good example of how meat need not predominate in the meal.

In the same way, lean cuts of meat can be used in a variety of recipes that are probably near and dear to you and your family. Soups, stews, casseroles, and other dishes need no more than 4 ounces per person. You'll note that in almost all cases meat is browned first, then other ingredients are added. When you do that, just remember to drain off the fat rather than keeping it in the pan. You really won't miss it at all.

Cooking with seafood

For many reasons, you'll want to start including more seafood in your meal planning. First, of course, fish and shellfish have the least amount of fat of any selection from the meat group. Second, the fat they do contain is particularly useful to those wishing to reduce cholesterol levels. Salmon, especially, is a great source of the alpha-three fatty acids, which have been shown time and again to lower lipid levels. Third, and possibly just as important as any other reason, fish offer an almost incredible variety to choose from in selecting dish after dish. Don't just stick with your favourites, but rather start to experiment with new and exciting types you come across at the seafood counter.

The following recipes happen to be favourites of mine that I've developed over the years. But you'll also want to get at least one good seafood cookbook.

But before getting into the recipes, I want to mention the importance of selecting fresh fish. Tne frozen types just aren't as good. Find a fish seller you can trust and ask his opinion about which fish is best on a particular day. Fish should have a fresh, not fishy aroma. If whole, the eyes should not be sunken and the fins should not be shrivelled. Fillets must not have a dried appearance.

Frozen Fish Fiesta

1 medium-sized onion, sliced
   thin
1 cup water
2 teaspoons chilli powder
1 teaspoon ground cumin
1 teaspoon oregano
1 large bay leaf
1 large garlic clove, crushed
6 stuffed olives, sliced
1 lb frozen cod (or other fish)

There are always times when you have to settle for frozen fish, and it's a good idea to have some in the freezer ready for an 'emergency'. One of the fish that freezes best is cod. Store it in 1-lb pieces in plastic storage bags.

Combine all ingredients except the fish in a saucepan and heat to a bubbling boil. By this time the fish should be partly thawed, enough to cut into 2-inch chunks. Toss in the chunks with the sauce and reheat to boiling, then simmer 20 minutes or less, until fish flakes easily. Serve over noddles for a hearty meal. You'll also want some big chunks of bread to soak up the sauce—this is hearty eating, so go ahead and get primitive.

Pescatori (Italian-Style Shellfish)

1 medium-sized onion
1 tablespoon olive oil
1 large clove garlic, minced
¼ teaspoon each oregano,
     thyme, and crushed red
     pepper
2 medium tomatoes, cut up
1 large clove garlic, crushed
8 oz raw clams
8 oz raw scallops

In a saucepan place all ingredients except the shellfish, and cook over medium heat for 4 to 5 minutes, until the pieces of onion and green pepper become tender and a saucelike consistency is reached. Then add the shellfish and simmer for just another 5 minutes, no more or the fish will be overcooked. *Serve over pasta for 4.*

Fish Baked in Paper

1 lb fish fillets such as sea bass
1 cup carrots, sliced into strips
1 small onion
2 teaspoons each dill weed and
     thyme leaves (or 1 tablespoon
     of each fresh)
Freshly ground pepper

Cut 4 circles of parchment paper (not waxed paper) about 15 inches in diameter. Place the fish, cut into equal pieces, on the 4 pieces of paper, and cover with vegetables. Season to taste with herbs and pepper. Fold the paper and crimp to seal. Place on a sheet and bake in a preheated oven at 350°F (180°C/Gas Mark 4) for about 12 minutes. *Serves 4, with small boiled potatoes and bread.*

Mexican Fish Delight

1 tablespoon olive oil
Juice of 1 fresh lime
1 lb fish fillets, such as sea bass
Freshly ground pepper
Chopped parsley
Chopped black olives
Chopped tomatoes

Preheat the oven to 450°F (230°C/Gar Mark 8). Mix the oil and lime juice together and rub over the fish fillets. Season to taste with pepper. Bake uncovered for 15 minutes without turning. Meanwhile, chop the parsley, black olives, and tomatoes and mix to form a garnish to top the fish with when the fillets come out of the oven.

Serves 4, with vegetarian refried beans, rice, and warm tortillas.

Polynesian Scallops

*½ cup diced green bell pepper
(or mix with red bell pepper)*
*1 tablespoon chopped spring
onion*
¼ cup sliced water chestnuts
¼ cup pineapple cubes
1 teaspoon Worcestershire sauce
1 teaspoon wine vinegar
¼ cup pineapple juice
Juice of 1 lime
1 lb scallops

Mix all ingredients except the scallops in a flameproof casserole and heat on the stove top until the vegetables are tender. Thicken, if you wish, with cornflour, added a bit at a time. Add scallops and mix. Cover the dish and bake in a preheated 350°F (180°C/Gas Mark 4) oven for just 5 minutes—more will overcook the delicate scallops. *The recipe serves 4.* Try it served with rice and Oriental vegetables.

Baked Salmon Loaf

1 1-lb can salmon
½ cup chopped celery
¼ cup chopped onion
¼ lb chopped fresh mushrooms
¼ cup skimmed milk
2 egg whites
*1 ½ tablespoons dill weed (fresh
is best if possible)*
*1 cup breadcrumbs or oat-bran
cereal*

Mix all ingredients well in a bowl. Place in a meatloaf pan large enough to accommodate the mixture. Bake in a 375°F (190°C/Gas Mark 5) oven for 45 minutes. Cut into slices and serve four with potatoes and vegetables of your choice.

While you're at it, you might as well make 2 loaves and freeze one for a future meal when you don't have time to cook.

Teriyaki Salmon

1/4 cup soya sauce
2 tablespoons brown sugar
2 tablespoons grated fresh ginger
1 lb salmon fillets or steaks

Mix the soya sauce, sugar, and ginger together in a plastic food-storage bag. Marinate the salmon for at least 30 minutes, preferably 1 hour. Grill the salmon in the grill or over charcoal. Figure 10 minutes per inch of thickness for broiling time.

Salmon Patties

1 1-lb can salmon
4 egg whites
2/3 cup oat-bran cereal
1 medium onion, minced fine
1 tablespoon finely chopped
  parsley
1 tablespoon fresh-squeezed
  lemon juice

Mix all ingredients together and make 8 patties shaped like hamburgers. Put them in a non-stick pan and fry until crisp. I love these best with mashed potatoes, canned sweetcorn, and a dash of ketchup—just the way we ate them as children in my family. *Serves four.*

Halibut Marengo

2 cups canned whole tomatoes,
  chopped
1/2 orange, sliced
1/4 cup each mushrooms, celery,
  green pepper
1/4 teaspoon each thyme and
  white pepper
2 tablespoons chopped onion
1 lb halibut (this is a nice, firm
  fish)

Mix all ingredients except fish and bring to a boil in a medium saucepan. Place the fish in a glass baking dish and pour the sauce over. Bake 15 minutes in a 375°F (190°C/Gas Mark 5).

Tuna- or Salmon-Salad Sandwiches

1 tin tuna or salmon
¼ cup finely chopped apples
6 stuffed green olives, sliced
1 green onion, minced
¼ teaspoon dill weed (or 1
    teaspoon fresh)
¼ cup chopped celery
3 drops Tabasco
Juice of ½ lime
Just enough reduced-fat
    mayonnaise to hold it all
    together

Even people who flat-out don't like fish enjoy these sandwiches. Choose tuna packed in water. Mix all the ingredients together, refrigerate long enough to cool, and serve on lightly toasted slices of sourdough bread.

This might sound a bit unusual; most people wouldn't think of including apples in tuna salad, but give it a try. Even my fish-hating wife thinks it's delicious enough to serve for dinner, when we don't want a big meal.

Seafood Kebabs

Juice of 2 lemons
¼ cup white wine
3 large garlic cloves, minced
3 tablespoons parsley, finely
    chopped
1 tablespoon vegetable oil
2 teaspoons oregano
½ teaspoon white pepper
1 lb scallops or fish chunks or
    both

Combine all ingredients except fish or scallops to form a marinade. Add scallops or fish and marinate 1 hour. Drain and skewer. Grill 10 minutes in the oven grill or over charcoal. You may wish to alternate the chunks of fish on a skewer with chunks of green pepper, mushrooms, or other vegetables for variety and colour. Baste with the marinade as you're grilling to keep the fish moist.

Cherished family recipes

It's important to stress that Life After Cholesterol can go on much as it did before. By all means one should continue to eat similar kinds of foods. It would be practically impossible to expect lifelong success eating nothing but foods foreign to what you're used to.

Maybe people in California can go on day after day eating grilled fish and boiled artichokes. But in everywhere else people have got used to many kinds of ethnic foods.

The trick is not to give up such foods, but rather to alter them sufficiently to eliminate as much fat and cholesterol as possible. Use egg whites for yolks; broth instead of oil for sautéing; turkey instead of beef or veal; skimmed milk or yogurt instead of cream.

Everyone has his or her own family recipes that shouldn't be forgotten. One of the things my mother used to make many years ago when I was growing up in Chicago was called *galumki*, with the 'l' pronounced as a 'w'. It's Polish stuffed cabbage. It calls for eggs and beef in the original recipe, but with a couple of simple substitutions, we have a perfect low-fat, low-cholesterol meal that's hearty and satisfying. The same kinds of substitutions can bring almost any recipe right into line with the prudent approach to eating. The following is mother's altered recipe.

Galumki (Polish Stuffed Cabbage)

1 head of cabbage, cored
Rice
1 ½ lb minced turkey breast
2 medium onions, chopped
Ground pepper
2 egg whites

Boil the cored cabbage head in water sufficient to cover for 10 minutes. Cook enough rice to make 2 cups. Cook turkey in a pan, stirring until the pinkness is gone. Combine the turkey, rice, onions, papper, and egg whites in a bowl. Cool the cabbage and remove the leaves whole. Divide the mixture and place on cabbage leaves, wrap, and secure with wooden toothpicks. Place in a casserole dish, cover, and bake in a 325°F (170°C/Gas Mark 3) oven for 1 hour.

Other family recipes for similar dishes include sour cream. Instead, use non-fat yogurt

sweetened with a bit of sugar and
dollop over the stuffed cabbage
leaves. You may also wish to baste
the stuffed cabbage with some
tomato juice while cooking. My
mother never did, but other
families did so.

Serve with chunks of hearty
bread. It's a meal in itself.

Wake up tomorrow morning and look at the sky. Even if it's raining
or gloomy, it's beautiful because you're there to experience it. Like
the words in the song, stop to smell the roses.

Every man and woman in the world is lucky in one way or another.
You have to define your own luck. You have to count your own
blessings. If you can honestly say there is nothing you enjoy anymore,
no one you care to hug today or tomorrow, then by all means, don't
make another batch of muffins. Throw your niacin tablets away. Forget
the diet and gorge on butter and eggs. Maybe you'll even want to
start smoking, or smoke more, to speed the process.

No thanks, not for me. Jenny's smile makes the gloomiest day bright.
Ross's every success and milestone is important to me. You never saw
two more terrific kids. Or maybe you have. Maybe they're yours.
Maybe they're your grandchildren. Or the children you haven't had
yet. Maybe your children are your work, your hobbies, your church,
your friends. All of these are important. All of them are the *most*
important.

What's your reason for tomorrow? And tomorrow? And tomorrow?

17. TO TOMORROW AND TOMORROW AND TOMORROW

Call it an instinct for survival. Call it a love of life. There is a desire, a burning need to survive, to live for tomorrow and tomorrow and tomorrow.

I have my own reasons. Their names are Ross and Jenny. You have your reasons. All of them are worthwhile and defy description on the printed page.

I'll never forget that day I came back from the surgeon's office when he told me of the mortality risk of the surgery. All I could think of was leaving my little children behind, with them not understanding why.

Think of it: by taking some vitamins, eating some muffins, and following a sensible, delicious diet, you and I can cut our risk of heart disease in half. We don't have to undergo 'heroic' measures. We'll never be written about in *Time* magazine, but we'll be pioneers nonetheless, proving that heart disease *can* be defeated.

No, I don't deny that I often envy those who dig into a gooey piece of chocolate cake, apple pie with crust made from lard, prime ribs of beef, and even the burgers and fries from the fast-food stands here in Southern California. There's a place here that serves, as I recall, the most scrumptious double cheeseburger in Los Angeles. The memories of those burgers are tempting and strong, but they don't stand a chance when I look at the faces of my two kids.

Ross and Jenny are my fortification. Each time I might be tempted to bite into one of those burgers, or a thick slab of prime rib, or a cheeseladen pizza I think that I might miss a day with them. Maybe I'd miss the graduation. Or the special award ceremony. Or the wedding. Maybe even the grandchildren!

You have to find your own reasons. It takes more than just a momentary decision to carry on a lifetime of commitment.

Think of those deeply committed to religious beliefs. The decision to attend those Sunday services on a day the sun is shining is based on deep commitment. It goes beyond a logical, scientific decision.

We all have our disappointments, and times when we think it may not be worth it. Those are the times when the temptations to forget the oat-bran muffins, the daily doses of niacin, the low-fat diet are the strongest. It's so easy to feel sorry for oneself, to give oneself a 'consolation prize' in the form of a dozen doughnuts or a 24-ounce sirloin steak.

I had the opportunity to consult for a weight-loss group for two years. Many of the clients failed to achieve their intended 'goal' weight or to stay with it once they reached that goal. Why? Often because they didn't have a good enough reason to become slender or to stay slender. Their excuses could fill a book. But those made it who came to realize that their own satisfaction was the ultimate reason for success.

If you skimmed over or skipped Chapter 7, on weight loss, go back and read it. I discuss a lot of the motivational drive needed to succeed. Those motivations are the same for *anyone* who sincerely wants to make a change in his or her life.

Face it: the changes you need to make could be the difference between living and not living. The next time you think that the flush you get from the niacin is uncomfortable and not worth it, think again. The next time you feel that a doughnut or a croissant would be better than another oat-bran muffin, think again. The next time you'd rather select the tournedos with béarnaise sauce over the grilled swordfish, think again.

Think about whether those choices are worth a year, a month, a week, or even a day. I think about that time with my kids. You think about the time with whomever or whatever.

NOTES

Chapter 2. Cholesterol: No More Controversy

1. Stamler, J. 'Diet and Coronary Heart Disease'. *Biometrics*, 1982: volume 38 Supplement, pages 95-118.
2. Friedman, M., and Rosenman, R. *Type A Behavior and Your Heart*. A. A. Knopf, New York, 1974.
3. Cooper, R., et al. 'Seventh-Day Adventist Adolescents—Life-Style Patterns and Cardiovascular Risk Factors'. *Western Journal of Medicine*, 1984: volume 140, number 3, pages 471-77.
4. Caggiula, A. W., et al. 'The Multiple Risk Intervention Trial (MRFIT) IV. Intervention on Blood Lipids'. *Preventive Medicine*, 1981: volume 10, pages 443-75.
5. Lipid Research Clinics Program. 'The Lipid Research Clinics Coronary Primary Prevention Trial Results. II. The Relationship of Reduction in Incidence of Coronary Heart Disease to Cholesterol Lowering'. *Journal of the American Medical Association*, 1984: volume 251, number 3, pages 365-74.
6. Pritikin, N., and McGrady, P. M. *The Pritikin Program for Diet and Exercise*. Grosset & Dunlap, New York, 1979.
7. Schaefer, E. J., et al. 'The Effects of Low Cholesterol, High Polyunsaturated Fat, and Low Fat Diets on Plasma Lipid and Lipoprotein Cholesterol Levels in Normal and Hypercholesterolemic Subjects'. *American Journal of Clinical Nutrition*, 1981: volume 34, pages 1158-63.
8. Rifkind, B. M., and Segal, P. 'Lipid Research Clinics Reference Values for Hyperlipidemia and Hypolipidemia'. *Journal of the American Medical Association*, 1983: volume 250, number 14, pages 1869-72.
9. Weidman, W. H., et al. 'Nutrient Intake and Serum Cholesterol Level in Normal Children 6 to 16 Years of Age'. *Pediatrics*, 1978: volume 61, number 3, pages 354-59.
10. Uhl, G. S., et al. 'Relation Between High Density Lipoprotein Cholesterol and Coronary Artery Disease in Asymptomatic Men'. *American Journal of Cardiology*, 1981: volume 48, number 5, pages 903-10.

11. Oster, P., et al. 'Diet and High Density Lipoproteins'. *Lipids*, 1981: volume 26, pages 93-97.

12. Kannel, W. B., et al. 'Is Serum Total Cholesterol an Anachronism?' *Lancet*, 1979: volume 2, pages 234-44.

13. Council on Scientific Affairs. 'Dietary and Pharmacologic Therapy for the Lipid Risk Factors'. *Journal of the American Medical Association*, 1983: volume 250, number 14, pages 1873-79.

14. *Dietary Guidelines for Americans*. U. S. Department of Agriculture and U.S. Department of Health, Education and Welfare, Washington, D.C., 1980.

15. Stamler, J., et al. 'Is relationship between serum cholesterol and risk of premature death from coronary heart disease continuous and graded?' *Journal of the American Medical Association*, 1986: volume 256, pages 2823-2828.

16. Colditz, G. A., et al. 'Menopause and the risk of coronary heart disease in women'. *New England Journal of Medicine*, volume 316, number 18, pages 1105-1111.

17. Brown, W. V., et al. 'Treatment of Common Lipoprotein Disorders'. *Progress in Cardiovascular Diseases*, 1984: volume 27, number 1, pages 1-20.

Chapter 4. Getting the Scoop on Oat Bran

1. Burkitt, D. P., et al. 'Effects of Dietary Fibre on Stools and Transit Times, and Its Role in the Causation of Disease'. *Lancet*, 1972: volume 2, pages 1408-11.

2. Anderson, J. W., and Chen, W. L. 'Plant Fiber: Carbohydrate and Lipid Metabolism'. *American Journal of Clinical Nutrition*, 1979: volume 32, pages 346-63.

3. Trowell, H. 'Fibre: a Natural Hypocholesterolemic Agent'. *American Journal of Clinical Nutrition*, 1972: volume 25, pages 464-65.

4. DeGroot, A. P., et al. 'Cholesterol-Lowering Effect of Rolled Oats'. *Lancet*, 1963: volume 2, pages 303-304.

5. Fisher, H., and Griminger, P. 'Cholesterol-Lowering Effects of Certain Grains and of Oat Fractions in the Chick'. *Proceedings of the Society for Experimental Biology and Medicine*, 1967: volume 126, pages 108-111.

6. Anderson, J. W. et al. 'Hypolipidemic Effects of High-Carbohydrate, High-Fiber Diets'. *Metabolism*, 1980: volume 29, pages 551-58.

7. Kirby, R. W., et al. 'Oat-Bran Intake Selectively Lowers Serum Low-Density Lipoprotein Cholesterol Concentrations of Hypercholesterolemic Men'. *American Journal of Clinical Nutrition*, 1981: volume 34, pages 824-28.

8. Anderson, J. W., et al. 'Cholesterol-Lowering Properties of Oat Products'. In press. Presented at the American Association of Cereal Chemists' annual meeting, 1982.

9. Anderson, J. W., et al. 'Hypocholesterolemic Effects of Oat-Bran or Bean Intake for Hypercholeratrolemic Men'. *American Journal of Clinical Nutrition*, 1984: volume 40, pages 1146-55.

10. Anderson, J. W., et al. 'Mineral and Vitamin Status on High-Fiber Diets: Long-Term Studies of Diabetic Patients'. *Diabetes Care*, 1980: volume 3, pages 38-40.

11. Anderson, J. W. 'Medical Benefits of High-Fiber Intakes'. *The Fiber Factor*, August 1983. Quaker Oats Company, Chicago.

12. *Dietary Guidelines for Americans*. U.S. Department of Agriculture and U.S. Department of Health, Education and Welfare, Washington, D.C., 1980.

Chapter 5. The Amazing Story of Niacin

1. Council on Scientific Affairs. 'Dietary and Pharmacologic Therapy for the Lipid Risk Factors'. *Journal of the American Medical Association*, 1983: volume 250, number 14, pages 1873-79.

2. Hotz, W. 'Nicotinic Acid and Its Derivatives: a Short Survey'. *Advances in Lipid Research*, 1983: volume 20, pages 195-217.

3. Wahlqvist, M. L., 'Effects on Plasma Cholesterol of Nicotinic Acid and Its Analogues (Niacin)'. In *Vitamins in Human Biology and Medicine*. CRC Press, Boca Raton, Florida, 1981, pages 81-94.

4. Hunninghake, D. B. 'Pharmacologic Therapy for the Hyperlipidemic Patient'. *American Journal of Medicine*, 1983: volume 74, number 5A, pages 19-22.

5. Paoletti, R., et al. 'Influence of Bezafibrate, Fenofibrate, Nicotinic Acid and Etofibrate on Plasma High-Density Lipoprotein Levels'. *American Journal of Cardiology*, 1983: volume 52, number 4, pages 21B-27B.

6. Kane, J. P., et al. 'Normalization of Low-Density Lipoprotein Levels in Heterozygous Familial Hyperscholesterolemia with a Combined Drug Regimen'. *New England Journal of Medicine*, 1981: volume 304, number 5, pages 251-258.

7. Nessim, S. A., et al. 'Combined Therapy of Niacin, Colestipol, and Fat-Controlled Diet in Men with Coronary Bypass. Effect on Blood Lipids and Apolipoproteins'. *Arteriosclerosis*, 1983: volume 3, number 6, pages 568-73.

8. Kane, J. P., and Malloy, M. J. 'Treatment of Hyperscholeratolemia'. *Medical Clinics of North America*, 1982: volume 66, number 2, pages 537-50.

9. Hoeg, J. M., et al. 'An Approach to the Management of Hyper-

lipoproteinemia'. *JAMA*, 1986; 255(4):512-521.

10. U.S. Defines Cholesterol Hazards and Offers Treatment Guidelines. *The New York Times*. October 6, 1987, page 1.

11. Blankenhorn, D. H., et al. 'Beneficial effects of combined colestipol-niacin therapy on coronary artherosclerosis and coronary venous bypass grafts'. *Journal of the American Medical Association*, 1987: volume 257, pages 3233-3241.

12. *Family Practice News*. Volume 16, number 2, page 65, 1986.

13. The Coronary Drug Project Research Group. 'Clofibrate and Niacin in Coronary Heart Disease (the Coronary Drug Project)'. *Journal of the American Medical Association*, 1975: volume 231, pages 360-81.

14. Cohen, L., 'Successful Treatment of Hypercholesterolemia with a Combination of Probucol and Niacin'. Presented at the Annual Meeting of the Federation of American Societies for Experimental Biology, April, 1985.

15. Mevacor R., advertisement. Merck, Sharp and Dohme. *Journal of the American Medical Association*, 1987: volume 258, pages 1884 A-H.

INDEX

Note: **bold** entries refer to tables.